D1546218

THE LOAN PUSHERS

THE LOAN PUSHERS
The Role of Commercial Banks in the
International Debt Crisis

WILLIAM DARITY, JR.
and
BOBBIE L. HORN

BALLINGER PUBLISHING COMPANY
Cambridge, Massachusetts
A Subsidiary of Harper & Row, Publishers, Inc.

International Standard Book Number: 0-88730-067-7

Library of Congress Catalog Card Number: 88-6181

Printed in the United States of America

Library of Congress Cataloging-in-Publication Data

Darity, William A., 1953–
    The loan pushers.

    Includes index.
    1. Loans, Foreign. 2. Debts, External. 3. Banks and banking,
International.   I. Horn, Bobbie L. II. Title.

HD3891.D36   1988   332.1′5   88-6181
ISBN 0-88730-067-7

To our families

CONTENTS

Introduction

As we go to press, the international debt crisis still is very much with us. Columnist Jack Anderson is expressing worries over American bankers lending heavily to the Soviet Union at low spreads; for example, First Chicago has now completed arrangements for a loan to the USSR of $200 million at a mere one-eighth of 1 percent over cost. Rumors still are alive of prospects of a default by a major COMECON nation.[1] A news weekly in Uganda regularly reports, as do many African news weeklies, on Brazil's posture with respect to its foreign debt. The article applauds Brazil's temporary stoppage on interest payments as "a qualitative leap in the debt crisis" that "should result in substantial change in the approach to the problem by Washington, the IMF, the banks and creditors."[2]

Brazil, of course, is not alone. Peru and Ecuador have not met their interest payments for many months.[3] Prospects for near-term improvement are dampened by evidence of a global economic slowdown that will hinder export growth from the developing country debtors. Commercial banks in the United States and Britain have been building both their capital bases and their loan loss reserves, implying that they will be increasingly reluctant to make new loans to the indebted nations. Among U.S. banks, Citicorp and the Bank of Boston have been most aggressive in raising loan loss reserves for their developing country loans. The magnitude of the debt crisis for developing countries also is reflected in the fact that more than 15 percent of Mexico's planned $92 billion 1988 budget has been designated for payment of its foreign debt.[4] Even this sum is not sufficient to service Mexico's accumulated debt. The debt-equity exchange recently agreed to by Mexico and J.P. Morgan—in which a portion of the loans will be swapped for new marketable Mexican securities—is tantamount to an admission by both Mexico and J.P. Morgan that the debt will never be fully repaid. Fears remain strong that the outright refusal to meet their obligations by large debtors like Mexico, Brazil, and Argentina could lead to "the collapse" of the international financial system.[5]

This book approaches the debt crisis from the standpoint of what may be called "the banking problem"—the classic tension between the alleged benefits associated with the capability of private financial intermediaries to allocate credit efficiently and the dangers associated with the capability of those same institutions to destabilize domestic and international economic relationships through their lending practices. Correspondingly, regulating financial intermediaries presumably inhibits their capacity to allocate credit efficiently but failing to regulate them opens the door for immense economic traumas. The apparatus of regulated banking contains the seeds of extensive state planning, but a gravitation toward "free banking" unleashes the bankers, with disastrous effects.

An indecisive or mixed posture toward the commercial banks and financial intermediaries typically yields to pressure to swing in one direction or the other. Indecision eventually gives way to greater regulation, perhaps even to thoroughgoing state control of credit creation, or to extensive deregulation, perhaps to complete dominion for the bankers. The ostensibly temperate "middle path" (and, indeed, its temperateness is questionable) is unlikely to be sustainable indefinitely.

Moreover, some observers have detected a pattern of overlending cycles repeating at approximate half-century intervals since the early nineteenth century. Finance moves in large volume from the more advanced to the less advanced regions with a fifty-year periodicity. Understanding these cyclical waves of credit flows from center to periphery is crucial in the study of the history of capital in financial form.

The debt crisis of the developing countries, the performance of the unregulated Eurocurrency market, and the current momentum to liberalize financial markets in the more developed countries and to lift "financial repression" in the developing countries forcefully bring the contradictions of private banking practices home to roost. Should the bankers of the world be viewed as loan pushers, possessing an addictive fix of credit that routinely becomes the agent of economic disturbance? This book is about commercial bank loans to developing countries and the implications of commercial bank loans both for economic theory and the world in which we live.

Debt woes on a global scale compel attention to many ongoing, unresolved theoretical problems for economists. The problems broadly include the appropriate theory of the firm, the appropriate theory of banking behavior, the proper analysis of the formation of contracts, the correct treatment of the formation of individual and market expectations, and the nature of trade cycles and financial crises. These problems surface dramatically in international credit arrangements—a world of big banks, second-line banks, multinational guardian institutions, allegations of neo-imperialist conspiracies, borrowing governments of questionable competence and incorruptibility, and persistent poverty among the populations of many of the borrowing nations.

While addressing aspects of all these problems, this book focuses in-depth on a particular controversy that has arisen in the midst of the international debt crisis—the controversy over the extent to which multi-national banks are responsible for the current situation. The claim that the commercial banks in some sense "pushed" loans on the less developed countries constitutes the indictment. Proponents of the loan push notion suggest that the banks have victimized themselves by their absurd lending decisions, advancing credit to foreign borrowers who have less than a prayer of making repayment.

This view of bank lending lies at an opposite pole from the view articulated by Irving Friedman. Friedman depicts banks as waiting patiently for foreign loan applications and evaluating each individually on its merits regardless of its country of origin. For example, Friedman writes:

> . . . the response of the banks is the response to a demand. Bankers do not make loans to countries, or entities within countries, that do not ask for a loan. The fact is that someone comes to a bank and asks for a loan. Then the banker judges whether to do it. Banks compete for attractive loans, but the borrower is essentially the genesis of the loan.[6]
>
> It is sometimes said that banks are "reaching" for loans. This is a concept that is often found, even in periodicals which are considered friendly to the private banks. I do not think it is right.[7]

Thus, on *a priori* grounds, applications for loans from two private businesses, one in Brazil and another in Chad, would be considered on an equal footing. The application from the Brazilian enterprise would not be actively sought and encouraged because of its relatively attractive country of origin, nor would the application from the Chadian business be dispensed with immediately because of its less attractive location. For Friedman the banks are passive actors in the game. The borrowers must take the initiative. Each application is weighed carefully on the basis of its own merits. A Chadian firm would be refused consideration only if it failed to submit a loan application.

Between Friedman's view, which might be called "debt pulling," and the loan pushing view is a position that sets mutual responsibility between both parties to the contract. The volume of indebtedness incurred by less developed countries (or LDCs) in the 1970s can be readily understood in light of the ordinary supply and demand apparatus. Loan pushing is simply a more colorful term for loan supply while, debt pulling is no more than a colorful term for loan demand. In this intermediate view the predominant effect—debt pull or loan push—in the 1970s varied from loan to loan and country to country.[8]

We believe, instead, that the concept of loan pushing provides a superior vehicle for exploring the contradictory aspects of private lending. From this perspective, bankers as loan pushers become active door to door salesmen (albeit in pinstripe suits). They persuade borrowers to agree to credits when the borrowers have no thoughts of obtaining a loan at all, or at least, not a large one. Moreover, from this perspective, in euphoric times banks will sell loans to borrowers in regions they (the banks) customarily leave alone.

NOTES

1. Jack Anderson, "Bank Loans to Russia Could Backfire," *Durham Sun*, 5 September 1987.
2. Roberto Alvarez Quinones, "Brazil's Action Represents Qualitative Change in Debt Crisis," *Weekly Topic* (Kampala, Uganda), 22 April 1987.
3. Peter Truell, "Despite Progress, World Still Gropes for Debt Solutions," *Wall Street Journal*, 14 August 1987.
4. "Mexican Budget Approved; 54 Percent Goes to Debt Payment," *Wall Street Journal*, 30 December 1987.
5. Truell, "Despite Progress."
6. Irving Friedman, "Emerging Role of Private Banks," in Stephen S. Goodman, ed., *Financing and Risk in Developing Countries* (New York: Praeger, 1978), p. 20.
7. Ibid., p. 20.
8. Representative of this ambivalent position is Carlos Massad in "Debt: An Overview," *Journal of Development Planning* no. 16 (1985): 3–24. Massad (p. 4) observes in commenting on the foreign borrowing boom in the LDCs that "Both creditors' push and debtors' pull played a role, although in different degrees in different countries, that is difficult to disentangle."

CHAPTER 1

Loan Pushing
Parallels between the 1920s and 1970s

LOAN PUSHING IN THE 1920s

The idea that banks force loans on borrowers emerges in the literature exploring financial flows in the 1920s from lenders in the United States to borrowers in Germany and Latin America. Max Winkler's provocative exposé on the underwriting practices of U.S. banks with respect to foreign bonds provides some remarkable anecdotes illustrating loan pushing. Winkler described a Bavarian hamlet that was reported to be seeking $125,000 to improve the town's power station. He reported further:

> How could a loan of so small an amount be offered to the American investor who had by now learned to 'invest' by the tens and hundreds of millions? After much persuasion, the mayor of the town in question was convinced of the desirability of contracting a larger loan. The result was a $3,000,000 issue, successfully sold in the American market.[1]

Winkler adds that after the necessary additions were made to the power plant, the balance was used "towards . . . various projects . . . ordinarily termed non-productive."[2]

An Impulse Toward Overlending

In a more general vein, Winkler observed that "[d]uring a period of prosperity there is a tendency to extend loans for nonproductive purposes or upon dubious security. . . ."[3] But Winkler warned that even if the loans were made "for so-called productive purposes," during "good times" there is still an impulse toward overlending.[4] Plus, Winkler made explicit his opinion that loan pushing took place when he observed that ". . . at times even pressure has been brought to bear to induce foreign governments and municipalities to contract loans which they did not want or need."[5] This was the outcome of voracious competition among the underwriters to be first in line to handle bond issues.[6]

Cleona Lewis also provided several examples from the 1920s that are compatible with images of overlending. The following passage describes the intensity of the rivalry among U.S. banks for foreign business:

> Whereas in the middle decades of the nineteenth century American promoters had scoured Europe in search of foreign lenders, in 1925–29 they were searching the world over for foreign borrowers. At one time, according to testimony before the Senate Committee on Finance investigating the sale of foreign securities on the United States, there were 29 representatives of American financial houses in Colombia alone trying to negotiate loans for the national government, for the departments, and for other possible borrowers. Some 36 houses, most of them American, competed for a city of Budapest loan and 14 for a loan to the city of Belgrade. . . . In Peru, a group of successful American promoters included one Peruvian, the son of the President of that republic, who was after tried by the courts of his country and convicted of 'illegal enrichment.' In Cuba the son-in-law of the President was given a well-paid position in the Cuban branch of an American bank during most of the time the bank was successfully competing against other American banks for the privilege of financing the Cuban government.[7]

Funding American Exports

Lewis's work highlighted another feature of the loan push doctrine—the creation of foreign markets for U.S. producers. Lewis found that numerous overseas loans were arranged for public works projects in the LDCs of the 1920s and that " . . . big American construction companies sometimes helped finance public works in foreign countries, sometimes secured their contracts on a competitive basis after the financing had been arranged."[8] She concluded that infrastructural "loans and contracts provided a considerable market for American materials and services."[9] The stimulus for products of U.S. origin had far-reaching dimensions:

> The roadbuilding contracts, for example, expanded the demand for American steam shovels and grading machinery; and also called for cement and asphalt

from the South American and Cuban subsidiaries of American companies. The building of sanitation, gas, and waterworks systems called for metal pipes and plumbing supplies. Railway building called for steel rails, engines and cars. The execution of all these contracts gave employment abroad to a large number of American engineers, and also called for additional numbers of employees in the home offices of the companies concerned.[10]

Henry Wallich, a long-time governor of the U.S. Federal Reserve Board, perceived that in the aggregate, the expansionary boost to American production in the 1920s from the Latin loans was sufficiently large to make the loans a net benefit for the U.S. economy, despite the subsequent defaults.[11]

However, from the standpoint of the bondholders, the ultimate lenders of the 1920s, the situation was bound to be unpleasant. As Wallich noted: ". . . it is obvious that by far the heaviest part of the burden, if not all of it, rested upon the security holders."[12] The ultimate lenders could delay the day of reckoning by extending additional credit to foreign borrowers but at that stage, as Max Winkler suggested "the lender becomes a slave to the borrowers."[13] Wallich's concept of net gain to the American economy stemmed from his presumption that the Latin loans did not contribute significantly to the propagation of the Great Depression in the United States.

At some point, when the record of default by foreign borrowers crosses an intolerable threshold, Charles Kindleberger's "phase of revulsion" sets in. The ultimate lenders will swallow their losses and retreat *en masse* from the international capital markets. By the early 1930s it had become virtually impossible for the less developed countries to float new bond issues. Lewis dated the revulsion from the time of credit contraction in the United States associated with the 1929 collapse of share prices on the New York Stock Exchange.[14] Wallich argued that the worldwide depression of the 1930s was the fundamental event that brought down the house of cards of foreign loans, simultaneously aggravating the borrowers' inability to pay and the lenders' refusal to continue to finance the debt.[15]

The Phenomenon of Loan Pushing

Six major features emerge in the literature on the loan adventures of the 1920s related to the loan "pushing" phenomenon: (1) There was the promotional-cum-persuasion aspect, where the initiative to borrow comes from the lenders. Borrowers received more credit than they themselves conceived as feasible or necessary at the outset. Like unnecessary surgery prescribed by some physicians, bankers generated a supplier-induced demand for incurring indebtedness. (2) Concomitantly, it was implied that a surplus of funds existed, that unable to seep into normal outlets made its way into the less developed regions. This notion is plainly evident in Cleona Lewis's description of the shift on the part of U.S. promoters from a search for overseas lenders in the mid-1800s to a search for overseas borrowers during the mid-1920s. (3) The foreign lending wave involved nepotistic connections and corruption in the arrangement of the loans. (4) The loans performed a market-making function for numerous U.S. producers since the loans created financial capacity in the less developed countries to purchase the output of U.S. enterprises. One might expect to find evidence that the U.S. Department of Commerce took a hand in assisting with the arrangement of such loans, given the nature of its constituency. Certainly the U.S. Department of State sought to encourage investors by vetting foreign bond issues for "political appropriateness" in a special division.[16] (5) When concrete evidence of softness in the ability of the borrowers to meet their obligations became visible, the lenders initially tried to resolve the situation by continuing to lend. (6) Eventually, the lenders withdrew altogether from providing funds ("revulsion" took hold).

FROM BOND FINANCE TO
BANK LOAN FINANCE

In contrast with the loans of the 1920s, when the commercial banks played an underwriting function and thereby transferred the risks of lending onto the bondholders, the credits issued in the 1970s have been outright commercial bank loans. That is, the banks and their depositors—which may be other banks, depending upon the structure of interbank relations—directly share the loan risks today. There is some controversy over why the lending of the 1920s, characterized by bond finance, gave way to bank loan finance in the 1970s. The switch is peculiar given the default experience on the loans of the 1920s, since banks are unable to shift the risks entirely away from their own portfolios when they make commercial loans. This switch puzzles economic theorists, who presume that economic actors—and by all means, bankers—behave rationally in seeking to maximize monetary gain.

Contract Theory

In an excellent survey of the literature on international capital markets and dynamic contract theory, Vincent Crawford has identified an argument for the transition from bond finance to bank loan finance. He advances the claim that the transition resulted because there are "increased benefits of renegotiation in response to debt crises." Such renegotiations are ruled out in the case of bond finance "because of the large number of bond-holders whose consent would be required." In the absence of a well-developed bondholders' organization, renegotiation would be unlikely if not impossible. However, Crawford muddies this explanation a bit by pointing to Hellwig's theoretical finding that there can also be benefits associated with a "precommitment not to renegotiate in some circumstances." Crawford concludes: " . . . in general, the superiority of bank lending over bond lending depends on the relative importance of default-risk moral-hazard problems and uncertainty that cannot be dealt with adequately by contingent contracts."[17] Bond lending actually might be superior in an environment where "moral-hazard problems predominate," making it desirable to minimize reschedulings. Still unclear is the reason why the transition occurred from bond to bank lending on the grounds of "pure" economic theory.

Charles Kindleberger has indicated that the explanation for the transition lies in (1) investors' continued skittishness about low-grade foreign dollar bonds, (2) the impact of the Glass-Steagall Act of 1933 (Sections 16, 20, 21, and 32 of the Banking Act of 1933) that separated commercial and investment banking, (3) the impact of the Interest Equalization Tax over 1963 through 1974, and (4) the general preference of Eurocurrency banks for sovereign loans over "Eurobond" issues.[18] Indeed, the latter preference might be shared on both sides of the loan contract due to the greater flexibility associated with shorter term commitments.

Insurance and Innovations

More developed country (MDC) lenders invested in LDCs in the interval between the 1930s and the 1970s. As David Folkerts-Landau points out, there were virtually no new international bond issues after 1931 and, by 1974, bond finance constituted only about 10 percent of external private debt for developing countries.[19] But bond finance yielded to direct investment in the interregnum between the two major twentieth century debt crises. Thus the shift toward bank finance in the 1970s meant not only a shift away from bond finance (a shift that had begun during the Great Depression) but also a shift away from direct investment.[20]

Folkerts-Laudau therefore seeks to explain the movement toward commercial bank loans to finance development, and the movement out of both bond finance and direct investment. He contends that the transition has been due "to comprehensive advantages gained by international bank lenders over the more traditional sources of development finance" attributable to two major factors:

> First, financial authorities were perceived as being increasingly willing to protect the deposit liabilities of their large money-center banks. . . . The cost of deposit liabilities for banks, therefore, became largely independent of the banks' choice of assets, which combined with low capital requirements to provide the incentives to expand into new areas of lending. Second, international banking markets generally proved better equipped to deal with the risk of lending to sovereign borrowers than the markets for foreign bonds and direct investment. In particular, international bank lenders were able to form credible coalitions designed to deny borrowers access to refinancing in the banking markets.[21]

According to Folkerts-Landau,[22] the latter factor facilitated the substitution of rescheduling negotiations for explicit debt repudiation. However, he also reveals that there were cases where bondholder organizations managed to accomplish similar objectives in the 1930s, "albeit imperfectly."[23] As Folkerts-Landau notes:

> There was a substantial number of defaults in the early 1930s but in almost all cases borrowers subsequently offered bondholders readjustment plans providing for partial payment of debt service. By December 1935, debt-service had been paid in full on 62 percent of all foreign dollar bonds outstanding, while interest was in default on 37 percent of the total owed, and principal and sinking funds were in default on 1 percent of the total.[24]

It remains to be seen whether the contemporary bankers' coalitions prove to be more effective than the mid-1930s bondholders' coalitions in arranging repayment after troubles are manifest.

And even these apparent bondholders successes were temporary. Folkerts-Landau neglects to mention that by 1949, 50 percent of the Latin American loans were in default. Almost the entire remaining half of the loans was "serviced on an adjusted basis," leaving less than 2 percent "to be serviced on the terms originally contracted."[25]

LOAN PUSHING IN THE 1970s

Although the mechanisms of finance have changed since the 1920s, the six characteristics of the loan pushing episodes of the 1920s have been well represented in the lending wave of the 1970s.

First, with respect to the promotional aspect, or the process of creation of borrowers, consider T.H. Donaldson's nervous warning about the pattern of lending toward the end of the previous decade:

> There is a developing feeling . . . that some banks are so concerned with finding borrowers—any borrowers—that they are occasionally *overpursuading* countries who should sensibly be cautioned against too much borrowing. If this fear proves justified, the banks concerned are storing up trouble not only for themselves and the borrowers involved, but for many other banks and borrowers who will suffer from the repercussions of future problems.[26]

Charles Kindleberger's rhetoric conveys an even more dramatic picture:

> . . . contemplate the enormous external debt of the developing countries, built not only since the rise of oil prices but importantly—a widely ignored fact—in the several years before that time, as multinational banks swollen with dollars tumbled over one another in trying to uncover new foreign borrowers and practically *forced* money on the less-developed countries.[27]

At least by early 1978 Kindleberger already perceived that the foreign loans might be "going bad." He wrote: "Some of the chickens have already come home to roost, in defaults by Zaire and Peru; others such as Petamina in Indonesia have had close calls."[28]

And the following passage appeared in an article in an early 1983 issue of the journal *Eurocurrency*: "They [the banks] lent $12 to 15 billion to Mexico over 12 to 15 months when the situation was clearly going wrong," gloated an American monetary source. And even a senior banker in Luxembourg was prepared to ask: "Who should be punished more? The addict or the money-pusher?"[29]

Surplus Funds and the Eurodollar Market

The image of multinational banks gorged with dollars is consistent with the second feature of the loan push doctrine—the existence of surplus funds that eventually gravitate toward unorthodox recipients. Excess dollars in the late 1960s and early 1970s can be attributed to the explosive development of the unregulated Eurocurrency market. Softening demand for commercial bank funds by the banks' preferred clients that began in 1971, coupled with the growth in the funds the banks wished to make available to borrowers led, in this view, to the cultivation of borrowers from regions customarily ignored by the bankers. For instance, then U.S. Federal Reserve Governor Andrew Brimmer observed in his October 25, 1973 Westerfield address delivered at Atlanta University: "The main explanation [for the sharp rise in bank lending to the LDCs] appears to lie in the abundant supply of funds to the Eurodollar market and the failure of demand for loans from borrowers in developed countries to keep pace with the expansion of credit availability."[30] This decline in loan demand at the center spurred " . . . the Eurocurrency banks (especially in London) . . . to push loans to the developing countries with considerable vigor."[31]

The recycling of the Organization of Petroleum Exporting Countries (OPEC) surpluses in the aftermath of the first major oil price increases in 1973 and 1974 are seen only as aggravating the surplus funds condition, and not fundamental to the beginnings of the situation. Again in the Westerfield address, prepared prior to the bite of the first oil shock, Brimmer said that the seeds already had been sown for an international debt crisis: " . . . there was a growing awareness in the late 1960s and early 1970s that the developing countries as a group, had incurred very large foreign debts and were faced with heavy debt service requirements in the years ahead."[32] As early as 1969, Brimmer informed his audience, a Commission on International Development headed by Lester Pearson warned about the difficulties posed for short- and long-term debt management problems for LDCs.[33]

Additionally, the World Bank reported that by the late 1960s and early 1970s several countries already "were unable to continue meeting their debt servicing obligations." These countries included Chile, Ghana, India, Indonesia, Pakistan, Peru, and Turkey seeking debt relief on a multilateral basis, and Afghanistan, Egypt, and Yugoslavia seeking relief on a bilateral basis.[34] In these latter cases, much of the indebtedness was attributable not to commercial bank loans but to loans from international agencies or foreign governments on concessional (less-than-market) terms. Nevertheless, the evidence suggests that commercial banks had begun to turn their attention toward the LDCs well before the oil price boom, despite the fact that some LDCs already were having debt servicing problems—even on loans received on concessional terms!

The growth of the Eurocurrency market must be perceived as lying at the heart of the recent creation of surplus funds. Expansion of the

Eurocurrency market represents "free banking" at its cosmopolitan best, since there are no substantive regulations on the operations of these transnational financial enterprises. Even reserve requirements are absent, so that the only authentic limits on lending by banks participating in the Eurocurrency market are fixed by the prudence of their respective managements. Since the start of the 1970s managers of these multinational banks progressively began to shift their asset base away from corporate lending toward sovereign lending, especially concerning the LDCs.[35] Of course, all LDCs were not the objects of the bankers' favors; there were still some "red lines" never to be crossed, particularly those drawn around the poorest of countries. But the medium income LDCs were to be transformed from ugly ducklings into the most preferred of gilded swans.

American Exports Once Again

Specifics on nepotistic-corrupting elements in contemporary loan making are harder to detail than the facts that surfaced in the 1920s. But former banker S.C. Gwynne's confessional exposé on his own involvement in arranging a $10 million loan from an anonymous "medium-sized Midwestern bank with $5 billion in assets" to a Philippine construction company drops many hints in this direction as the author describes his maneuvers in 1978 in southeast Asia.[36]

Gwynne's article does provide explicit evidence of the loan performing a market-making function. A major depositor with Gwynne's bank—an "earth-moving equipment company, a subsidiary of a major auto company and an old client of the bank"—emerges as the principal force pressuring for the loan.[37] The earth-moving company anticipated, correctly, that the loan would finance shipments of its product to the Philippine construction company. As Gwynne reports, once the loan had been approved formally:

> Three weeks later, we disburse $5 million, the first in a series of "drawdowns" that will correspond to shipments of earth-moving equipment. Although our transfer bank, Chase Manhattan, manages to lose the $5 million for a few frantic days, the money eventually lands in the right account.[38]

It would be interesting to learn how many instances of commercial bank loans involved financing demand for products made by their major customers. The impression given by Lewis and Wallich on bond finance in the 1920s was that of a broad—albeit temporary—external stimulus to U.S. aggregate demand.[39] A similar impression appears in connection with the *Wall Street Journal*'s description of the effects of the recent wave of U.S. bank loans to Mexico. In fact, the following passage contains the entire mix of corruption, market-making, and loans soon to go bad:

> In the late 1970s salad days when the oil looked inexhaustible, the [Mexican] government's development plans focused on massive capital projects that were heavily dependent on *imported materials*; steel mills, oil installations and electrical power plants were prominent. Imports soon began rising at a faster rate than exports, and the deficit in trade and services grew.
>
> Much of the investment went to notoriously inefficient state-owned agencies and companies. That led to wasted money. Corruption drained further resources. Allegations of corruption at Pemex alone run into billions of dollars. The architect of its expansion, Jorge Dias Serrano, is in jail awaiting trial on charges of fraud.[40]

Indirect statistical support for the proposition that U.S. commercial banks followed their customers, nonfinancial corporations, abroad comes from an interesting study conducted by Arvind Jain of McGill University.[41] Jain regressed the ratio of the assets of U.S. commercial banks over the assets of all banks on the U.S. share of total trade and the U.S. share of total direct foreign investment in each of the countries in the study sample of forty-six countries. Using data from 1982, he reported the results of his estimated equation and found a strong statistical relationship between U.S. bank loans to a country and contemporaneous U.S. investment and trade activity. Jain observes: "If these ties were not important, U.S. as well as non-U.S. banks would determine their exposure in each country solely upon the characteristics of the loan, which . . . should not change with the lending bank's country of origin."[42]

Involuntary Lending and Revulsion

As for the fifth and sixth features of the loan push story—initially continued lending to support unstable borrowers and then revulsion on the part of the borrowers—that are apparent in the stories of the 1920s, the first response has been more in evidence with respect to major borrowing nations. The situation in the 1980s is more difficult to interpret than that a half century earlier because of the existence today of both multinational institutions and national institutions in the developed countries that play an active role in international financial markets. These institutions include the International Monetary Fund (IMF), the World Bank, and the central banks in the West, especially the U.S. Federal Reserve Board. Would the revulsion stage have already leapfrogged the stage of continued lending if these institutions had not prompted further syndications—individual banks joining together to subscribe to a loan—to continue to provide credit to the major borrowing nations during their current period of difficulty? Did the phenomenon of so-called "nonspontaneous" or "involuntary" lending that followed the crystallization of crisis in 1982 prove that the revulsion occurred at that time? Would the banks be able to maintain their hard line on the terms for reschedulings and new credits if not for the existence of the IMF and its austerity program for troubled debtor nations?[43] Whatever the proper responses to these questions, by 1983–84, U.S. banks had significantly reduced their lending to the developing countries.[44]

Overall, the parallels between the loan adventures of the 1920s and the 1970s are strong. The evidence suggests that the view of banks as aggressive credit promoters is superior to the view of banks as passive recipients of loan applications. The bankers are better seen as the active agents, literally covering the globe to find new borrowers.

It is this perspective—inclusive of the six features identified above as components of a broader loan push doctrine—that is the subject of inquiry in this book. The following chapter will further explain the idea of loan pushing. Succeeding chapters will consider loan pushing in the context of competing explanations for the current international debt crisis toward both understanding the banking problem and exposing the limitations of conventional economic theory in explaining the crisis.

NOTES

1. Max Winkler, *Foreign Bonds: An Autopsy* (Philadelphia: Roland Swain Company, 1933), pp. 86–87.
2. Ibid., p. 87.
3. Ibid., p. 47.
4. Ibid.
5. Ibid.
6. Ibid., p. 87–88.
7. Cleona Lewis, *America's Stake in International Investments* (Washington, DC: The Brookings Institution, 1938), pp. 377–88. The history of lending to Cuba prior to the 1959 revolution was especially notorious. For details on the "dance of the millions" see Leland Hamilton Jenks, *Our Cuban*

Colony (New York: Vanguard Press, 1928) and Henry Wallich, *Monetary Problems of an Export Economy: The Cuban Experience 1914–1947.* (Cambridge: Harvard University Press), 1950.

8. Lewis, *America's Stake*, p. 378, offered the examples of (1) Ulen and Company's contract to build the port works in Colombia; (2) Frederick Snare and Company's financing of public works contracts in Peru; (3) Warren Brothers road-building contracts in Argentina, Chile, Colombia, Cuba and Guatemala; and (4) Foundation Company building roads, sanitation works, and public works in Peru and Bolivia and public works in Argentina, Chile, and Colombia. She does not detail the extent to which the contracts were completely fulfilled.

9. Ibid., p. 379.

10. Ibid.

11. Henry Wallich, "The Future of Latin American Dollar Bonds," *American Economic Review* 33 (June 1943).
Wallich (pp. 326–27, emphasis added) observed:

> It was pointed out by Professor Hansen in his testimony before the Temporary National Economic Committee that the American prosperity of the 1920's was due not to any inherent characteristics of our economic system but to the cooperation of a number of stimulating factors. One of these factors was the high level of our exports, paid for in part with the proceeds of our loans. It cannot, of course, be proved that the loans increased exports by an equal amount. Since, however, most countries had only limited exchange reserves of their own, insufficient to permit a continuously passive current balance, a fair presumption exists that the increase in exports was roughly equivalent to our loans. These additional exports produced an *export multiplier* effect and thus tended to raise national income by a multiple of their own value. From this gross gain in national income we must, of course deduct the losses suffered through the default of the loans, in order to arrive at the net gain attributable to the loans. But these losses have been smaller than the loans themselves, since the defaulted bonds still retain some market value. Hence their subtraction from the gross gains, which were larger than the loan-induced exports (which we have assumed to be equal to these loans), still leaves a considerable margin of net gain for the United States.

Wallich's comments indicate that foreign lending can be analyzed in terms of the transfer problem so popular in the pure theory of international trade. See, for example, Harry G. Johnson, "The Transfer Problem and Exchange Stability," *Journal of Political Economy* 44 (June 1956): 212–25. For a contemporary discussion of debt and the transfer problem see Rudiger Dornbusch and Stanley Fischer, "The World Debt Problem: Origins and Prospects" *Journal of Development Planning* no. 16 (1985): 71–75.

12. Ibid., p. 327n.4.

13. Winkler, *Foreign Bonds*, p. 88.

14. Lewis, *America's Stake*, passim.

15. Wallich, *Dollar Bonds*, pp. 322–23.
16. Marcello de Cecco, "The International Debt Problem in the Interwar Period," *Banca Nazionale Del Lavoro Quarterly Review* 38 (March 1985): 58.
17. Vincent P. Crawford, "International Lending, Long-Term Credit Relationships, and Dynamic Contract Theory" (Discussion Paper 84–14, University of California at San Diego, 1984) 33–34.
18. Authors' personal correspondence, July 6, 1984.
19. David Folkerts-Landau, "The Changing Role of International Bank Lending in Development Finance" *IMF Staff Papers* 32 (June 1985): 320.
20. Ibid.
21. Ibid., p. 318.
22. Ibid.
23. Ibid., p. 321. On the activities of international councils of bondholders Folkerts-Landau refers to Edwin M. Borchard and William H. Wynne, *State Insolvency and Foreign Bondholders* (New Haven: Yale University Press, 1951).
24. Ibid., p. 321 n.2. Folkerts-Landau indicates that "[t]heir shares were computed by Corporation of Foreign Bondholders, various *Annual Reports*, 1930–36 [and] does not include defaults on foreign bonds that had been issued before 1920."
25. Rudiger Dornbusch, "International Debt and Economic Instability," in *Debt, Financial Stability and Public Policy* (Kansas City, MO: Federal Reserve Board, 1987), p. 63. For a more detailed autopsy on the returns obtained on bonds issued in the 1920s and 1930s by developing countries see Barry Eichengreen and Richard Portes, "Debt and Default in the 1930s: Causes and Consequences," *European Economic Review* 30 (1986): 599.
26. T.H. Donaldson, *International Lending By Commercial Banks* (New York: Wiley and Sons, 1979), p. 159 (emphasis added).
27. Charles P. Kindleberger, *Manias, Panics, and Crashes: A History of Financial Crises* (New York: Basic Books, 1978), pp. 23–24 (emphasis added). In a similar vein Ronald McKinnon refers to "overlending" by the commercial banks during this period in "The International Capital Market and Economic Liberalization in LDCs," *The Developing Economies* 22 (September 1984): 476–81.
28. Ibid., p. 24.
29. Peter Field, David Shirreff, and William Ollard, "The IMF and Central Banks Flex Their Muscles," *Euromoney*, January 1983, p. 35.
30. Andrew Brimmer, "International Capital Markets and the Financing of Economic Development," in *Addresses, Essays, Lectures of Andrew Felton Brimmer* 13 (Washington, DC: Federal Reserve Library 1973): 17. Similar positions have been taken by such disparate observers as Cheryl Payer, "Will the Government Bail Out the Banks?" *The Bankers Magazine* 160 (Spring 1977): 84 and Stephen I. Davis, *The Management Function in International Banking* (New York: John Wiley and Sons, 1979), pp. 19–20.

31. Brimmer, "International Capital Markets," p. 17.
32. Ibid., p. 15.
33. Ibid., p. 16.
34. The World Bank, *World Debt Tables: External Public Debt of LDCs,* December 15, 1974, p. xvii.
35. Davis, "The Management Function," pp. 23–25. Davis provides estimates that indicate that from the end of 1974 to the end of 1977 banks in the Group of Ten countries and Switzerland raised their net exposure in Brazil by 335 percent, in Mexico by 317 percent, in South Africa by 197 percent, in the Soviet Union by an astonishing 8,457 percent (although the initial base was negligible), in Poland by 284 percent, and in Peru by 285 percent.
36. S.C. Gwynne, "Adventures in the Loan Trade," *Harper's,* 267 (September 1983): 22–26.
37. Ibid., pp. 25–26.
38. Ibid., p. 26.
39. When the banks stop lending the stimulus ceases, and the banks will try to stop lending when repayment difficulties emerge. See James R. Barth and James Pelzman, *International Debt; Conflict and Resolution* (Fairfax, VA: George Mason University, 1984), pp. 21–27.
40. Steve Frazier, "Oils Lure Led Mexico and Banks into Payment Woes," *Wall Street Journal,* 15 May 1984 (emphasis added).
41. Arvind K. Jain, "International Lending Patterns of U.S. Commercial Banks," *Journal of International Business Studies* 17 (Fall 1986): 73–88.
42. Ibid., pp. 76–79. Elsewhere Jain reports that relatively smaller U.S. banks seem to have stayed even closer to their clients than the relatively larger banks engaged in foreign lending. See Arvind K. Jain, "Bank Size and International Lending Patterns," *Economics Letters* 22 (1986): 55–59.
43. See "A War of Nerves over Latin Debt," *Business Week,* 18 June 1984.
44. Henry S. Terrell and Rodney H. Mills, "U.S. Banks' Lending to Developing Countries: A Longer-Term View," International Finance Discussion Paper No. 255 (Washington, DC: Board of Governors of the Federal Reserve Board, July 1985).

CHAPTER 2

Loan Pushing and the Global Debt Crisis

The loan push doctrine was depicted in the previous chapter as a complex of attributes. But the specific act of "pushing" or "forcing" loans requires elaboration. Obviously, it does not mean that bankers force officials in LDCs at gunpoint to accept loan contracts. The act of pushing a loan must involve the structure of incentives offered to potential borrowers—incentives that are out of step with the risk characteristics possessed by the borrowers.

THE BRIMMER CONCEPT

Brimmer states that pushing loans entails a drastic softening of terms related to the expectations of potential borrowers. When the Eurocurrency banks turned their attention toward the developing countries, the banks reduced the spread between their cost of funds, the London Interbank Offering Rate (LIBOR), and the loan rate they offered LDC borrowers. In addition, they lengthened the maturities on the loans and substantially raised the amounts they were willing to lend. From Brimmer's perspective, in an effort to dispose of their surplus funds in the periphery, the commercial banks made their terms particularly attractive to LDC borrowers.[1]

The pattern of declining spreads and lengthening maturities is especially clear between the final quarter of 1975 and the final quarter of 1979 for both non-OPEC LDCs and OPEC nations at the aggregate level. (See Table 1; all tables appear in the Appendix.) The pattern is also

15

plain for the major debtor nations. (See Table 2.) Signs of reversal became visible in 1980 and 1981 as repayment difficulties accelerated and as reschedulings were negotiated on harsher terms than the initial loans.

The key point in the Brimmer concept of loan pushing is the implied segmentation of the global financial market between borrowers in the developed and developing countries. The commercial banks turn toward the LDCs only when loan demand from sources in the developed world weakens sufficiently, at the terms required to bring forth additional demand, to be perceived as unprofitable. To make the new loans in the countries on the "outskirts" of dense industrialization may necessitate comparatively soft terms for borrowers there, but the lenders still perceive those terms as sufficiently adequate to produce a desired degree of profitability.

Whether such a perception was reasonable or rational is an open question that we shall take up in greater detail below. The Brimmer concept finds reinforcement in the fact that although there was a downward trend in the average spread over LIBOR charged to LDC borrowers by the commercial banks in the late 1970s, the spread was consistently higher than that offered to borrowers in the developed countries. (See Table 3.) Whether or not the spreads charged to LDC borrowers were sufficient to cover the risks is also an open question; but insofar as the spreads remained higher than those charged borrowers in advanced countries they at least bore a semblance of being an outlet for preserving profitability.[2]

THE KINDLEBERGER CONCEPT

Kindleberger, while acknowledging that his observation (quoted in Chapter 1) about banks " 'forcing' loans on the LDCs is a bit hyperbolic," has also attempted to give precision to the concept of loan "pushing." He argues that sharp differences exist in opportunities to contract for interest rates across borrowers with varying risk characteristics.[3] Kindleberger constructs a position for the shape of the supply curve for loanable funds that resembles the implications of the ancient mercantilist doctrine of the utility of poverty for the labor supply function: ". . . when interest rates decline sharply *for any reason*, lenders look around to make loans at high interest rates and take greater risks, in a sort of backward-bending supply curve, to preserve their old incomes."[4] The mercantilists, in parallel fashion, believed that falling wage rates would induce more effort (or greater labor supply) from workers who were seeking to maintain their target incomes.

Reconciling the target income idea with profit-maximization remains unclear, but the Kindleberger concept still has merit if one simply assumes that differential demand elasticities for credit exist across the two regions. The commercial banks' movement toward LDC borrowers with respect to terms could have been due to the elasticity of loan demand by "center" borrowers being much greater than the elasticity of demand by borrowers from the periphery. Therefore, a point is reached on a phase of loan expansion when the commercial banks perceive that they will have to make unacceptably large reductions in the terms to continue lending to the center borrowers. But Kindleberger's model shows the banks facing softer terms at the center for *any* reason, presumably including central bank monetary policy, will turn to a new set of borrowers.

In fact, Kindleberger argues that the recent buildup of LDC indebtedness was triggered by former Federal Reserve chairman Arthur Burns's "cheap money efforts . . . in the early part of 1971;" this depressed interest rates in the Eurodollar market and led the participating banks to chase down potential borrowers in the LDCs, particularly in Latin America.[5]

THE ESSENCE OF LOAN PUSHING

Thus, the commercial banks are portrayed as attempting to avert reductions in their profitability or earnings by shifting toward LDC borrowers. The banks were unwilling to accept a decline in terms great enough to achieve full absorption of their loanable funds at the center. On the other hand, softening the terms for periphery borrowers to a sufficient degree, stimulating their consent to contract for large sums of indebtedness, would still leave the banks, rightly or wrongly, with what they considered to be adequate margins for profitability.

"Loan pushing," then, amounts to the design of loan packages that attract borrowers who were formerly denied access to international credit markets altogether or who were, at a minimum, denied such large amounts of funds. The LDC borrowers' risk characteristics, which presumably were responsible for their previous exclusion from easy credit terms, remain unchanged. But suddenly, instead of being pariahs for the major international lending institutions they find creditors clamoring for their attention. As Richard Bernal puts it, the medium-income LDCs became the targets of ferocious competition on the part of the transnational banks, so much so that especially after the OPEC boom the

". . . banks, in 1974–75, [abandoned] their conservative tenets of banking and [assumed] an aggressive attitude of offering loans to countries at attractive terms. . . ."[6] However, in light of recent events and discoveries, one wonders how conservative bankers are in the first place.

To clarify the relationship between loan pushing and the current international debt crisis, we need first to examine some facts and statistics. For example, precisely which countries are in trouble? Which banks are in trouble? How can we tell? A series of indicators are frequently used to identify nations that have lost their creditworthiness and banks that have made imprudent loans. The theoretical basis for these indicators is typically obscure, but they nevertheless are used repeatedly as guideposts for those engaged in the debt watch. This chapter examines these indicators to determine their implications for nations or lending institutions whose credit practices have crossed bounds of reasonableness.

DANGER SIGNS FOR COUNTRIES?

Criteria used to identify problem countries include (1) their total external debt, (2) their per capita external debt, (3) their debt to GNP (or GDP) ratio, (4) their debt-export ratio, (5) their debt-service ratio, and (6) their consistency (or inconsistency) with Simonsen's interest rate rule (explained later in this chapter).

Taken in isolation, a nation's total external debt reveals nothing about its capacity to meet its debt obligations. But to the extent that claims on a nation are held by a group of commercial banks, this measure does help identify the countries that are likely to warrant the greatest attention from bankers. The column on total external debt of fourteen major LDC borrowers in 1985 shown in Table 4 should make it clear why Brazil, Mexico, Argentina, and Venezuela—the big four of Latin American debtor nations—figure so prominently in news about the global debt crisis. Brazil and Mexico, in particular, must rank high on the list of countries on the multinational banks' watch list. Their absolute levels of foreign indebtedness are twice as great as those of any other developing countries. Bankers also might be more accommodating when these countries experience repayment difficulties, since they can figure so prominently in the lending institutions' portfolios. (Table 12 will demonstrate that U.S. banks are the major lenders to Latin borrowers.)

Table 4 also distinguishes between external public debt and total external debt of each of the countries shown. External public debt includes loans taken by public sector enterprises, loans taken by governments to finance fiscal deficits, and publicly guaranteed loans—all drawn at year end, and net of repayments of principal and write offs at year end. (Obviously this distinction is meaningless in Poland's case since its private sector is negligible.)

In contrast with total external debt, per capita external debt is a measure that suggests the magnitude of the task if a government was to tax each member of its population by an equal sum to pay off its entire foreign debt. This measure, of course, ignores distributional considerations as well as the age composition of the population, but in a crude way describes the mean debt burden faced by a nation.

Ratios, Ratios, and More Ratios

The first column of Table 5 reports on the external debt per capita for selected nations. In this case the list is not limited to LDCs nor to major borrowers in terms of absolute levels of external debt. Some surprises are evident. For instance, if per capita external debt is taken as the relevant gauge of a country's creditworthiness, the biggest trouble spots in 1983 would have been several countries in Scandinavia, as well as the countries of Israel, Ireland, Switzerland, and Canada. The recently wealthy oil-exporting principality of Kuwait also ranks high on this list, but the first "true" developing countries to appear on the list are Venezuela, Panama, and Costa Rica.

Table 5 also reports estimates of per capita GNP or GDP for each of the same countries, which makes it possible to calculate debt-GNP (or GDP) ratios. The results of the latter calculation appear in column three of Table 5. Intuitively, the debt-GNP ratio permits one to ask what are the requirements if a nation was to surrender a portion of its annual product in a given year to pay off its entire foreign debt. A possible (albeit arbitrary) criterion for concluding that a nation's repayment prospects are viable is to hold that a country with a debt-to-GNP ratio below 50 percent is in good fiscal shape. As the estimates in Table 5 indicate, nations such as Israel, Ireland, Portugal, Costa Rica, Chile, Morocco, and Jamaica would have exhausted their entire national product in 1983 if for some reason they had sought to pay off their entire foreign debt out of their GNP (or GDP).

Table 6 provides a companion list of the twenty countries with the highest estimated total external debt-to-GNP (or GDP) ratios in 1983 as well as comparative data for 1985. Virtually all the countries that appear on this "top twenty" list are customarily classified as LDCs. Among the big four Latin borrowers, Argentina and Mexico make it onto the list in 1983 with rankings of seventeen and nineteen, respectively. Both Brazil and Venezuela came in below the 50 percent cutoff in 1983, and do not make the list (although by 1985 their ratios were 57 and 65 percent respectively). Plainly, the "worst" cases by 1985 are Jamaica, the Ivory Coast, Bolivia, and Morocco. Jamaica would have had to double its GDP to pay off its entire external debt at once. Poland, another nation that underwent repeated debt renegotiations in the early to mid-1980s, had a debt-GNP ratio of only 29 percent in 1983. From a strictly empirical standpoint a close fit between the debt-GNP ratio and creditworthiness is not apparent, although most of the nations listed in Table 6 have undergone recent debt reschedulings.

In Table 7, the ratios are updated to 1984 from an even more comprehensive list of nations. But here the numerator is restricted to estimates of long-term external debt, i.e., debt with an original maturity of at least one year. The numerator includes long-term public debt, publicly guaranteed debt, and private nonguaranteed debt. This particular "top twenty" list is dominated by African, Central American, and Caribbean nations. None of the big four Latin borrowers make the list (even Mexico, grading out worst among the four with a 54 percent ratio is not included). Virtually all the countries on the 1984 top twenty list have experienced debt repayment difficulties, but so have various nations that do not come close to reaching the group.

The same table also shows how debt-GNP ratios have changed since 1970. For every country on the 1984 top twenty list, the long-term debt-GNP ratio has increased over the course of about fifteen years. In some cases, e.g., Mauritania and Nicaragua, the increase has bordered on the fantastic (also see the notes for Table 6). There can be no doubt that a remarkable change took place in the relative external debt positions of many LDCs between 1970 and 1984. The loan pushing view suggests that the countries themselves were not remarkably different between 1970 and 1984, aside from the ramifications of their accumulated foreign indebtedness. All that had changed was the posture of the international banks toward them as potential borrowers. In fact, although none of the big four Latin borrowers appear in Table 7 they too display a similar, marked (although somewhat less dramatic) growth in long-term external debt-GNP ratios between 1970 and 1984. Brazil's ratio rose from 11.7 to 44 percent, Mexico's from 17 to 54 percent, Argentina's from 23.6 to 46.8 percent, and Venezuela's from a meager 8.7 percent to 52.7 percent.[7]

A major conceptual problem exists in addition to the empirical anomalies associated with use of the debt-GNP ratio. Typically, external debt is denominated in foreign currencies, and aggregate measures like GNP do not isolate the sources of foreign exchange for LDCs. Total GNP certainly does not measure the availability of foreign exchange that can be used to meet claims held by foreigners.

It is often assumed that export earnings are the critical source of foreign exchange for developing countries. Of course, a nation need not earmark all of its export earnings to meet debt obligations, and if a nation runs up a net trade deficit its stock of foreign debt will increase. Modellers such as William Cline or Dornbusch and Fischer, seeking to analyze prospects for debt repayment, assume that all trade surpluses attained will go in full toward debt payments, but if foreign trade is the key source of foreign exchange the trade surplus may set no more than an upper boundary on viable debt payments.[8]

But the emphasis on export earnings as the critical source of foreign exchange has led to the use of the debt-export ratio as an alternative to the debt-GNP ratio as a gauge of creditworthiness. In Table 8 debt-export ratios for major LDC borrowers in 1985 are reported. It is striking that among the four large Latin borrower countries the ratios range from 261 percent for Venezuela to 576 percent for Argentina. If foreign debt must be paid in foreign currency, and if foreign currency is obtained via export earnings, Nigeria was the only nation in the table that could have had any possibility of paying its entire foreign debt in 1985.

Of course, the entire foreign debt does not come due at once, since the annual interest bill plus a portion of the principal is due in any year. This means, in turn, that a debt-export ratio above 100 percent need not be a cause for worry, although exactly which ratio should trigger alarms remains a mystery. William Cline has suggested that a "debt/export range of 200 per cent [is] required for normal creditworthiness."[9] But Dragoslav Avramovic, a long-time student of creditworthiness indicators, immediately expressed skepticism about Cline's cutoff, observing that: "This 200 percent is an arbitrary number . . . and one might just as easily say 100 per cent or 300 per cent."[10] Still, it may be significant that eight out of the twelve countries on which estimates are available had debt-export ratios in excess of 200 percent in 1985 (see Table 8).

Some Complaints

We emphasize that debt-export ratios above 200 percent *may* be significant because there are conceptual limitations associated with this measure as well. Dornbusch and Fischer have highlighted three limitations. First, they say that an improved measure would have a nation's true interest bill in the numerator.[11] Receiving interest payments from borrowers is a banker's primary concern in assessing their ongoing creditworthiness. This modification presses toward use of the debt-service ratio rather than the debt-export ratio. Second, while they acknowledge that the debt-export ratio may be a useful measure of an economy's "liquidity needs," Dornbusch and Fischer propose that if concern is aimed toward "the vulnerability of an economy to a cutoff of lending, it would be preferable to have a variable in the denominator representing the economy's potential net earnings of foreign currency."[12] Certainly, total annual exports do not capture the net foreign exchange concept; perhaps a statistic such as the net change in central bank reserves of foreign exchange would come closer to the denominator Dornbusch and Fischer have in mind. Certainly the denominator typically would be a much smaller number than gross annual exports. Third, Dornbusch and Fischer point out that the debt-export ratio is a snapshot indicator of the economy's performance that fails to incorporate potential "future developments that would affect a country's ability to pay its debts."[13]

Dornbusch and Fischer go on to add that: "In some instances, a transitorily rising debt/export ratio may be entirely consistent with improvement of a country's ability to service its external debt." This would be the case when "debt accumulation has investments and future export earnings as counterparts;" then "a rising debt/export ratio is a leading indicator of future prosperity, not catastrophe." But Dornbusch and Fischer do not foresee such a benign outcome on the horizon today because the recent debt growth in LDCs has not been, in their words, "productive."[14]

The Debt-Cycle Hypothesis

The benign vision of increasing debt-export ratios is imbedded in the standard version of the Avramovic "debt-cycle hypothesis." In a 1964 volume, Avramovic and coauthors proposed that as it undergoes economic development, each nation typically goes through a debt cycle spanning thirty-six years. During twenty-five of these years a nation would face growing indebtedness.[15] The Avramovic cycle was advanced as the stylized characterization of debt and growth, paralleling Simon Kuznets' characterization of a general pattern of income distribution and economic growth, and Raymond Goldsmith's characterization of a general relationship between financial layering and economic growth. Summarized in the World Bank's *World Development Report* for 1985, the debt-cycle hypothesis proposes that growing nations pass through five stages, three of which encompass Avramovic's stylized thirty-six years.[16]

The debt cycle hypothesis treats nations as biological entities that pass through stages. First a nation is a "young debtor" as its growth process begins—facing a trade deficit, incurring a net outflow of interest payments, receiving a net inflow of "capital," and experiencing increasing debt. Here its debt-export ratio presumably is rising, perhaps dramatically. In the second stage, it becomes a "mature debtor." Its trade deficit declines and a surplus emerges on current account in this stage, and it continues to have a net outflow of interest payments while its "capital" inflow continues to be positive although at a declining rate. Similarly, its debt continues to grow (as does its debt-export ratio), but also at a declining rate. In stage three it moves into the final eleven years of Avramovic's thirty-six year cycle where it becomes a "debt reducer." Now the country's trade surplus grows, the outflow of interest payments drops, it becomes an exporter of "capital," and its net foreign debt (and debt-export ratio) falls.[17]

The final two stages—the "young creditor" and "mature creditor" stages—lie beyond the thirty-six years of Avramovic's cycle. The *World Development Report* for 1985 displays more confidence in the broad validity of the cycle than the exact Avramovic time frame, indicating that "The debt cycle model does not predict reliably how long a country may remain in any given stage of the debt cycle."[18] There may be, in fact, some frictions in passing on to the next (higher) stage, requiring appropriate policy choices. But the message is clear. To the extent that all nations—at least those that are capitalistic—develop in this fashion, the current debt problems of various LDCs are nothing more than "growing pains." A dramatic increase in the debt-export ratio is no more than a signal that a nation is truly on the way to sustained real economic growth via foreign borrowing.

Of course, Dornbusch and Fischer's observation that the recent wave of loans has not been used "productively" is problematic for the applicability of the hypothesis. One also might wonder what type of cycle the Latin American borrowers are riding since their debt-export ratios rose sharply in the 1920s and 1930s and then fell to relatively low levels for three decades, only to rise again in the 1970s and 1980s. Avramovic himself has little to say about his own hypothesis today and much to say about the weaknesses of institutional arrangements for coping with the debt crisis.[19]

Service for the Debt?

What about using the debt-service ratio in place of the debt-export ratio? It can also be used, as it was by Avramovic and his coauthors in 1964, to chart their hypothesized debt cycle.[20] The projected movements of debt-service would be much the same as those of the debt-export ratio. But even in the early 1960s, Avramovic and his coauthors doubted its effectiveness "as a meaningful indicator of the *long-run* aspect of debt servicing capacity," arguing instead that the "only important factor from the long-run point of view is the rate of growth of production."[21]

Earlier in the same volume, Avramovic and the others expressed bewilderment over when a debt-service ratio is at the " 'critical' level— 5%, 10%, 15%, or 20%?"[22] They cited a study by Raymond Mikesell that identified several empirical paradoxes associated with the debt-service ratio. For example, Mikesell reported that Argentina had a debt-service ratio of 40 percent in the 1890s and maintained loan payments, but with a ratio of 35 percent in 1933 it defaulted on public debt obligations. In 1947 it set limits on foreign transfers despite a debt-service ratio of ten percent.[23] The debt-service ratio is limited conceptually, Avramovic and his coauthors argued, because it is comprised of only two of nine variables they believed were relevant for assessing a nation's debt-service capability. Therefore, the critical level for the debt-service ratio was hard to identify.[24]

Nevertheless, for completeness, we have examined data on debt-service ratios. Tables 9 and 10 provide estimates of debt-service ratios in 1985 for the major borrowers listed in Table 4 with the exception of Poland, for which no estimates were available. Here the rule-of-thumb criterion is that a country in trouble often has a debt-service ratio in excess of 20 percent. Table 9 reports ratios of payments made on external public debt to exports of goods and services, while Table 10 reports ratios of payments made on total long-term debt to the same numerator. By the 20 percent rule, all of the big four Latin borrowers except for Venezuela should have been experiencing problems servicing their debt. Mexico's situation plainly appears to be the rockiest.

It is noteworthy that several subsaharan African nations whose total *absolute* external debt is too low for them to appear in Table 4 look to be in major difficulty using *relative* indicators of overindebtedness. For example, Somalia had a ratio of total long-term external debt to GNP of 53.5 percent and a debt-service (long-term debt) ratio of 44.8 percent in 1985. Comparable figures for Togo were 121.1 percent and 27.5 percent, respectively. Both Nigeria and the Ivory Coast are included in Table 4, although at the low end of major borrowers. For Nigeria the ratios were a remarkably low 17.8 percent for the debt-GNP ratio but 32.1 percent for the debt-service ratio in 1985. Nigeria's low debt-GNP ratio, coupled with its problems in making payments, reveals again the empirical anomalies associated with these indicators. Because absolute external indebtedness is not unusually high for the African nations (individually or even as a group) they are unlikely to extract significant concessions from commercial bank lenders. Nonetheless, these nations can still be faced with immense policy conflicts in trying to service the loans their leaders have taken on without the leverage the large Latin borrowers can exercise on occasion. All of these African nations have experienced problems in making debt payments.

The Simonsen Rule

The final criterion for identification of problem countries we consider here is the Simonsen rule. Mario Simonsen, a one-time planning minister in Brazil, has proposed that the growth rate of a nation's exports ought to exceed the interest rate at which it can currently borrow.[25] According to Simonsen, if this situation does not exist, a country with a significant prior debt accumulation is liable to run into trouble. This criterion, however, is not particularly different from the debt-service ratio, except that the Simonsen criterion emphasizes the direction and rate of change of the debt price and an indicator of foreign exchange accumulation. Table 11 reports the average annual growth rates for the period 1980 through 1985 for exports and the average interest rate in 1985 on external public borrowing for the countries listed in Table 4, again with the exception of Poland.

By this summary measure, the only countries in Table 11 that should have been free of debt worries were Mexico, Turkey, and South Korea. Venezuela and Nigeria evidently would be courting disaster. Mexico's difficulties in meeting annual debt payments, in fact, probably have superseded Venezuela's by at least one order of magnitude. Simonsen's criterion may prove to be more consistent with the facts concerning which countries actually have experienced major problems in making good on their debts if comparable data had been available for export growth in 1985 alone, rather than an annual average for the entire interval 1980–85. On the other hand, the annual average for half a decade should be more representative of the customary recent export performance of each country. However, one might then prefer data on the annual average interest rate on external debt over the same interval for a more valid comparison.

Cline has compared nominal export growth with LIBOR plus 1 percent for six major borrowing nations—Brazil, Mexico, Argentina, Korea, Venezuela, and Chile—for 1973 through 1982. He finds that generally, export growth exceeded LIBOR plus 1 percent for all the countries in that time period with the exception of (1) the depression year 1975, when only South Korea displayed a positive differential and (2) especially 1982, where the differential turned negative for all six countries. Moreover, in both 1981 and 1982 for non-oil LDCs (taken as a group), export growth lagged well behind Cline's interest rate measure. In 1982 export growth rates were typically negative.[26] This is, of course, consistent with the fact that repayment problems became evident in this period. However, renewed export growth in 1983 and 1984 led Cline to reach excessively optimistic conclusions about prospects for repayment thereafter.[27]

An Infallible Summary Statistic?

Dornbusch and Fischer have also considered a variety of these summary statistics to assess the status of developing country indebtedness. They have estimated debt-export ratios (total external) for Latin American nations as a group for selected years and have found that in 1929 the ratio was 149, by 1935 it reached an extremely high 224, but had fallen by 1955 to 60. In 1973 the debt-export ratio had climbed to 176, by 1978 was up to 212, and by 1983 reached 243, surpassing the 1935 estimate.[28] To the extent that 1935 was a period in which Latin nations were experiencing widespread default on loans contracted in the 1920s, Dornbusch and Fischer can argue that the 1983 estimate gives cause for alarm.

They also have examined a measure of the "real" prime rate for developing countries, which was defined as the U.S. prime rate minus the rate of increase of the dollar price of non-oil developing country exports over the course of the *subsequent* year. They legitimately depicted the early 1970s as "a debtor's paradise," since their measure of the real prime rate for LDCs was hugely negative during that period, e.g., −27.1 percent in 1972 and −27.4 percent in 1973. Aside from the depression year 1974, the real prime rate whether negative or positive stayed low for the developing countries throughout the remainder of the 1970s. However, in 1980 it turned sharply positive at 20.3 percent and by 1981 had reached 25.5 percent, the last year for which Dornbusch and Fischer report an estimate. It is notable that late 1979 was the point when the U.S. central bank officially adopted a money targeting policy, which amounted *de facto* to a high nominal interest rate-disinflation policy.[29]

In addition, Dornbusch and Fischer observe that between 1973 and 1983 the total nominal growth in LDC external debt was 446 percent. Even adjusted for inflation, the rate of growth was still a spectacular 165 percent (or 9.3 percent per annum) in real terms over the same period. Real debt growth far exceeded real income growth, so that the debt-GDP ratio across LDCs in general rose by 67 percent.[30] Although Dornbusch and Fischer both readily acknowledge—unlike Cline—that there is an ongoing debt crisis, they are uncertain about the summary statistic that can genuinely separate debtor countries likely to be facing payment problems from those likely to be making payments smoothly. They note, correctly, that the theory of summary measures of external indebtedness is not complete.[31]

DANGER SIGNS FOR BANKS?

Have particular banks overlent to less developed countries? Unfortunately, the theory of summary measures for identification of banks with imprudent LDC lending practices is similarly incomplete. There is uncertainty not only about the correct measures that will distinguish the solvent from the insolvent lender to developing countries, there is a shortage of data.

In terms of actual commercial bank practice, again particularly in the Eurobanking sector, certain conventional rules have evolved that are used to assess the status of the lenders. For example, Stephen Davis refers to a 50-50 rule that some Eurobankers consider—50 percent of loans should be interbank loans and 50 percent should be customer loans.[32] Or, "sound" bankers may seek to set a maximum limit of 10 to 20 percent of stockholders' funds on exposure to one borrower or related groups of borrowers.[33] This is one type of capital adequacy criterion that might be used to insure that risk is adequately diversified. In a similar fashion, a bank may seek to assure that no more than 10 percent of its total portfolio involves loans to one country, or no more than 50 to 100 percent of net worth to LDC loans.[34] When Davis surveyed Eurobankers about appropriate levels of loan loss reserves, they responded with percentages that varied from 0.75 percent to 5 percent, with the typical figure falling around 1.5 percent of outstanding customer loans.[35]

With adequate data it would be possible to ask which banks adhered to these rules as they expanded their loans to developing countries in the 1970s and 1980s. Those banks that did not follow these rules while increasing their exposure in lending to the periphery would be problem banks. It is not possible to obtain detailed data on individual banks or all these potential indicators; however, there is some aggregate data that is interesting and suggestive. If anything, the available data points broadly toward evidence of vulnerability in the asset structure of large U.S. banks.

Loan Clusters

Jain and Gupta report that the nine largest banks in the United States at the close of 1982 held 29.8 percent of the total assets of the U.S banking industry—but were carrying 63.5 percent of total U.S. loans to developing countries. Their ratio of relative exposure in LDC lending to their relative share in total U.S. banking assets was a remarkable—and potentially disturbing—213 percent. In contrast, the next fifteen banks, while holding 12.8 percent of U.S. banking assets in 1982, possessed 19.1 percent of U.S. bank loans to developing countries. In turn, their ratio of relative exposure to asset share was 149 percent. Over 125 regional banks held 21.3 percent of total U.S. banking assets and a 17.4 percent share of U.S. international loans. Their relative exposure to asset share ratio, therefore, was less than 100 percent.[36] The critical level for the percentage of the exposure to asset share ratio, however, remains unknown.

U.S. and British banks played an especially large role in the recent wave of lending. As Andrew Brimmer has observed: ". . . at the end of 1981, banks in the United States accounted for 29 percent of all loans by commercial banks to borrowers in developing countries outside the BIS [Bank for International Settlements]) reporting area [and] United Kingdom banks [accounted for] 20 percent."[37] Brimmer adds that from the perspective of the borrowing nations, reliance upon U.S. and U.K. banks appears even greater:

> LDCs that had no oil income had $314 billion of bank credit outstanding at the close of 1981. About 39 percent of this amount (or $123 billion) had been supplied by United States commercial banks. These LDCs had borrowed $50

billion from banks in the United Kingdom, representing 16 percent of their total indebtedness to commercial banks. Thus, over half (55 percent) of these countries' total indebtedness to commercial banks was owed to institutions in the United States and the United Kingdom.[38]

Based again upon 1981 data, Table 12 indicates the percentage of loans to major LDC borrowers, attributable to U.S. and to U.K. banks, for both non-oil exporting and oil-exporting developing countries. The critical role of both sets of banks in lending to these nations is directly evident from the table. One can imagine the potentially frantic discussions in major U.S. and U.K. bank boardrooms in the midst of the 1982 Argentine-British war. Furthermore, given the fact that only twenty-four U.S. banks are responsible for more than 80 percent of U.S. bank loans to developing countries, these banks must have a substantial stake in loans to each of these countries. Poland appears as a marked exception, only because other Western European banks played a large role in lending to Poland.

Reserving the Losses

Finally, consider the ratio of LDC indebtedness to U.S. and U.K. banks relative to their respective bank capitals in 1981. With respect to oil exporting countries taken as a group, the percent of LDC indebtedness for U.S. banks was 31.6 and for U.K. banks it was 23.8—but for oil importing countries, the figures were 192.5 percent for U.S. banks and 137.6 percent for U.K. banks. Particularly striking is the exposure data for Brazil and Mexico. The amount of debt due to U.S. banks relative to bank capital from Brazil alone in 1981 was 28.5 percent, while it was 18 percent for U.K. banks. For Mexico the percentage for U.S. banks was 34.2, and for U.K. banks it was 21.4 percent.[39]

The data points toward a marked emphasis in U.S. and U.K. bank portfolios on LDC loans by the start of the 1980s. Although LDC loans had not come to absolutely dominate loans to borrowers in MDCs, a relative shift toward much greater lending to LDCs had plainly taken place. These loans also were proving by the mid-1980s to have been, in retrospect, imprudent.

As recently as April 20, 1987, Chase Manhattan bank reported "a 28 percent drop in its net income for the first quarter, largely because of problem loans to Brazil."[40] Both Brazil and Ecuador suspended interest payments in March 1987, leading Chase to place $2.6 billion of its medium- and long-term loans to the two countries on a nonaccrual basis. Simultaneously Chase took the step of adding $34 million to its loan-loss provision. This lifted its total loan-loss provision to $160 million and raised its total reserve for potential losses to $1.1 billion, or 1.69 percent of total loans,[41] slightly above Davis's 1.5 percent rule for loan-loss reserves. Should Chase have been there all along? Did it arrive at that percentage too late? Perhaps the loan-loss reserve decision provides the best key to glimpsing the degree to which banks have been imprudent lenders—or, loan pushers.

More dramatic still was Citicorp's announcement on May 19, 1987 that it was raising its loan-loss reserves by $3 billion to a total of $5 billion, or a hefty and unprecedented 39 percent of the $12.8 billion in loans to its six largest developing country borrowers. Citicorp's decision under new Chairman John S. Reed can be interpreted as a repudiation of the posture (and posturing) of his predecessor, Walter Wriston, who often spoke as though developing country loans were riskless assets. Citicorp may have bitten a sufficiently large bullet to avoid future write-offs and to engage its borrowers more aggressively in rescheduling negotiations, since its loan-loss reserves now are quite substantial.[42]

In addition, if Citicorp was the lead bank in LDC loan syndications, its marked increase in loan-loss reserves puts competitive pressure on other syndicate participants to follow suit. After all, if the lead bank signals such skepticism about the quality of the syndicated loans to developing countries, other creditors cannot maintain a credible air of confidence in these assets. Citicorp is probably the only major bank with the financial resources to provide loan-loss reserves for such a large share of its loans to Third World countries. Citicorp's lead role in loan syndications seems to be indicated by the fact that William Rhodes, a senior vice president at Citicorp, served as chairman of an advisory committee to reschedule the Mexican debt during 1982 through 1984, and as chairman or co-chairman of advisory committees for Brazil, Argentina, Peru, and Uruguay during the same interval.[43] At a minimum, Citicorp's decision suggests its current management acknowledges that the recent lending wave to developing countries was imprudent.

An alternative but related tactic for the banks, given the existing debt overhang, has been advocated by Morgan Guaranty Senior Vice President Rimmer de Vries; that is, for the banks "to build capital several times faster than exposure to the major debtors."[44] He emphasizes that this step will also enhance the lenders' ability to act from a position of strength in further negotiations with the debtor nations. Further, de Vries comments:

> Even though the banks' LDC exposure-to-capital ratios have come down in the last few years—they are now below end-1977 levels—the bankers generally regard these ratios as uncomfortably high. For the large money center banks, exposure to the four largest borrowers in Latin America—Argentina, Brazil, Mexico, and Venezuela—ranged between 75 percent and 135 percent of primary capital at the end of 1985.[45]

He adds, somewhat smugly, that the percentage "was lowest for Morgan and around the middle of the range for most of the others."[46] But certainly even Morgan's 75 percent figure far exceeds the target exposure-to-capital ratio limits of 10 to 20 percent of stockholders' funds suggested previously by Stephen Davis. Moreover, how effectively can institutions with admittedly questionable portfolios raise additional equity "to build capital?"

WHAT INDICATORS DID THE BANKERS CONSIDER?

When they moved toward increased lending to developing countries, the commercial bankers presumably used some criteria to determine which countries ought to be the major beneficiaries of their desire to acquire assets in LDCs. Even if many banks simply followed some subset of "leading" banks, the leaders must have had some basis for selecting which countries to anoint with loans.

The Arida and Falk Hypotheses

Several possibilities—some provocative, some obvious—are available. One of the more provocative indicators the bankers may have used is implicit in an observation made by the Brazilian economist Persio Arida. Arida argues that there is a strong connection between those nations that have pursued liberalization policies and those nations that have become overindebted.[47] Arida's liberalization-debt nexus hypothesis, if valid, could be motivated by the tendency of bankers with ideological commitments to *laissez faire* economics to be predisposed to lend to countries that are engaged in freeing their markets. In the 1980s, U.S. and British bankers also might have felt a political push to lend to liberalizing regimes given the philosophical orientation of the Reagan and Thatcher administrations. Regardless, Arida's hypothesis suggests that the more liberalized a nation, the greater its external indebtedness.

In a similar fashion—with the political aspects predominant in his argument—Richard Falk has proposed a militarization-debt nexus hypothesis.[48] Militarized regimes, according to Falk, are most likely to have been recipients of large lines of credit.

Two remaining factors might have influenced bankers' lending practices: (1) the actual growth rate of a country as an indicator of prospects for repayment and (2) the extent of industrialization as a guide to prospects for economic development.

Some Regression Results

A simple regression analysis permits us to jointly examine the relative strength of these factors. We have used as the dependent variable in an ordinary least squares regression the growth in external public debt between 1970 and 1983 in current dollars. To assess the Arida hypothesis, World Bank economist Ramgopal Agarwala's distortion index is employed as an independent variable in the regression analysis.[49] Our sample is necessarily restricted to those countries for which Agarwala estimated the degree of distortion. There are problems with the Agarwala index, not the least of which is the fact that Argentina, Uruguay, and Chile all appear to be highly distorted economies despite the major liberalizations they undertook in the early 1980s. This is because Agarwala's index is calculated on data from the interval between 1970 and 1980, prior to extensive liberalization in the southern cone of Latin America. If anything, use of the Agarwala index would be weighted against supporting the Arida hypothesis, since Arida's hypothesis implies *less* distorted economies will experience *greater* credit inflows.

To assess the Falk hypothesis, defense expenditure as a percentage of total government expenditure is used as a second independent variable in the regression. The third independent variable utilized is the average annual growth rate of GDP between 1972 and 1983. The final independent variable is the percent of GDP attributable to industry in 1983.

The data is reported in Table 13 and the regression results for various combinations of variables are reported in Table 14. The only parameter that consistently has a statistically significant *t*-ratio is the estimated coefficient associated with the Agarwala index. Note also that the sign on the estimated coefficient is always negative, providing robust support for the Arida hypothesis. There appears to be an inverse relationship between distortion and indebtedness—or, the less "distorted" an economy the more rapid the rate of growth of its external public debt. The Falk hypothesis is called into question on the basis of these regressions, plus the remaining two independent variables, particularly when included in multivariate regressions.

More on the Falk Hypothesis

However, if reconsidered from the standpoint of the relationship between a country's receipt of U.S. military aid and its external indebtedness the Falk hypothesis seems to find slightly stronger support. Table 15 provides evidence of the external debt of the twenty largest recipients of U.S. military assistance ranging from Israel to Indonesia, in 1983. Nine out of the twenty countries had debt-GNP or GDP ratios in excess of 50 percent and eleven out of twenty had ratios in excess of 40 percent.

In a study prepared for the Rand Corporation in 1983, Walter Kitchenman detected a strong relationship between arms transfers and growth in external public debt, implying that borrowed funds were used to purchase weapons. Indirectly at least, some portion of commercial bank loans were being used to finance arms transfers. Kitchenman roughly estimated that arms purchases accounted for 16 percent of the average yearly flow of medium- and long-term credits from lenders to borrowing countries in the 1970s.[50]

Market-Making Once Again

But perhaps the most important consideration for the bankers was the location of their customers' sales. The potential tie between liabilities and assets (deposits and loans) is all too often ignored; loans that support purchases of customers' products can increase the volume of deposits and extend the banks' ability to make new loans. This is a special case, specific to banking, of the joint product phenomenon. The evidence advanced by Jain mentioned in Chapter 1 is consistent with this presumption.[51] Still unknown are the considerations used by the banks' customers to identify specific LDCs as sites for profitable penetration, thereby seducing their bankers into developing country lending.

LIQUIDITY VERSUS SOLVENCY

The magnitude of the world debt problem is reinforced by the unparalleled incidence of debt reschedulings by developing countries. A survey conducted by the World Bank found that there had been eighty-four multilateral reschedulings between 1975 and 1983. Out of about $90 billion in debt payments due between those years, over $75 billion was rescheduled.[52]

The fact that payments were typically rescheduled rather than declared in default by the lenders or repudiated by the borrowers is taken by some observers as a sign that the debt problem is manageable. From such a perspective the problem amounted to a temporary crisis of illiquidity for the countries. The developing countries were faced with a large-scale cash flow problem in 1982 and 1983 due largely to the contraction in their export income. They were illiquid in the sense that they were unable to convert their wealth into the form that would be required for them to meet their obligations. Illiquidity may cause short-term stress, but rescheduling is a reasonable solution since the countries have the intrinsic, long-term ability to pay.

In contrast, if countries are diagnosed as insolvent—as unable to meet payment sums even if their assets could be converted into the currency required by the loan contracts—then a quite different response is in order. The loans should then be written off. There would be no point in rescheduling, or sending good money after bad.

Cline Versus Dornbusch and Fischer

But is there a sharp dividing line between illiquidity and insolvency? Can a clear-cut distinction be made between instances when a country is illiquid and when it is insolvent? William Cline has proposed an empirical criterion based upon projections of balance of payments and the stock of the country's debt over a future time period. He has argued that "[i]f (using reasonable projections about the path of the international economy) such projections indicate a steady and substantial improvement in the debt situation, the premise of illiquidity is supported." On the other hand: "this premise would be challenged if further deterioration appears likely."[53]

On the basis of his 1983 forecasting model—a model created on the assumption that LDC growth is a function of MDC growth via trade relations and applied to the nineteen largest debtor countries, Cline concluded that the world debt problem is primarily a matter of illiquidity. Both balance of payments deficits and debt-export ratios for the major borrower nations would fall with global economic expansion. To preserve such an eventuality, Cline acknowledged that a 2.5 to 3 percent rate of real economic growth in the Organization for Economic Co-operation and Development (OECD) countries would be needed to provide the required export growth in the LDCs, to meet debt obligations.[54]

Data presented by Dornbusch and Fischer, however, indicates that in exactly one-half of the fourteen years between 1970 and 1983 the average real growth rate of GDP in the industrial countries exceeded the 3 percent threshold.[55] They also express skepticism about the validity of the three percent cutoff rate for maintaining the viability of developing countries' ability to pay. For Dornbusch and Fischer it is not merely the real growth rate that matters, but also the character of growth: "It is also important how growth comes about. The favoured combination is growth and a collapse of the dollar. The fall of the dollar would raise dollar prices in world trade and thus write down debts in real terms."[56] Indeed, Cline's formulation offers no assurance that 3 percent OECD growth rates will be achieved by a falling dollar.

The Fishlow View: An Invalid Distinction

But Albert Fishlow has argued that the liquidity-solvency distinction is inappropriate for nations. The distinction is drawn from an analogy with assessments of the status of business enterprises. Fishlow contends that ". . . it is not entirely adequate to speak of countries as if they were firms."[57] After all, Fishlow observes:

> For a firm, solvency is defined by an excess of assets over liabilities; otherwise it is bankrupt, and its creditors may be driven to seek its dissolution. Countries, on the other hand, cannot go bankrupt *in the same sense.* Their assets cannot be seized by a court and liquidated. Countries are solvent if they can manage to pay back their debts over some undefined future. They are liquid if they manage to service them now. What is of interest is whether developing countries will be liquid in the future, not whether they will have paid back their debts.[58]

Fishlow advocates a focus on the size of prevailing external debt relative to the general interest rate on the debt and the export growth rate. A country with balanced trade in a given year still will have to borrow to finance its existing interesting obligations. The rate of increase of its stock of external debt will equal the annual rate of interest. The rate of export growth versus that of the interest rate determines whether or not the debt-export ratio falls. When interest rates exceed export growth rates, a nation's debt-export ratio can be contained only by the euphemistically titled tactic of "import compression"—reducing import demand by lowering domestic income. Restraining imports permits the country to run a trade surplus. But success in achieving a trade surplus in this fashion appears no more attractive a prospect to Fishlow. (This "success," achieved in dramatic fashion by several LDC borrowers in 1984, led observers such as Cline to claim that the debt crisis had turned the corner.) A trade surplus accomplished by "import compression," Fishlow argues, "is not a good index of solvency," since it merely indicates that "developing countries pay more in interest than they receive in new loans."[59] Restraint on imports typically entails the unpleasant adoption of austerity measures in the countries involved.

Thus, Fishlow dismisses as impractical efforts to determine whether countries are illiquid or insolvent. Their long-term capacity to service their debt depends on interest rates and export growth rates. His criterion for country creditworthiness amounts to the equivalent of the Simonsen rule.

Since separation between liquidity and solvency originally was made in the analysis of the creditworthiness of business enterprises, presumably the distinction should have greater applicability to commercial banks than to their debtors. Judgement of whether a bank is illiquid or insolvent due to its developing country loans could serve as the basis for response by regulators. An illiquid bank justifiably may receive assistance from its nation's central bank or other possible lenders of last resort. In contrast, an insolvent bank may justifiably be subject to bankruptcy proceedings and dissolution.[60]

But the condition of banks with significant loans to developing countries is contingent on the capacity of the countries to pay their debt over time. Therefore, even if a sharp line could be drawn to determine if banks are illiquid or insolvent, a prior assessment of the ongoing creditworthiness of their debtors must be made. That assessment merely presses the regulators back onto the ambiguous terrain we covered at the beginning of this chapter.

Notes

1. Andrew Brimmer, "International Capital Markets and the Financing of Economic Development," in *Addresses, Essays, Lectures of Andrew Felton Brimmer* 13 (Washington, DC: Federal Reserve Library, 1973): 17.

2. See the discussion in Richard Bernal, "Transnational Banks, the International Monetary Fund and External Debt of Developing Countries," *Social and Economic Studies* 31 (1982): 72–73.
3. Authors' personal correspondence, July 6, 1984.
4. Ibid.
5. Ibid.
6. Bernal, "Transnational Banks," p. 72.
7. The World Bank, *World Development Report 1986* (New York: Oxford University Press, 1986), pp. 212–13.
8. See the model used by William Cline in "International Debt: Analysis, Experience and Prospects," *Journal of Development Planning*, no. 16 (1985): 25–55. Cline defines debt growth as the sum of interest obligations on the accumulated stock of debt and the trade deficit. A trade surplus implicitly reduces debt by the full amount of the surplus. Why Cline is willing to make such an assumption is not altogether clear. Cline is by no means unique in making such an assumption; despite their rejection of Cline's optimistic reading of prospects for debt crisis resolution, Dornbusch and Fischer also adopt a framework of analysis where the entire trade surplus is used to finance external debt. See Rudiger Dornbusch and Stanley Fischer, "The World Debt Problem: Origins and Prospects," *Journal of Development Planning*, no. 16 (1985): 57–81. There is no model of which the authors are aware that attempts to determine what percentage of a trade surplus, if achieved, will be devoted to financing external debt.
9. Ibid., p. 51.
10. Dragoslav Avramovic, "Debts In Early 1985: An Institutional Impasse," *Journal of Development Planning*, no. 16 (1985): 105.
11. Dornbusch and Fischer, "World Debt," p. 63.
12. Ibid., p. 63.
13. Ibid.
14. Ibid.
15. Dragoslav Avramovic et al., *Economic Growth and External Debt* (Baltimore: Johns Hopkins Press, 1964), pp. 47–84.
16. The World Bank, *World Development Report 1985* (New York: Oxford University Press, 1985), pp. 47–48.
17. Ibid., p. 47.
18. Ibid.
19. Avramovic, "Debts in Early 1985," pp. 105, 114–18.
20. Avramovic et al., *Economic Growth and External Debt*, pp. 64–69.
21. Ibid., p. 67.
22. Ibid., p. 39.
23. Ibid., p. 40.
24. Ibid., pp. 40–41.
25. William Cline, *International Debt: Systemic Risk and Policy Response* (Washington, DC: Institute for International Economics, 1984), p. 7.
26. Ibid., pp. 6–7.

27. Cline, "International Debt: Analysis," passim. Peter Nunnenkamp bluntly says that Cline "fail[ed] to correctly predict future developments in debt servicing difficulties." See Nunnenkamp's review of Cline's book, *International Debt: Systemic Risk and Policy Response* in *Weltwirtschaffliches Archiv* 122 (1986): pp. 601–3.

28. Dornbusch and Fischer, "World Debt Problem," p. 58.

29. Ibid., p. 58. Dornbusch and Fischer use the subsequent year's inflation rate for LDC export prices because their (Irving) Fisherian decomposition of the real rate requires them to measure the expected rate of inflation. They assume perfect foresight on the part of economic "agents" when they use the actual rate in the subsequent year as the measure of the expected rate.

30. Ibid., p. 60.

31. Ibid., p. 81n.5. The empirical case also remains unsettled. In a statistical study, Philippe Callier used several indicators estimated between 1971 and 1975, including the public external debt to GDP ratio and the ratio of current account to GDP, in a logit model (with cross-section data from a sample of sixty-two countries) to identify the probability that a country would (1) undergo a rescheduling of maturities falling due between 1977 and 1982, (2) impose a moratorium on debt service, or (3) go into arrears on payments on imports or interest during 1977–82. He found that all of his independent variables had the expected signs. All were significant at the 5 percent confidence level with the exception of his capital productivity indicator. Still, even his relatively successful model indicated a probability of default of less than 50 percent for 9 percent of the countries in his sample that experienced debt payment problems in 1977–82, and a greater than 50 percent probability of default for 19 percent of the countries in his sample that met external commitments on time. See Philippe Callier, "Further Results on Countries' Debt-Servicing Performance: The Relevance of Structural Factors," *Weltwirtschaffliches Archiv* (*Review of World Economy*) 121 (1985): 105–15.

32. Stephen I. Davis, *The Euro-Bank: Its Origins, Management and Outlook* (New York: John Wiley and Sons, 1976), p. 41.

33. Ibid., p. 43.

34. Ibid., p. 44.

35. Ibid., p. 49.

36. Arvind K. Jain and Satyadev Gupta, "Some Evidence on 'Herding' Behavior of U.S. Banks" *Journal of Money, Credit, and Banking* 19 (February 1987): 83n.12. The relative exposure to asset share ratio is the authors' statistic constructed from the Jain and Gupta data.

37. Andrew F. Brimmer, *The World Banking System: Outlook in a Context of Crisis* (New York and London: New York University Press, 1985), p. 36.

38. Ibid., pp. 36, 41.

39. Ibid., p. 39.

40. Leonard Sloane, "Chase's Net Falls: Latin Loans Cited," *New York Times* 21 April 1987.

41. Ibid.
42. "Banking Gamble: Citicorp Sharply Lifts Loss Reserves, Putting Its Rivals on the Spot," *Wall Street Journal* 20 May 1987.
43. Marko Milivojevic, *The Debt Rescheduling Process* (New York: St. Martin's Press, 1985), pp. 68, 74–75, 208. The advisory committee on Yugoslavia was chaired by a representative of Manufacturer's Hanover.
44. Rimmer de Vries, "Commentary on 'International Debt and Economic Instability,' " in *Debt, Financial Stability, and Public Policy* (Kansas City: Federal Reserve Bank, 1987), p. 94.
45. Ibid., pp. 94–95.
46. Ibid., p. 95.
47. Persio Arida, "Macroeconomic Issues for Latin America," *Journal of Development Economics* 22 (1986: 182–83. Ronald McKinnon's view that banks rush to lend to newly-liberalized LDCs is consistent with Arida's hypothesis. See his "The International Capital Market and Economic Liberalization in LDCs" *The Developing Economies* 22 (September 1984): 476–81.
48. Richard Falk, "Militarism and Human Rights in the Third World," in Charles Wilbur ed., *The Political Economy of Development and Underdevelopment* (New York: Random House, 1981), p. 457.
49. Ramgopal Agarwala, *Price Distortions and Growth in Developing Countries* (Washington, DC: World Bank Staff Working Papers No. 575, July 1983.
50. Walter F. Kitchenman, *Arms Transfers and Indebtedness of Less Developed Countries,* Rand Note N-2020-FF (Santa Monica, CA: Rand Corporation, 1983), p. 16.
51. Arvind K. Jain, "International Lending Patterns of U.S. Commercial Banks," *Journal of International Business Studies* 17 (Fall 1986): 73–88.
52. Dornbusch and Fischer, "World Debt Problem," pp. 57–58.
53. Cline, "International Debt: Analysis," p. 29.
54. Ibid. The OECD nations are essentially the Western industrial nations and Japan.
55. Dornbusch and Fischer, "World Debt Problem, p. 59.
56. Ibid., p. 78.
57. Albert Fishlow, "The Debt Crisis: Round Two Ahead?" in Richard Feinberg and Valeriana Kallab, eds., *Adjustment Crisis in the Third World* (New Brunswick, Canada: Transaction Books, 1984), p. 39.
58. Ibid., p. 39.
59. Ibid.
60. Milivojevic, "Debt Rescheduling," p. 97.

CHAPTER 3

Loan Pushing and Economic Models of the Banking Firm

E conomists who analyze bank behavior customarily seek to model bank "as a microeconomic firm that attempts to maximize an objective function in terminal wealth."[1] In effect, banks—most usefully defined as institutions that issue transaction accounts—are typically treated as another instance for application of the textbook theory of the firm.[2] Over the relevant time horizon a bank, like any other microeconomic firm, sets marginal revenue equal to marginal cost to maximize profits.[3]

Does such an apparently straightforward treatment of bank behavior preclude loan pushing? Would a bank be expected to suddenly make large loans to a borrower that was previously neglected, refused, or ignored—despite the fact that the borrower's characteristics that indicate creditworthiness have not changed—on the basis of the model of the bank as "microeconomic firm?"

First, it is not clear that the orthodox model of the firm sets any substantive limits on the types of actions we might expect from banks. Equating marginal cost to marginal revenue does not, in and of itself, set any obvious constraints on the practices a bank might pursue. The exact nature of both implicit and explicit costs and revenues remains open for the analyst to specify. The existence of risk and/or uncertainty when decisions are made renders profit-maximization prospective; the consequences of decisions made now will be realized only in the future. Hence the bank ought to be characterized as setting prospective marginal revenue equal to prospective marginal cost. Any observed pattern of behavior—regardless of its actual results—can be reconciled with

microeconomic optimization by the obvious claim that the firm's decisionmakers *expected* it to be profitable when they made the commitment. Perhaps the bank's managers had reason to expect a future
(favorable) change in the economic outlook of their newly-acquired borrowers that was not evident at the time of the loan, but their forecast
simply proved to be wrong.

Compounding matters is the environment in which the bank oper-
ates—both from the standpoint of challenges from rival institutions and
the impact of the regulatory apparatus. Is the bank a perfect or imperfect
competitor? What limitations and incentives are created by regulations?
Merely saying that banks are profit-maximizing firms does not carry
us very far in determining their precise course of action in making loans.

ARE BANKS SPECIAL?

Furthermore, it is unclear that banks fit within the framework of the
"microeconomic firm" at all. The Federal Reserve Bank of Minneapolis
devoted an entire annual report to the question of whether banks sufficiently differ from other types of firms to justify the unique and extensive regulatory environment under which they operate in the United
States.[4] The report displayed a belief that the regulatory structure is too
extensive, but also that there are particular dangers associated with a
loss of public confidence in banks, resulting in "sudden drains of bank
deposits," that do not apply to firms in other industries.[5]

Of Banks and Butcher Shops

The late Carlos Diaz-Alejandro wondered whether or not runs on banks
and runs on butcher shops are really distinct events:

> Are banks special and really all that different from butcher shops? Neither type
> of firm is *exactly* like the textbook idealization of the atomistic firm operating
> in a perfectly competitive market, where spot prices summarize all informa-
> tion relevant for buyers and sellers of product. Customers at a butcher shop
> will not only look at price, but will also attempt to ascertain quality; in some
> countries they will be aided by government-established quality categories and
> certifications. Breakdowns in the trust consumers have in their butchers or in
> government certification, say because of rumors regarding meat tainted by
> poisonous substances, could produce a kind of "run" on butcher shops, and
> widespread failures among them.[6]

Loss of trust in the butcher shops sounds much the same as the Federal Reserve Bank of Minneapolis' description of the cause of a bank run: "Sudden drains on bank deposits occur when depositors conclude that loan losses or other circumstances might jeopardize a bank's ability to meet its deposit obligations."[7]

However, Diaz-Alejandro acknowledged that his "comparison is surely being forced."[8] He then catalogued several reasons why the bank is indeed different from the butcher shop:

> Few butcher shops will deliver meat of standard quality out of town to third parties on instruction from a customer. Few externalities could be expected from a "run" on a butcher shop under suspicion. Furthermore, a butcher will seldom turn down a customer who wants to buy with cash everything in sight at the price announced by the butcher . . .; a banker will surely not lend all a customer wants to borrow at the going interest rate. The former is a spot transaction; the latter involves a promise to repay in the future which may or may not be sincere or wholly credible. Enforcing the loan contract or liquidating collateral property will involve costs, and even with speedy enforcement the bank may be unable to get all of its money back. The bank will incur costs to explore the credit-worthiness of borrowers; the butcher will not care much for the reputation of cash-carrying customers.[9]

The Federal Reserve Bank of Minneapolis gave pride of place to the "externalities" accompanying "sudden drains on bank deposits" as the decisive factor that distinguishes banks from other firms. From the viewpoint of prudent regulation, the bank's report included the following observation: ". . . even when 'problem' bank situations have been resolved with a minimum of costs to the individual institution, these situations have, on occasion, involved high costs in terms of generalized financial market disruption."[10]

There is ostensibly a severe ripple effect that bank failures would induce across the economy that a string of butcher shop failures could not begin to replicate. But is such a ripple effect due to the inherent characteristics of a bank or because of the size of those banks that might fail? If there was a butcher shop of the magnitude of the Chrysler Corporation, its possible failure would probably be a source of alarm for those concerned with the performance of the U.S. economy. Still, it is unlikely that a plan would be inaugurated to monitor the fiduciary soundness of *all*, or even most, butcher shops. Indeed, Continental Illinois and Penn Square were treated quite differently by regulators—the failure of the former perceived as having much greater significance than that of the latter. Nevertheless, there is a sense that one bank failure can trigger others in the absence of the regulatory-cum-deposit insurance environment that now prevails. Even failure of a small bank could start a financial contraction and propagate a general economic downturn, given a particular structure of interbank linkages. (In fact, Penn Square had an upstream link to Continental Illinois!)

Both Diaz-Alejandro and the Federal Reserve Bank of Minneapolis annual report indicate that at a minimum banks are special because when they fail the adverse external effects are potentially large and widespread. Since banks are unique—not really like other firms—they require their own regulatory apparatus. They are to be regulated because they are special.

Regulation and Uniqueness

There is, of course, the antithetical view that banks are special only because they are regulated. The regulatory apparatus gears their structure and performance, and often engenders perverse incentives. Robert Taggart, Jr., for example, has argued that a separate theory of the banking firm *is* required, but primarily because the bank regulatory structure makes banks unique.[11] Although Taggart does not make such a leap, others might argue that the regulatory apparatus is the source of the problem with respect to bank performance. Lawrence White, in an Austrian-spirited study of the "free banking" period in Britain, suggests that in the absence of state regulation–intervention in banking, the discipline of the market and rivalry among bankers would preclude the occurrence of monetary instability (or debt crisis, for that matter).[12]

Those who take the position that banks are special only because they are regulated can easily explain loan pushing as an outcome of the moral hazard problem created by the regulatory structure. The public provision of deposit insurance and the existence of a lender of last resort ostensibly combine, spurring banks to take riskier positions with respect to their assets than they might otherwise. Loan pushing is induced by the regulatory system itself.

Such reasoning fails to explain why loan pushing occurred at earlier times when the regulatory structure was quite thin. For example, there was no federal deposit insurance in the United States until the mid-1930s. Such reasoning also fails to explain why financial liberalization often simultaneously unleashes financial instability. Several countries in Latin America in the early 1980s—Chile, Colombia, Argentina, and Uruguay—are prime examples of this situation.[13]

On the other hand, those who see banks as regulated because they are special seem to acknowledge that banks under *laissez faire* have a predisposition toward imprudential lending. Why would such imprudence continue after regulation? Here, one would look toward inadequate monitoring by the examiners; regulation-induced innovations that permit the banks to proceed as if they are not subject to supervision or restriction; or the ability of the banks to move into geographic areas beyond the legal or effective reach of the examiners. It even has been argued that the emergence of the (unregulated) Eurocurrency market was a regulation-induced innovation.[14]

SPECIAL THEORIES OF THE BANKING FIRM

If banks are unique, they then require their own models that are distinct from the standard model of the firm. Much economic research in this area has been conservative in the following sense: essentially *ad hoc* adjustments have been made to the textbook model to account for the stylized facts of banking. None of these modifications rule out loan pushing as a possible consequence of the particular profit-seeking strategy arrived at by the "banking firm."

One set of variations on the theme of the bank as microeconomic firm involves development of a series of imperfect competition models. Models that ascribe price-setting capabilities and some degree of monopolistic power to banks are especially popular among those economists who perceive that there are significant economies of scale in banking operations.[15] For those who want to maintain the assumption that individual banks must offer all borrowers the same interest rate—but do not observe banks meeting all borrowers' demands at the prevailing interest rate—more refined intellectual "pyrotechnics" are required. The argument shifts entirely into a world where risk and informational asymmetries are used to explain observed outcomes.[16]

The Theory of Adverse Selection

A specific example of the latter style of modeling bank behavior is the somewhat ingenious theory of adverse selection. Adverse selection has been employed to explain how credit rationing can occur when all lenders are "perfect competitors," in the sense that they must offer all borrowers the same rate of interest. The uniformity of the offered interest rate is reinforced by the inability of the lenders to discriminate among potential borrowers on the basis of their default propensities. The borrowers themselves, but not the lenders, know their own likelihood of default. Moreover, "[t]he potential borrowers of a bank lack signals to demonstrate their varying degrees of default propensity."[17] Banks are unable, on informational grounds, to practice price discrimination among borrowers.

If there are rationed borrowers, the customary presumption is a forthcoming general rise in interest rates. But "[u]nder an information asymmetry scenario . . . an increase in the interest rate has the undesired adverse selection effect that borrowers with low risk default propensities leave the market."[18] Although banks are unable to identify the default propensities of each potential borrower, they do know that as interest rates rise, proportionately more high-risk borrowers will remain in the pool of credit customers. Lower-risk borrowers will simply have withdrawn their loan demands as interest rates increase. Banks may opt to avoid interest rate increases, despite the presence of a large fringe of unsatisfied borrowers, to preclude the adverse selection effect that can reduce the expected return on their loans.

Folkerts-Landau has explicitly applied the theory of adverse selection via supply and demand curves to the international loan market, with a subtle twist. An individual borrower's own default propensity may not be fixed, but may instead be sensitive to variations in the interest rate. As Folkerts-Landau notes, ". . . the average riskiness of the projects and policies the borrower chooses to finance with external loans rises with the lending rate."[19] The pool of borrowers need not change as interest rates rise; the borrowers' intended uses of the funds will change instead. If—following the best dictates of mean-variance portfolio analysis—there is an inverse relationship between the expected profitability of a loan and its riskiness, "the expected profits from raising the lending rate may not be sufficient to make up for a decline of expected profits due to riskier loans."[20]

If banks can only exercise incomplete discrimination among borrowers, this leads to an alternative explanation for Kindleberger's purported backward-bending bank loan supply function to developing countries. (See Chapter 2.) If the loan demand function intersects the loan supply function *above* the "bend" (the point where profits are maximized or where supply begins to contract), the market will not move to the position that equates loan supply and demand. Borrowers would obtain less total credit and the banks would receive less profits at the market-clearing interest rate. Credit rationing supplants price (interest rate) adjustment.[21] This means, in turn, that banks will limit credit for some countries rather than allow interest rates to rise when there is an excess demand for loans.[22] The countries facing such limits would be those that fall into higher risk categories at each interest rate. For loan supply to equal loan demand, or for the market to clear, the backward-bending loan supply schedule would have to shift rightward until the demand schedule cuts the supply schedule *below* the optimal rate. Folkerts-Landau thus argues that the LDCs moved from a credit-constrained position in the early 1970s to an unconstrained position by 1981 as the bank loan supply schedule shifted to the right due to "financial innovations and institutional developments that reduced some of the difficulties in monitoring and enforcing loan terms." He then suggests that "[a]fter the end of 1981 innovations can be presumed to have slowed and may have somewhat reversed, though the good experience, with rescheduling over the past two years [1983 and 1984] may have prevented a substantial leftward shift of the supply curve for credit."[23] By the late 1970s, credit available to LDCs could increase without interest rates rising.

Rationing LDCs?

Folkerts-Landau's claims about rightward shifts in the loan supply schedule seem to be consistent with a body of research on the extent to which LDCs have been rationed on credit markets. Eaton and Gersovitz conducted an investigation utilizing nonmarket-clearing research methods that led them to conclude that 80 percent of developing countries they sampled experienced an excess demand for credit in 1970 and 1974.[24] A subsequent re-estimation of the Eaton-Gersovitz model by John Morgan using 1977 and 1981 data indicates that the LDCs were not as credit constrained in the late 1970s and early 1980s as they had been beforehand.[25]

Obviously there could be alternative explanations for the change in the relative access to credit on the part of LDCs that need not rely upon supply and demand curves to such an intricate degree. But both Folkerts-Landau's application of the theory of adverse selection and the empirical evidence on credit constraints for developing countries are quite consistent with loan pushing, which is now interpreted as a "supply-leading" phenomenon in credit markets. This is particularly true if once again, economic prospects for LDC borrowers did not look distinctly different in 1974 than in 1979.[26]

This broad consistency may be insufficient to maintain the theory of adverse selection as a credible explanation of bank behavior. Broll and Gilroy propose that collateral requirements would enable the banks to increase the information they have about borrowers' default propensities, thus reducing the extent of credit rationing.[27] Ironically, though, the developing country loans made by commercial banks generally were noncollateralized. Reputation, a borrowers' past history of performance, etc., all presumably could assist banks in discriminating among borrowers. As long as banks do not in fact have to charge all borrowers a common loan rate, the need for such an ingenious construct as adverse selection theory becomes weaker.

It is interesting that whether persuasive or unpersuasive, none of these *ad hoc* amendments to the standard treatment of the bank as a "microeconomic firm" are inconsistent with loan pushing. These variations are open to the theoretical possibility of loans descending in clusters on previously deprived borrowers. Economies of scale (or of *super*scale) could lead the largest banks to reach a stage where their perceived "marginal costs" of additional loans are so low that they look for relatively high-risk borrowers on relatively easy terms. Plunging toward developing country borrowers could also result from bankers, for whatever reason, moving from a risk-averse toward a risk-taking posture. These models do not establish an inherent inclination by the bankers to engage in loan pushing, but neither do they preclude such behavior.

ASSET MANAGEMENT?

Banks may also be treated as portfolio managers confronted with a number of potential risks when they make loans. Each of these risks can presumably be managed by appropriate measures. Adequate management would also presumably reduce the likelihood of a bank being faced with a series of loans on which they incur losses, *even* if they have "pushed" loans.

Risky Business

These potential risks to a lending bank include (1) credit (or default) risk, (2) liquidity risk, (3) foreign exchange risk, (4) interest rate risk, (5) regulatory risk, (6) fund availability risk, and (7) country risk.

Credit risk involves the possibility that the borrower simply will be unable to repay the loan—the possibility of outright failure to pay. Liquidity risk involves a circumstance where the borrower has a sound asset base but one that is not easily convertible into the form required for loan payments. Foreign exchange risk constitutes a situation where a bank has a net open position in foreign currency due to its own speculative practices or to currency mismatching. Interest rate risk involves unexpected movements in interest rates over the course of a loan. Related to this type of risk are unexpected changes in the purchasing power of currencies that can significantly alter the real value of interest payments or principal. Regulatory risk involves unforeseen changes in the regulatory requirements, e.g., reserve requirements, capital-asset ratio requirements, in the country in which the debtor country has operations over the course of a loan. Fund availability risk, similar to liquidity risk, arises when a large customer abruptly withdraws deposits from a bank, reducing the bank's reserve base. Country risk involves the factors influencing loan quality arising from a country's political or economic structure. This risk includes as subcategories sovereign risk (political/military measures that may block loan payment) and transfer risk (difficulties borrowers may face in obtaining foreign exchange).[28]

Bank Coping Strategies

How do the banks cope with such risks? To manage credit or default risk, banks typically (a) seek collateral, (b) diversify their portfolios, or (c) seek to participate in a syndicate rather than lend individually to a large borrower. Again, most LDC loans were noncollateralized. So, in the recent wave of lending, if this default risk was being managed, it was done via strategies (b) and (c). Stiglitz even doubts that the banks have been able to diversify adequately in an *ex post* sense, referring to: ". . . recent episodes of large banks becoming overly committed to certain classes of correlated risks (oil and gas loans; loans to LDCs)."[29] Syndication obviously can work at cross purposes with diversification if the syndicates all point toward similar sets of borrowers, while giving the lenders the possibly false sense of security of travelling with a pack.

Liquidity risk can be managed by the bank (a) holding more liquid assets or (b) borrowing funds in the money markets, for example, the federal funds market and overnight Eurodollar market.[30] The former step means reducing the expected return on the bank's portfolio while the latter step may reduce confidence in the bank if it is observed dipping into the money markets too frequently.[31] Foreign exchange (or currency) risk is handled by (a) setting limits on each branch office's net exposure, either currency by currency or on total; (b) setting limits on global operations with the head office performing an offset function; and/or (c) shifting risk to the borrowers by denominating and funding loans in the same currency.[32] The first two steps reduce the flexibility of the banks to the extent that exposure limits become rigid. The latter step changes the form of the risk the bank faces into either a default risk by the borrower or transfer risk.

Interest rate risk might be managed by incorporating floating rates into loan contracts. In domestic contracts in the United States, the reference rate typically is the Treasury bill rate, while abroad LIBOR is typically used.[33] Given uncertainty about inflation, however, this incorporation of floating rates may generate an increase in credit risk for the borrower if the nominal rates rise higher than the inflation rate. Regulatory risk could be contained via contingency contracts that allow the lender to charge the borrower for changes in regulations.[34] Of course, unless the regulatory change reduces the borrower's loan expenses, this tactic may reduce the capacity of the borrower to meet payments.

To cope with fund availability risk, banks may (a) try to discourage big depositors from holding highly liquid accounts by offering higher interest rates on less liquid accounts and (b) structure loan agreements to contain fund availability clauses.[35] Such procedures can be workable in the absence of intense rivalry among the banks for depositors and borrowers. Rivalry is muted by effective regulation, regulation that is largely absent from the Eurocurrency market.[36]

Finally, to counter country risk, banks can utilize their presence within syndicates to threaten borrowers with permanent exclusion from access to international loans if they repudiate their debts. Diversification, syndication, and more careful study of economic and political developments in LDCs are other possible options.[37] Outright economic imperialism is another resort. Of course, the tension between diversification and syndication still persists. If the banks are confident that their home governments are willing to enforce payment of the loans by force, they may be encouraged to take on riskier loans.

Rational asset management is no guarantee of prudent lending. Containment of one type of risk typically promulgates another. Since these "risks" are not quantifiable, bank managers can only "guesstimate" whether reducing one type of risk more than compensates for the increase in another. No internal response to risk is foolproof for the banks. Reliance on the home government as an ultimate "insurance" agent merely engenders incentives for banks to be less cautious in their lending practices.

POLITICS AND COMMERCE

The theory of the banking firm is particularly underdeveloped with respect to the interaction between a national government's broadly constituted policies and the profit-seeking activities of the banks. It also is quite underdeveloped with respect to the relationship between the commercial interests of individual bank customers, account management, and foreign lending. These facets of the climate in which commercial banks operate are not readily incorporated into models of bank behavior from the standpoint of a theoretical reduction to the individual, representative banking firm.

Credit and Empire

Nevertheless, the often intimate links between private banks and national governments suggest that there is frequently a symbiotic pressure to engage in foreign loan adventures. The difficult and perhaps unresolvable issue is: do banks lead their governments abroad or do governments lead their bankers abroad?[38] If governments are pulled in by loan default, given the potential repercussions of bad foreign loans and bank failures on their domestic economies then, in a sense, the bankers hold their governments hostage. The governments function as insurers of the last resort, using their powers of coercion to make the loans good. If governments lead the banks in, given a particular foreign policy agenda, then the banks legitimately can expect a *quid pro quo*; the governments are obligated to make the loans worthwhile to the banks. In either case, the banks can look to their governments as a prop in the foreign loan trade.

Private banking has rarely maintained a steadfast separation from either the public sector or purported national interests. A fascinating early essay by the brilliant economic theorist Piero Sraffa provided a case study of the spectacular growth of the Banca Italiana di Sconto, a growth that was entirely derivative from the bank's loans to the state-supported munitions industry that had flourished during World War I.[39]

Marcello de Cecco recently argued persuasively that the surge in American lending during the early interwar years was prompted in large part by the conscious attempt of New York to supplant London as the leading center of international finance. If the cities are treated as metaphors for nations, American bond finance was a critical route the United States took to replace Britain as the global imperial center.[40] The banks were agents of international geopolitical rivalries.

Red Loans Across Red Lines

Recent loans by Western banks across the "red line" into Poland evoke the same set of themes concerning the interdependence of national politics and commercial banking practices. Journalist Anthony Sampson contends that Poland has long held a special attraction to Western investors. Its vast mineral resources served as a special lure, for Poland's mineral wealth exceeded that of all other Eastern European nations (except for the Soviet Union).[41] There were certain reservations, however. As Sampson notes, Poland "also had more headstrong leaders, more determined workers, . . . inefficient industries, [and] a tradition of industrial backwardness."[42] On the other hand, Western observers felt that aside from the anomalous case of Yugoslavia, strikes were virtually unknown in Eastern Europe.[43]

Perhaps most important was the bankers' embrace of "the umbrella theory," the expectation that the COMECON group of nations were under the protective hegemony of the Soviet Union and therefore, would not be allowed to default on their loans.[44] The bankers expected the Soviet Union to perform a function of lender of last resort similar to that performed by the IMF and central banks for Western countries experiencing external debt and payments difficulties. The Polish case is a prime example of unfulfilled expectations.

The chronology of events relevant to the Polish debt crisis can perhaps be dated from the late 1960s, although the acceleration of Western bank lending did not occur until the mid-1970s. The first contemporary phase of credit flows to the Polish regime took place in the later years of the Gomulka regime. Although the magnitude of the initial loans was unspectacular, the basis for the loans was no less slippery:

> Buyers and sellers, lenders and borrowers were all so anxious to please in the early years that business was negotiated on eggshells. "Who would have asked Gomulka critical questions about a steel plant?" pleads a Western banker. He was referring to the intimidating Polish leader of the 1960s.[45]

But is it not the bankers' business to ask critical questions about any project? Why would the bankers have been intimidated by Gomulka, since they held the funds? Were they already revealing an anxious predisposition to acquire new assets—or had their home governments already greased the pig?

Gierek became Poland's prime minister in 1970 after food riots brought down Gomulka's regime. It was Gierek who opened Poland's doors wide to foreign funds. Willy Brandt, West Germany's prime minister at the time and a major architect of East-West detente, encouraged Western banks to pursue Gierek's call. Gierek expressed the desire for Poland to achieve rapid economic growth, fueled by foreign borrowing. The external debt would be paid off with the fruits of growth.

The amount of prodding Western bankers needed is not certain. What is certain is the fact that loans to Poland ballooned during that period, "many of them" in Sampson's words, for "dubious industrial projects."[46] Sampson further reports: "The First Chicago Bank, in the midst of a Polish-American stronghold was especially active in Warsaw, and set up its own office there."[47]

Letting Poland Be Poland?

Poland then underwent an episode of marked improvement in the material standard of living, symbolized by a consumer goods boom. But it began to become evident that the credits were proving to be pure consumption loans rather than industrial production loans, leaving the sources of repayment afloat like castles in the air. Matters were compounded in 1976 when Poland was beset by an agricultural crisis, precipitating food shortages. This led Gierek to increase food prices, which sparked another round of food riots, ironically the same circumstances that had helped make Gierek the prime minister in the first place.[48]

At this point signs of nervousness began to emerge in the banking community. Some spokespersons for American banks began to suggest that no new loans to Poland would be forthcoming. But the screw had yet to turn completely. In 1977 ". . . Chase Manhattan was lending $600 million to Eastern Europe, including Poland, to finance a new gas pipeline with little information about how the new money would be used . . ." and in 1978 ". . . Poland raised a new syndicated loan worth half a billion dollars."[49] Between 1970 and 1980 the "hard-currency indebtedness" of the COMECON nations had grown from

$7 billion to over $65 billion. By 1980 Poland alone had accumulated $26 billion in external indebtedness, more than one-half of which was owed to commercial banks.[50] West German banks held the largest share among commercial banks, followed by British and American banks. The day of reckoning was on the horizon, although in commercial banking days of reckoning can be deferred indefinitely.

Early in 1980 the Polish government was negotiating for an additional one-half billion dollars in loans. This was, however, the year in which the Solidarity trade union movement came into open confrontation with the regime. The strikes that could never happen did, in fact, take place.[51] The structure of the Polish social system hung in the balance. The threat of Soviet invasion was a continuous theme of media reports throughout the tense summer.

For some commercial banks holding Polish loan paper, a Soviet invasion was not an altogether unsavory idea. If the Polish regime could not discipline the Polish workers, perhaps the Soviets could do so more effectively. At a minimum, the Soviet Union was better situated to meet Poland's debt obligations.[52]

An Umbrella With Holes

No Soviet invasion came, nor did any Soviet commitment to function as Poland's lender of the last resort. There was instead a "capitulation to higher wages"[53] followed by internal efforts under the direction of General Jaruzelski to contain the ongoing impact of Solidarity. The net result in the West was a cacophony of unusual political postures:

> The Western attitudes were full of paradoxes. American conservatives who abominated labor unions were now boundless in their admiration of the Polish strikers. American labor unionists were refusing to import Polish goods in support of their Polish comrades, while Polish Americans pressed for more credit.[54]

The bankers were concerned primarily with how to insure that their debts were paid—at least that their interest payments were met. The banking community would accept whatever political configuration in Poland would insure that payment. The bankers even moved to arrange new loans for Poland to rollover the existing debt, well aware that Poland's payment obligations in 1981 would be larger than the total dollar value of its exports.[55]

The bankers also sought aid from their governments. Indeed, the banks reasoned, if their governments had led them into Poland they (the banks) were in a position to make an ethical case for support. Even if the reverse was closer to the truth, the bankers certainly were able to mobilize such support. Despite the Reagan administration's strong rhetorical posture on behalf of Solidarity, the decision was made "to rescue Poland and the banks—to the tune of $344 million in 1982 alone—rather than countenance a formal default."[56] Perpetual reschedulings and rollovers are the remnants of that Polish debt.[57]

Poland has shown unequivocally that (1) strikes can occur in Eastern Europe and (2) the Soviet Union will not fullfill the umbrella function the commercial bankers anticipated. Some more deeply paranoid observers propose that the Soviet leadership saw Western banks as a route toward entrapment of the capitalist world in financial crisis. From this vantage point, the Polish debt crisis is merely the leading edge of a Soviet plot to bring down international capitalism with the banks playing the suckers' role. The last thing the Soviet Union might do is help pay any of the COMECON nations' debts.

On the other hand, numerous Western strategists openly portrayed lending to Poland and other Eastern European nations as desirable to shift the countries' ties from the Soviet Union toward the West.[58] Given such conscious intent, it would be ironic if the Soviet Union had indeed set a deeper trap. Poland, for one, was no less reliant on the Soviet Union despite its huge accumulation of debt.[59] Still, trade relations had expanded between East and West in concert with the growth in lending. As the external debt of COMECON nations to Western sources grew, so did East-West trade. Between 1971 and 1981 the money volume of East-West trade rose from $6 billion to $40 billion annually.[60] The Polish economic boom of the first half of the 1970s was also a boom for Western consumer goods producers. Markets can be made by loans to countries outside of the capitalistic orbit, just as well as by loans to countries within the orbit. Loans in both regions can also go equally bad.

Souk the Banks

Bankers in the more developed countries are not alone in their infidelities and in their ties to governments. Everywhere, banks can get into trouble and governments can stand ready to bail them out. Consider the case of the 1982 crash of the Souk-al-Manakh, the unofficial stock exchange in Kuwait. This was a genuinely free market affair, with shares purchased by use of postdated checks—some postdated as late as 1991—and the banks were necessarily involved. But banks in the region, including some that were American owned, also had lent money on the basis of the "kited" checks. When the booming stock market's bubble burst, repayment became impossible and there was a direct transmission of the impact of the crash to the banking system.[61]

Almost three years later, the Kuwaiti government was still contemplating the use of public funds to assist banks and other financial institutions holding billions of dollars of bad debts since the crash of 1982.[62] The government already had taken steps immediately after the crash to "shore up" the banks.[63]

Somewhat ironically, to the west of Kuwait, Israeli banks were manufacturing their own financial crisis at about the same time. Between 1980 and 1983, Israel's inflation rate soared to around 100 percent per year. Bankers recognized that "a large number of ordinary Israelis [were] worried about losing the value of their savings [and] encouraged [them] to buy bank shares as a hedge against inflation."[64] In this case, the bubble burst in October 1983. Nervousness about a maxi-devaluation of the Israeli shekel led to "a panic by bank share holders."[65] Once more the government served as insurer of the last resort; its officials, troubled by prospects of collapse of the banking system "the government . . . guaranteed the shares at 15 percent below their market value."[66] According to international trade specialist David Eichorn, the situation poses familiar dilemmas for the public sector:

> The government's emergency action prevented a banking disaster. Now, the government faces the first major share redemption in October 1987 to the tune of $1.5 billion and the second a year later in the amount of $3.8 billion.
>
> The government is in a very difficult position. The cost of redeeming the bank shares is a budgetary nightmare. The cost of not redeeming them could be even higher. The loss of credibility and prestige if the government defaults would result in repercussions around the world. . . .[67]

Indeed, the optimal risk management strategy for the commercial banks often appears to shift the risk of default onto their governments.

Multi-Service Firms?

Suppose banks are characterized as pursuing a general profit strategy by providing multiple services to their customers. Loans of an apparent low quality may look unprofitable on their own terms, but may be quite profitable from the standpoint of broader commercial practices. Governments as insurers of last resort merely serve to "ice" an already lucrative "cake."

For instance, banks could issue loans that implicitly or explicitly, are export credits for foreign borrowers to promote sales by their customers. Bank lending to developing countries, and eventual exchange liberalization policies (from IMF conditions for those countries that get into trouble), could aid and abet capital flight from the LDCs. And, of course, capital fleeing the LDCs typically flows into the banks' accounts in the form of deposits.[68]

Robert Heller, a former vice president with Bank of America and now one of the governors of the Federal Reserve Board, carries the argument in just such a direction. He contends that: "the future of international bank lending to developing countries should be seen as a long-term strategic decision and not merely a credit judgment about a particular borrower at a given moment in time or the expected rate of return on a specific loan."[69] Believing that it is in the commercial banks' "long-term interest to maintain a business relationship with the developing countries," Heller does not seem to be unduly concerned about the performance of existing loans. After all, development of a long-term customer relationship with LDC borrowers is of paramount importance.[70] For Heller the debt crisis is a short-term difficulty that can be managed by (a) the MDCs promoting growth of their economies to raise their import demand from LDCs while simultaneously avoiding protectionism; and (b) by the IMF and the World Bank continuing to lend to countries in trouble as long as those nations implement "market-focused adjustment programs."[71]

From this latter standpoint, the loans to LDCs were simply one aspect of a broader profitability strategy being pursued by the bankers. The intent was to provide multiple services to existing customers and to build up a new customer base on the periphery. Only time will determine if such a strategy has been successful or has sown the seeds of disaster. One might think there are easier ways to build warm relations with new customers.

NOTES

1. Anthony M. Santomero, "Modeling the Banking Firm," *Journal of Money, Credit, and Banking* 16 (November 1984): 580.
2. Such a definition of banks is suggested, for example, in the Federal Reserve Bank of Minneapolis, *Annual Report 1982: Are Banks Special?* (Minneapolis: Federal Reserve Bank of Minneapolis, 1982), p. 2. Specifically, the report says "a bank is any institution that is eligible to issue transaction accounts." Since *eligibility* enters the definition, the report brings the regulatory apparatus into identification of banks from the outset.

3. Santomero, "Modeling the Firm," pp. 580–99.
4. Federal Reserve Bank of Minneapolis, *Annual Report.*
5. Ibid., pp. 8–9.
6. Carlos Diaz-Alejandro, "Good-bye Financial Repression, Hello Financial Crash," *Journal of Development Economics* 19 (1985): 2.
7. Federal Reserve Bank of Minneapolis, *Annual Report,* p. 8.
8. Diaz-Alejandro, "Financial Repression," p. 2.
9. Ibid.
10. Federal Reserve Bank of Minneapolis, *Annual Report,* p. 9.
11. Robert A. Taggart, Jr., "Comment on 'Modeling' the Banking Firm: A Survey," *Journal of Money, Credit, and Banking* 16 (November 1984): 616.
12. Lawrence White, *Free Banking in Britain: Theory, Experience and Debate, 1800–1845* (Cambridge, MA: Cambridge University Press, 1984).
13. Diaz-Alejandro, "Financial Repression," pp. 9–24. For a detailed exegesis on the Chilean case see Jose Pablo-Arellano, "De la Liberalization a la Intervencion: El mercado de Capitales en Chile: 1974–83," in *Estudios CIEPLAN,* 11 (December 1983): 5–49.
14. Stephen I. Davis, *The Euro-Bank: Its Origins, Management and Outlook.* (New York: John Wiley and Sons, 1971), p. 22.
15. An example of an imperfectionist model of bank behavior is in Stephen Rousseas, "A Markup Theory of Bank Loan Rates," *Journal of Post Keynesian Economics* 8 (Fall 1985): 135–44. An example of recent empirical work on evidence of economies of scale in banking is in George J. Bentson, Gerald A. Hanweek, and David Humphrey, "Scale Economies in Banking: A Restructuring and Reassessment," *Journal of Money, Credit, and Banking* 14 (November 1982): 435–56. In a recent editorial Michael C. Keeley and Randall Pozdena take possible economies of large-scale operation as a given and a justification for repeal of the Glass-Steagall Act that prohibits uniting investment and commercial banking in the same institutions. See their article "Uniting Investment and Commercial Banking," *Federal Reserve Bank of San Francisco Weekly Letter,* 19 June 1987.
16. See Joseph E. Stiglitz, "Credit Markets and Control of Capital," *Journal of Money, Credit, and Banking* 17 (May 1985): 133–52.
17. Udo Broll and Michael B. Gilroy, "Collateral in Banking Policy and Adverse Selection," *The Manchester School of Economic and Social Studies* 54 (December 1986): 357.
18. Ibid., p. 357.
19. David Folkerts-Landau, "The Changing Role of International Bank Lending in Development Finance," *International Monetary Fund Staff Papers* 32 (June 1985): 344.
20. Ibid., pp. 344–45.
21. Ibid., pp. 345–46.
22. Ibid., p. 347.
23. Ibid., p. 348.

24. Jonathan Eaton and Mark Gersovitz, "LDC Participation in International Financial Markets," *Journal of Development Economics* 7 (1980): 3–21 and Jonathan Eaton and Mark Gersovitz, *Poor Country Borrowing in Private Financial Markets and the Repudiation Issue* (Princeton, NJ: Princeton Studies in International Finance, Princeton University, 1981).

25. John B. Morgan, "A Note on Eaton and Gersovitz's Model of Borrowing," *Journal of Development Economics* 25 (February 1987): 251–61.

26. On this point see the discussion in Arthur MacEwan, "International Debt and Banking: Rising Instability Within the General Crisis," *Science and Society* 50 (Summer 1986): 193–95.

27. Broll and Gilroy, "Banking Policy," pp. 358–66.

28. Laurie S. Goodman, "Bank Lending to Non-OPEC LDCs: Are Risks Diversifiable?" *Federal Reserve Bank of New York Quarterly Review* 6 (Summer 1981): 10–20. Sovereign risk appears to have been decisive in the destruction of loans made abroad by German and French savers in the pre-1914 period. The Russian revolution undercut French lenders, and their nation's defeat in World War I undercut German lenders. See H.W. Arndt and P.J. Drake, "Bank Loans or Bonds: Some Lessons of Historical Experience," *Banca Nazionale Del Lavoro Quarterly Review* 38 (December 1985): 384.

29. Stiglitz, "Credit Markets," p. 148n.50.

30. Goodman, "Bank Lending," p. 12.

31. Ibid., p. 12.

32. Ibid.

33. Ibid.

34. Ibid.

35. Ibid., p. 13.

36. On regulation limiting the extent of competition (as rivalry) among banks see MacEwan, "International Debt," p. 193.

37. Goodman, "Bank Lending," p. 13.

38. A noncommittal but fascinating inquiry into this issue is in Benjamin Cohen's *In Whose Interest? International Banking and American Foreign Policy* (New Haven: Yale University Press, 1986). Cohen concludes that sometimes banks, sometimes governments, take the lead. Phillip Wellons also has emphasized the interdependence between "transnational" banks and their home country governments. See Phillip A. Wellons, "Multinational Institutions in the Debt Crisis: National Interests and Long Term Consequences," in Michael P. Claudon, ed., *World Debt Crisis: International Lending on Trial* (Cambridge, MA: Ballinger Publishing, 1986), pp. 147–69.

39. Piero Sraffa, "The Bank Crisis in Italy," *The Economic Journal* 32 (June 1922): 178–97.

40. See Marcello de Cecco, "The International Debt Problem in the Interwar Period," *Banca Nazionale Del Lavoro Quarterly Review* 38 (March 1985): 52–62.

41. Anthony Sampson, *The Money Lenders: The People and Politics of the World Banking Crisis* (Middlesex: Penguin Books, 1983), p. 331. Poland possesses coal, sulfur, copper, zinc, silver, and lignite.
42. Ibid.
43. Darrell Delamaide, *Debt Shock: The Full Story of the World Debt Crisis* (Garden City, NJ: Anchor Books, 1985), p. 73.
44. Ibid., pp. 70–95. Also see Sampson, *The Money Lenders,* pp. 330–31. For a detailed examination of the "red" loans see Laura D'Andrea Tyson, "The Debt Crisis and Adjustment Responses in Eastern Europe: A Comparative Perspective," *International Organization* 40 (Spring 1986): 239–85.
45. Ibid., p. 71.
46. Sampson, *The Money Lenders,* p. 332.
47. Ibid., p. 332.
48. Ibid.
49. Ibid., pp. 332–33. Sampson adds on p. 333: "The Western bankers, after all, were short of reliable borrowers; and the Polish government negotiator, Jan Woloszyn, was one of the most respected of all international bankers." One wonders whether reliability was a major criteria in identification of borrowers in the first place.
50. Robert Reich, "The Loan Rangers," *The New Republic,* 8 December 1986, p. 44 and Sampson, *The Money Lenders,* p. 334.
51. Ibid., p. 333 and Delamaide, *Debt Shock,* p. 73.
52. Penny Lernoux, *In Banks We Trust* (Harmondsworth, England: Penguin Books, 1986), p. 238. Sampson, *The Money Lenders,* p. 334 adds "Several bankers privately admitted that they would feel much safer if the Russian tanks rolled into Poland."
53. Sampson, *The Money Lenders,* p. 333.
54. Ibid., p. 333.
55. Ibid., p. 334.
56. Reich, "The Loan Rangers," p. 44.
57. See Delamaide, *Debt Shock,* pp. 78–80 for a brief anatomy.
58. Sampson, *The Money Lenders,* pp. 334–35.
59. Ibid., p. 334.
60. Delamaide, *Debt Shock,* p. 83.
61. Edward J. Epstein, "Kuwait: Embassy Cables," *The Atlantic* 251 (May 1983): 16–19.
62. Barbara Rosewicz, "Kuwait Government Debates Aiding Banks Wounded in 1982 Market Crash," *Wall Street Journal,* 10 May 1985.
63. Fida Darwiche, *The Gulf Stock Exchange Crash: The Rise and Fall of the Souk-Al-Manakh* (London: Croom Helm, 1986). Darwiche reports on pp. 119–20:

    The government put at the disposal of the Central Bank several devices to help the commercial banks maintain their liquidity. The devices included discount operations, whereby commercial promissory notes maturing within a year could be swapped at special interest rates; and swapping facilities with local banks, which involved the exchange of local for foreign currencies for periods ranging from one week to three months. The Central Bank was empowered to issue bonds in periods of one week, one month or three months. Those bonds would provide the commercial banks with instruments bearing interest which could replace current account balances with the Central Bank itself! However, economic crises inevitably cast doubts on the integrity of the banking system. As the Al-Manakh crisis broke, doubts were reflected in the drying up of liquidity and a sharp and rapid rise in interest rates. When the Ministry of Finance and the Central Bank both announced they were standing by the banks, the declaration helped to restore confidence.

64. David Eichhorn, "Israel's Economy Must Surmount Serious Obstacles," *Washington Jewish Week,* 15 January 1987.
65. Ibid.
66. Ibid.
67. Ibid.
68. The connection between external debt and capital flight for LDCs is explored somewhat timidly and tentatively (for obvious reasons) by Mohsin Khan and Nadeem Al Haque, "Foreign Borrowing and Capital Flight," *IMF Staff Papers* 32 (1985): 606–28.
69. H. Robert Heller, "The Debt Crisis and the Future of International Bank Lending," *American Economic Review* 77 (May 1987): 172.
70. Ibid., p. 172.
71. Ibid., pp. 174–75.

CHAPTER 4

Rational Expectations and the Global Debt Crisis

A mainstream economist presumably would want to find an explanation for the massive build up of external indebtedness in less developed countries that is compatible with the belief that bankers possess rational expectations (or stochastic perfect foresight). Typically, from this standpoint, growth in periphery debt is either no object for alarm or is due to unforeseeable shocks.

One explanation for the buildup of external debt says in effect that the debt crisis is not really a crisis after all. Loans that appear to be going bad really are good loans. The bankers have acted wisely. The current traumas are only temporary. Profitability of the commercial bank claims on LDCs will be demonstrated eventually.

The second explanation says that there is indeed a crisis, but one attributable to random events and therefore could not be anticipated by the bankers. Here the bankers again acted reasonably, but the loans went bad due to entirely unforeseeable circumstances.

There is, however, a third possibility consistent with attributing rational expectations to the bankers. The bankers could have made bad loans knowing they were bad loans. Of course, the reason why this might have been the case requires a full argument. It must be shown that banks have some overall advantage from making bad loans.

THE FIRST VIEW: NO CRISIS

Michael Beenstock is perhaps the premier exponent of the first view.[1] Beenstock's "transition theory" says that the LDCs are now becoming the major global industrial centers. De-industrialization in the center and industrialization on the periphery—particularly in the so called newly industrializing countries (NICs)—has meant shifts in Beenstock's marginal product of capital schedules in each region. The downward shift in the center nations' schedules and the upward shift in the periphery nations' schedules raised the rate of return on capital in the developing countries relative to that in the developed countries. Short-term effects from the oil price hikes contributed to the increased indebtedness of the non-OPEC LDCs, but the structural change in the world economy that shifted industrial growth toward some of those nations becomes Beenstock's fundamental cause of the increase in debt.

Beenstock and Pangloss

Beenstock, to confirm his explanation, points to the fact that growth in LDC manufacturing has accompanied growth in their debt. He suggests that the situation is analogous, for example, to the indebtedness incurred by borrowers in the United States during nineteenth century industrialization. In his estimation, growth in LDC debt today is merely an equilibrium adjustment that reflects the necessary flows in finance from low return to high return regions. There is no reason for panic, according to Beenstock. He argues that the NICs will become industrial centers within twenty to thirty years and the current disarray is only a temporary period of pain that goes hand in hand with international structural transformation. The bankers' eagerness to loan to the LDCs during the 1970s was therefore reasonable.

Furthermore, it is argued the bankers can rely upon some natural safeguards inherent in their approach to lending. Specifically, Laurie Goodman has placed emphasis on the bankers' capacity to diversify their lending to reduce the degree of covariance (or interdependence) between the various credits issued. Goodman, writing shortly before the 1981 Mexican peso drama (the collapsing value of the peso on international markets) was so optimistic about the effectiveness of diversification that she could conclude "that the nightmares of bankers, regulators, and journalists of massive LDC defaults paralyzing the United States banking system are not warranted on economic grounds."[2] In the 1970s, the bankers simultaneously delivered funds to OPEC and non-OPEC LDCs on the presumption that they would be covered regardless of the direction of movement of oil prices.

Beenstock's explanation for the build up of LDC debt is intriguing, but it poses its own set of rhetorical questions. Is it believable that differentials in the interest rates that could be contracted on loans in the center and on the periphery were grounded in differences in the real return on capital? Even if Brazil is destined to be where the U.S. is today in terms of economic development by the year 2010, does it mean that the typical loan received by Brazilian borrowers will be utilized to generate sufficient earnings to pay the lender the prospective real return?

The Utilization of Development Loans

Kindleberger, for one, has a far less agreeable view of the uses of funds by LDC borrowers, contending that the historical record reveals that ". . . productive loans in the developing countries are not very productive and do not stay long out of default."[3] Indeed, one wonders why the grounds for optimism concerning the relative potential for economic development in Argentina in the 1970s ought to have been any greater than it was in the 1920s. "Development" loans do not have an impressive history of success. They rarely have produced any semblance of economic development and have often produced defaults. Metais contends that the 1970s constitutes the fifth wave of lending to the "backward" regions. He identifies the periods 1817–25, 1870–76, 1900–14, and the 1920s as the four previous waves. "Unfortunately," Matais concludes, "they all ended in widespread defaults." Some of the same countries were involved in the lending booms in the latter three waves—1900–14, the 1920s, and the 1970s: Argentina, Brazil, Egypt, Mexico, Spain, and Turkey.[4] If the past is a guide to the future (a possibility that the rational expectationists do not rule out altogether) commercial bankers in the 1970s should have forecast that their loans to the periphery were going to go into default.

There are those who claim that the loans of the 1970s were utilized productively in the LDCs that were major borrowers rather than wastefully or merely to sustain consumption. Jeffrey Sachs, in particular, argued on the basis of his 1981 econometric research that "much of the growth in LDC debt reflects increased investment."[5] Unfortunately Sachs, on the basis of this finding, went on to infer a conclusion that he should have known would return:

> If my analysis is correct . . . the growth in LDC debt . . . should not pose a problem of repayment. The major borrowers have accumulated debt in the context of rising or stable, but not falling, saving rates. This is particularly true for Brazil and Mexico, which together account for about 40 per cent of the net bank liabilities of the LDCs and about 20 percent of total debt of the LDCs.

The growth in debt might be a cause for concern if borrowing reflected an attempt to maintain consumption at unsustainable levels after the oil price increase.[6]

By August 1982 , of course, the Mexican government announced suspension of payments on its external debt, an event virtually all observers concede signalled the crystallization of the country's contemporary debt crisis. Moreover, the statistical correlation between borrowing and investment that Sachs detected for the period 1965–78 was not evident in the period 1979–83.[7] Correlation is obviously not causation.

William Cline, relying in part on Sachs's research, also reaches the conclusion that borrowed finance was used largely for productive purposes in LDCs. He points to various instances of ". . . significant investment projects (the Itaipu dam, domestic energy resources, and steel production in Brazil, oil development in Mexico, copper expansion in Chile)" as invalidating "the sweeping assertion that borrowed funds were wasted (although differences among countries were sharp, especially with respect to capital flight)."[8] Given the notoriety of the operation of Pemex, the national oil company, one can wonder, at least, about Cline's inclusion of "oil development in Mexico" on his list of laudatory investment projects. The World Bank's *World Development Report* for 1985 contends that commercial bank borrowings in the 1970s generally were used inefficiently or unproductively. Loans not "used to maintain consumption when commodity prices fell (such as in Zambia) . . . went to finance large public investments, many of which contributed little to economic growth or to generating the foreign exchange to service the debt" in subsaharan Africa.[9] Even in the East Asian "tigers," where the Bank's report generally applauds the quality of investment, the Bank identifies errors in public sector expenditures of commercial bank borrowings.[10] The more fundamental point is that even if borrowed funds are used for "productive purposes," there is no guarantee that the loans will achieve a profitable return for the lenders.

Consider Beenstock's suggestion that contemporary LDC indebtedness parallels the experience of the United States in the latter half of the nineteenth century. Many of those nineteenth century loans were made to state governments, and the funds often used for bonafide infrastructural development, such as roads, dams, bridges, railroad tracks, and the like. Yet numerous state governments repudiated their debts[11] —all in a period when the nation was experiencing unprecedented economic growth.

Advance Calculation of Real Returns

Furthermore, advance calculation of the real returns on loans—inclusive of an accounting for risks of repayment difficulties—is a dubious proposition. If a climate of non-calculable risk envelops lending decisions, uncertainty becomes subjective in that it precludes formulation of mathematical or even ordinal, systematic expectations. In his discussion of country risk analysis, Wallich says: "Practitioners of this activity are the first to point out that analysis of country risk is not a science. I hesitate to call it an art; perhaps it may be dignified by the term 'craft.' "[12] Wallich adds that a host of variables are typically examined to gauge debt service capability—export volume, GNP, level of foreign reserves, available credit facilities, and "compressibility of imports"— but warns:

> . . . these are very partial relationships. In some of them the variables are not even accurately defined. Far more subtle and detailed relationships and data can and need to be brought to bear on the problem. Even then different views can be supported by the same basic facts. . . .[13]

The effects of the actions of one debtor on others are especially difficult outcomes to forecast. If one defaults, will others follow suit?[14] The literature suggests that it is a devastatingly open-ended question that can only receive an unequivocal answer if stringent—and unrealistic—assumptions are employed.[15]

Stephen Dubrul, Jr.'s observation that "the only certainty in international finance is uncertainty"[16] is especially telling. There is no magic formula that permits bankers to calculate the real return on their loans. They are confronted with uncertainty in Keynes' most disturbing sense.[17] The bankers cannot tell the *real* return that will be earned on capital in the future. They cannot see the future. Their decisions must be made despite inherently frail predictions.

Debt-Service Ratios and Prospects for Crisis

It is also interesting to note that a more careful look at the variable Beenstock isolates to support his position—the debt-service ratio— actually could support the opposite case. Beenstock is probably a victim of the date of publication of his manuscript—his data on debt-service ratios is complete through 1979, but by 1981 the debt-service ratio had reached 20 percent for LDCs in general and was climbing. (Also see the discussion in Chapter 2.) Once the ratios crossed the 20 percent threshold, they were in the vicinity of Latin American debt-service ratios that prevailed between 1930 and 1937.[18]

A recent study by Dooley et al. reinforces how dramatically the debt-service ratios for LDC borrowers have changed since the publication of Beenstock's book. While admitting that they "do not know what level of this ratio is sustainable for any country nor . . . that it is the only relevant measure of country's debt position," Dooley and his co-authors contend that the ratios of real net interest payments to exports "clearly show a deterioration in the external position of several of these countries to levels that are very high by historical standards."[19] Note that the Dooley et al. measure of debt-service capability is more conservative than Beenstock's, because the former measure does not include payments on principal that would permit amortization of the debt. If anything, the measure understates the problems LDCs face in meeting their debt obligations.

By the measure of real net interest as a percentage of their exports, the situation is especially drastic for Mexico, Brazil, and Argentina. The Dooley et al. debt-service ratio was 16 percent for Mexico and 24 percent each for Brazil and Argentina by 1982.[20] Dooley and his co-authors suggest that the debt-service ratios were quite different before 1981 and 1982 because (1) "the dollar value of these countries' exports grew rapidly throughout the 1970s in both volume and value terms;" (2) "dollar prices of oil and other exports grew faster than the dollar prices of traded goods in general;" and (3) growth of the debt burden was contained "by generally low or at times negative real interest rates on dollar [denominated] debt." In 1981 and 1982 conditions changed. The rate of export growth tailed off due to the impact of worldwide recession. Plus: ". . . interest rates on floating rate dollar debt rose relative to inflation rates so that the real interest costs on existing debt increased substantially."[21]

Reporting Nonperforming Loans

It is true that losses on bank loans to LDC borrowers, for U.S. banks in particular, remain low relative to losses on loans to domestic borrowers. This may provide comfort to those who share Beenstock's view that the crisis is no crisis at all. But the figures on loan losses on foreign debts are deceptive. The large money center banks are able to avoid listing their nonperforming loans as "nonperforming" in their regulatory reports.

They can roll the loans over through automatic or near-automatic refinancing or rescheduling arrangements to avoid having to deduct them from their assets.[22] Makin provides details on how the major U.S. money center bankers "handled" their nonperforming loans to Brazil in 1983:

> Citicorp was not alone in facing heavy write-downs on Brazilian loans, where arrearages had mounted by the fall of 1983 to over $4 billion. Among Citicorp's fellow New York banks, Manufacturers Hanover had $2.0 billion in Brazilian loans, and development-loan-oriented Chase, $2.6 billion—both exposures comparable to Citibank's in view of their smaller net worth. It is likely that some judicious rolling over of loans had been required to avoid triggering the "nonperforming" alarm bell on Brazilian loans. We have already seen that loans that had a sixty-day nonperformance clause had in September 1983 been relaxed to a ninety-day clause to avoid the costly nonperformance designation. With respect to their LDC clients, the mighty banks were in the position of a bomb squad disarming a time bomb. Top priority at the moment was to disarm the nonperforming fuse—or worse yet, the default fuse—before it ignited the debt bomb. At such a critical moment capturing the bomber—like reflection on fundamental causes of, and long-run solutions to, the massive overhang of developing country debt—was a secondary consideration.[23]

Companies in Mexico did not pay any interest on their debts between August 1982 and January 1983 because they could not obtain access to U.S. dollars. The government inaugurated exchange controls on August 5, 1982, dictating that only the government could buy and sell U.S. dollars at a preferential rate of fifty pesos per dollar. But the Mexican government had no dollars to sell, regardless of the exchange rate. The commercial banks threatened to hold off new loans to the Mexican government until they received interest payment from private sector borrowers. But the banks' threat was a consequence of their fear that they would have to label many of their private sector loans to Mexican borrowers as nonperforming. By February 1983 the commercial banks had put together the largest syndication in financial history—a syndicate of 500 commercial lenders—to provide $4.8 billion in loans for 1983 to permit the financing of the prior interest obligations.[24] This was rollover in its highest form. The *quid pro quo* commercial banks demanded was harsher terms on refinancing the Mexican government's own debt. The government, according to the banks, did not want to contract for more than one point above LIBOR (which was at 15 percent in early 1983), but the banks insisted upon 1.5 percent above LIBOR.[25]

Bankers are loath to report any of their loans as nonperforming, which would require the loans to be recorded on a nonaccrual basis. It is easier for them to avoid such reports on foreign loans due to the nature of the existing regulatory arrangements.[26] The banks have interpreted the prevailing regulations as meaning that they can record loan interest although the interest remains unpaid. The banks assert that this is legitimate under existing rules as long as they "believe the loans are well-secured and in the process of collection."[27] Of course, the banks are largely free to determine whether or not a particular loan is "well-secured and in the process of collection." Only very recently has any evidence surfaced that the comptroller of the currency and the Federal Reserve Board have begun to attempt to "clarify" the accounting rules, tightening the conditions under which banks can continue to report interest on loans that are ninety days overdue, as if interest has been received.[28] Moreover, the observation that the loss rate is lower on foreign than domestic loans may be "damning" the foreign loans with faint praise, given the questionable quality of numerous domestic loans at present.

Other Bank Management Problems

A more difficult management problem for the money center banks than avoiding writing down their earnings on Latin debt may be preventing their stocks from losing heavily on the securities market. Investors may simply look through the accounting stratagems and make a negative judgment about the earnings position of the banks due to doubts about the banks' LDC loans.[29] The question remains whether or not investor reaction is a sufficient disciplining force to rein in excessive lending by the commercial banks. This issue will be treated in greater depth later in this text when the principal-agent dilemma approach to the international debt crisis is examined. To the extent that the current crisis actually shows fundamental weakness in the international financial system, the investor response appears only to have an impact after the fact—after the loans have already been made that eventually become nonperforming.

The bankers' natural safeguards—such as diversification, so enthusiastically endorsed by Goodman—certainly have not proven effective during this episode of lending to the LDCs. The banks made a special effort to lend simultaneously to non-oil exporting LDCs and oil exporting LDCs ostensibly to cover themselves regardless of what happened to petroleum prices. Additional increases in oil prices would hurt the balance of payments position of the non-oil exporting LDCs, but enhance the ability of the oil exporters to repay their loans. Decreases in oil prices would have the opposite effect.

But in an environment of softening petroleum prices during the start of the 1980s, *both* sets of countries began to experience serious difficulties in balance of payment. The falling petroleum prices would have an obvious adverse effect on the Latin oil exporters with large external debt—Mexico and Venezuela. Brazil and Argentina, the Latin oil importers, should have benefitted, but several factors combined to undermine that presumption. The combination of rising real interest rates, the drop in commodity prices for the oil importers' (non-oil) exports, and the generalized global downturn of 1980–82 pushed them into illiquidity as well. Plus, while the oil exporters had benefitted from the oil price rise of 1978 and 1979, the oil importers had already been placed in a difficult situation by the last oil price boom.[30] Retrospectively, important aspects of the "risks" of foreign lending were "non-diversifiable." There proved to be a strong rather than weak correlation between the poor growth experiences of the LDCs in the banks' foreign loan portfolios in the early 1980s.[31]

The current accelerated softening of oil prices is now having the anticipated adverse impact on the oil exporting debtor nations. By early 1986, an anonymous European banker was reported to be "terribly concerned" as oil prices spiralled downward toward $20 per barrel because Mexico was being pressed "into a 'desperate situation.'" Some Mexican officials were also reported to be admitting that if the price of oil were to fall under $20 per barrel, Mexico "simply [would] default on its interest payments."[32] There were no reports of offsetting improvements in the status of oil importing LDC borrowers.

Still, it is possible to maintain that the present problems are temporary and will reverse themselves in the normal course of events without a major intervention by national or multinational monetary authorities. One might continue to hold such a position despite (1) the historical precedents on LDC lending; (2) the statistical evidence on debt-service ratios for major LDC debtor nations; (3) the substantial record of nonperformance on these loans; (4) the obvious failure of the bankers' natural diversification safeguard to ensure that their portfolios show a reasonably balanced mix of developing nations with positive/negative rates of overall economic growth or net export growth; (5) and the apparent lack of the courage of their own convictions, evident in bankers' attempts to withdraw from lending after 1982.

THE SECOND VIEW: SURPRISED BANKERS

Alternatively, as suggested above, a rational expectationist can argue that the bankers made their decisions based upon rationally formed anticipations, but they were surprised by unforeseen and unforeseeable events that made the loans perform badly. The position that the existing debt crisis is the outcome of a random shock is most fully developed by Sachs in conjunction with Bruno.[33] They cite the oil price shock and its effects as the key random event that sent the borrowing nations into arrears on their debt payments. However, Sachs and Bruno probably have not selected the most convincing surprise. It would be difficult to support the view that the second oil price boost of 1978 and 1979 was a "shock." Loan portfolio diversification was intended to cope with just such an eventuality.

If anything, the failure of diversification is probably more suggestive of the bankers' ignorance about the structure of the world economy and the behavior of financial markets than of a surprise from a random shock.[34] Or perhaps the bankers were beset with the intractable problem of forming expectations of outcomes when their forecasts require prediction of the expectations of *other* participants in international credit markets, while the other participants seek to form their expectations in just the same manner.[35] That still does not explain the banks' rashness in response to such uncertainties.

The biggest surprise may have been the U.S. central bank's inauguration of a stringent disinflationary policy. A case can be made that no one—including the bankers—expected the Federal Reserve to staunchly maintain its tight money policy. Advocates of the Fisherian theory of interest rates were baffled, as retroactively measured real rates of interest on the dollar rose from low and even negative levels to historically unprecedented positive levels over the course of the past several years. John Makin, for one, places the onus of the international debt crisis on the doorstep of the Fed's great success in bringing down the U.S. inflation rate; he depicts Walter Wriston as one money center banker who was "shocked" by the Fed's vigilance:

> What remains is to determine what force on earth could bring to so sudden a stop the music that both borrowers and lenders had been so pleased to hear and dance to with such abandon from 1974 to 1981. In two words, it was Paul Volcker. Again Wriston is the spokesman who characterizes a transition from the banker's perspective. Asked in a 1978 interview whether he would welcome any restrictions on any U.S. lenders or borrowers, Wriston replied:

"I just want the opposite. Let us have their freedoms." "Which ones?" asked the interviewer. Wriston replied: "I believe the most important thing the bank will have to deal with over the next 10 years is not money policy, because the options are limited and there isn't much elbow room. [Rather] it's the revolution in the financial business of America." Five years later, asked the inevitable "what's gone wrong now" question in another interview just before the September annual meetings of the IMF and World Bank, Wriston replied: "We're beat upon the fact that we have imprudent moments. But I don't know anyone that knew Volcker was going to lock the wheels of the world."[36]

Simply put, the banks and their borrowers got caught in the left hand tail of the rate of return frequency distribution due to the random shock created by the U.S. central bank's unanticipated commitment to disinflation. The bankers' lending terms were reasonable and conditioned on their reasonable forecasts of the direction of the world economy. Floating rates on loan contracts—tied for reference to nominal rates designed to protect the lenders from high inflation—punished the carriers of dollar-denominated debt as inflation was wrung out of the U.S. economy. Fixed rate medium- to long-term loans fared no better, since the rates were set during a period of relative high U.S. inflation.

Magee and Brock take exception to this position, arguing instead that large money center bankers, themselves, urged the Fed to pursue a high real interest rate policy. The bankers' motive, according to Magee and Brock, was a "rent-seeking" gain to compensate for the fragility of their exposure on the periphery.[37] Lance Taylor, however, expresses doubt about the Magee-Brock claim, observing that: "The argument is not convincing, since banks make money from the spread between loan and deposit rates. Why increased rates would also raise the spread is not clear."[38] Nonetheless, Taylor does add: ". . . one cannot quibble with Magee and Brock's conclusion that no 'solution' to the Third World debt problem may be feasible if it is at variance with the economic interests of the large U.S. banks."[39]

The political clout of the large money center bankers is such that they could indeed exercise influence on central bank policy. In fact, they may have favored a high real interest rate policy to offset the low or negative retrospective real rates attained throughout most of the 1970s. What may have "surprised" them was the timing and duration of the Fed's disinflationary stance. Perhaps they were really surprised that their political clout was not quite sufficient to precisely dictate the time-path of the high real interest policy.

THE THIRD VIEW: BAD LOANS
ARE GOOD BUSINESS

Short of the cynical, but potentially defensible, position that the bankers intentionally made bad loans, the rational expectations hypothesis suggests either that there is *no* debt crisis or, if there is one, it has been due to a random shock. In either of these cases, if loan "pushing" occurred it was not overlending, given the well reasoned judgments of the lenders. If the terms were softened to encourage LDC borrowers, those terms were consistent with best estimates of the risks involved—country risk, credit risk, exchange risk, etc.—at the time the loan contracts were made initially.

Ironically however, loan pushing is most consistent, within the context of the rational expectations hypothesis, with the third possibility—that the bankers knowingly made bad foreign loans. This third position can be maintained—despite its idiosyncracies—if one carefully distinguishes between the potential interests of the large money center banks whose shares are publicly traded, and the comparatively smaller banks that are not publicly owned. The latter, it can be argued, were pressed into the foreign loan business by their major depositors' efforts to export abroad. It should be added that larger banks, through correspondent relationships, can exert leverage to pull second and third tier banks into foreign loan syndications.

There are a variety of reasons why foreign loans are of potential special benefit to large money center banks, regardless of loan quality. First, the money center banks can obtain loan fees initially for setting up the syndication. Second, as suggested above, the regulatory climate permits foreign loans to be kept on the books as performing far longer than domestic loans when foreign borrowers are in arrears. Third, when smaller banks withdraw from syndications at the point when problems appear, the larger banks can absorb their claims (presumably at a lower cost than the price of the initial commitment). Fourth, foreign loans to LDCs have potential international insurance agents, for example, in the form of the IMF. The World Bank has also been assuming more of this type of function lately. Fifth, LDC loans can contribute to an overall climate of financial pressure that facilitates greater dominance by large banks of the banking industry—partially because of the manner in which regulators respond to the crisis. Sixth, there might be a net gain on the stock market from the foreign loan commitment, depending on market participants' reaction over time to the loan.

The phenomenon of bankers opting to contract for loans that have a high probability of going into default also may rest upon the existence of public sector institutions (that is, governments) that the bankers anticipate will function as "guarantors" in their stead. The argument is reinforced when the incentives for lending, generated by the existence of these backup institutions, coexist with intense competitive pressure among financial intermediaries. Based upon evidence from the earlier lending waves to the less-developed countries, lending that existed prior to the FDIC, the IMF, or the World Bank, competitive pressure alone may be sufficient to bring on a debt crisis. But the modern regulatory apparatus might make it even easier for the bankers to forget any potential lessons to be learned from the past.

NOTES

1. Michael Beenstock, *The World Economy in Transition* (London: George Allen and Unwin, 1983).
2. Laurie Goodman, "Bank Lending to Non-OPEC LDCs: Are Risks Diversifiable?" *Federal Reserve Board of New York Quarterly Review* 6 (Summer 1981): 20.
3. Charles Kindleberger, "Debt Situation of the Developing Countries in Historical Perspective," in Stephen Goodman, ed., *Financing and Risk in Developing Countries* (New York: Praeger Publishers, 1978), p. 6.
4. Joel Metais, "Less Developed Countries' Rising Indebtedness and the Lender of Last Resort in International Context," in C.P. Kindleberger and Jean-Pierre Laffargue, *Financial Crisis: Theory, History, and Policy* (Cambridge, England: Cambridge University Press, 1982), pp. 222 and 234n.2.
5. Jeffrey Sachs, "The Current Account and Macroeconomic Adjustment in the 1970s," *Brookings Papers on Economic Activity* 1 (1981): 243.
6. Ibid.
7. The World Bank, *World Development Report 1985* (New York: Oxford University Press, 1985), p. 46.
8. William R. Cline, "International Debt: Analysis, Experience and Prospects," *Journal of Development Planning* (1985): 27.
9. The World Bank, "World Development," pp. 51–54. These wasteful public investments included: "large conference centers, administrative buildings, university centers, hotels, and highways, as well as projects in the industrial sector, such as oil and sugar refineries, steel mills, and textile and cement factors."
10. Ibid., p. 54. The "tigers" are the rapidly growing Asian nations of Singapore, Taiwan, Korea, and Hong Kong.
11. See William A. Scott, *The Repudiation of State Debts: A Study in the Financial History of Mississippi, Florida, Alabama, North Carolina, South*

Carolina, Georgia, Louisiana, Arkansas, Tennessee, Minnesota, Michigan, and Virginia (New York: Thomas Y. Crowell and Co., 1893).

12. Henry Wallich, "How Much Private Bank Lending Is Enough?" in Stephen Goodman, ed., *Financing and Risk in Developing Countries* (New York: Praeger Publishers, 1978), p. 15.

13. Ibid., pp. 15–16.

14. Ibid., p. 16.

15. See Vincent P. Crawford, "International Lending, Long-Term Credit Relationships and Dynamic Contract Theory" (Discussion Paper 84–14, University of California at San Diego, 1984).

16. Stephen M. Dubrul, Jr., "Management of Risk" in Stephen Goodman, ed., *Financing and Risk in Developing Countries* (New York: Praeger Publishers, 1978), p. 57.

17. J.M. Keynes, "The General Theory of Employment," *Quarterly Journal of Economics* (February 1937): 214 (emphasis added):

> By "uncertain" knowledge, let me explain, I do not mean merely to distinguish what is known for certain from what is only probable. The game of roulette is not subject, in this sense, to uncertainty; nor is the prospect of a Victory bond being drawn. Or, again, the expectation of life is only slightly uncertain. Even the weather is only moderately uncertain. The sense in which I am using the term is that in which the prospect of a European war is uncertain, or the price of copper or the rate of interest twenty years hence, or the obsolescence of a new invention, or the position of private wealth-owners in the social system in 1970. About these matters there is no scientific basis on which to form any calculable probability whatever. *We simply do not know.*

18. Neil J. McMullen, "Historical Perspectives on Developing Nations' Debt," in Lawrence G. Franko and Marilyn Seiber, eds., *Developing Country Debt* (New York: Pergamon Press, 1979) pp. 3–16.

McMullen also was an optimist about the LDC debt build up of the 1970s, based upon a comparison with the conditions of the 1930s. His comparisons may have been, like Beenstock's, premature. The only salient differences between the 1930s and the current situation that McMullen identified that still applies is the existence of international institutions that can make concessionary loans and grants, and because of loan finance instead of bond finance countries with debt problems may have more alternatives to formal default.

19. Michael Dooley, William Helkie, Ralph Tryon, and John Underwood, "An Analysis of External Debt Positions of Eight Developing Countries Through 1990," (International Finance Discussion Paper No. 227, 1984, p. 7).

20. Ibid., p. 7.

21. Ibid.

22. G. Christian Hill, "Lender Beware: List of Troubled Banks Shows Realty, Energy Lead Bad-Loan Areas," *Wall Street Journal*, 19 March 1984.

23. John H. Makin, *The Global Debt Crisis: America's Growing Involvement* (New York: Basic Books, Inc., 1984), p. 135 (emphasis added).

   It is interesting to note that the initial loan contracts included a contingency clause—the sixty day nonperformance clause—but that the banks effectively *recontracted* with the Brazilian borrowers by extending the nonperformance clause to ninety days. At first blush, recontracting may appear to be incompatible with the behavior associated with invocation of rational expectations on the part of the bankers. But in the context of strategic gamesmanship were both partners to the contract—lender and borrower—must form expectations about the other's reactions, the possibility of renegotiation and recontracting can mute the moral-hazard problem. See Crawford, "International Lending," pp. 19–42.

24. See Lawrence Rout, "Banks Want Interest From Mexico Firms: Institutions Threaten to Bar New Government Loans Unless Debt Is Paid Off," *Wall Street Journal*, 24 November 1982, and "Mexico Arranges over $4.8 Billion in Loans For 1983," *Wall Street Journal*, 9 February 1983.

25. Lawrence Rout, "Mexico's Debt Load Troubles Banks," *Wall Street Journal*, 21 April 1984.

26. Jane D'Arista makes a similar point in "Private Overseas Lending: Too Far, Too Fast?" in Jonathan D. Aronson, ed., *Debt and the Less Developed Countries*, (Boulder, CO: Westview Press, 1979), pp. 69–70.

   Despite fiascoes in Indonesia and elsewhere, some analysts argue that banks have not been reckless in their LDC lending. They cite as evidence a Federal Reserve Board study showing that loan loss experience on foreign loans has been significantly lower than on domestic loans. An obvious question arises: Is it possible that the same banks that lent $22 billion to REITs were miraculously more prudent when lending to foreigners? Albert Fishlow suggests that this could be so if banks are more willing to *accept* losses on domestic portfolios than on foreign. Domestic bankruptcy laws offer some protection unavailable abroad, especially where governments are involved. It may be rational for banks to accept refinancing or rescheduling of foreign loans rather than default.

   Thus, evidence of problems in international lending may lie elsewhere. The Securities and Exchange Commission has, in fact, turned over a stone ignored by other bank regulatory authorities. It requires bank holding companies to report aggregate nonperforming loans and sometimes has pressed banks to break out these loans by source and state their earnings' impact. At the end of 1976, a few U.S. multinational banks reported nonperforming foreign loans at levels almost as high as those for domestic borrowers. While much more information is needed to assess the source of international lending problems, it is clear that loan loss experience is an inadequate measure of foreign lending prudence.

27. Daniel Hertzberg and S. Karene Witcher, "New U.S. Rules on Latin Debt to Affect Banks," *Wall Street Journal*, 19 June 1984.

28. Ibid.

29. For example, Manufacturers Hanover, with heavy exposure in Latin America, experienced a major "battering" of its stock in 1984, well before the regulators took steps to encourage more stringent accounting practices.

30. Thomas O. Enders and Richard P. Mattione, "Latin America: The Crisis of Debt and Growth," Brookings Discussion Papers in International Economics, (Washington, DC: The Brookings Institution, 1983), p. 24.

Enders and Mattione also argue that the situation was made worse by the failure of the Latin debtor nations' regimes to engineer an "adjustment" to their balance of payments difficulties. "Adjustment" is a euphemism for the austerity of reducing consumption and imports. Of course, this leaves open the issue of who will bear the burden of "adjustment"—the wealthier strata of the debtor nation or the poor. There are sound reasons for believing that the brunt will be felt by the poor when such "adjustments" are enacted—particularly after a "successful" visit by an IMF mission.

31. Richard S. Dale, "Country Risk and Bank Regulation," The Banker, 133 (March 1983): 46.

Makin, The Global Debt Crisis, p. 142 observes:

> The argument for diversification was compelling—but not, it turned out, compelling enough to overcome two very serious problems. First, it overlooked the ability of governments to spend more than they have no matter how much they have. In this case governments proved to be wasteful intermediaries between banks and projects, out of carelessness or incompetence and sometimes out of downright dishonesty. Second, it forgot that the diversification argument relates only to the stability of earnings, not their level. The sad truth is that if a world recession—like the one that began in 1981—unites with waste to produce a widespread negative rate of return, it does not help much to have diversification to thank for its being a *stable* negative return instead of a volatile negative one. The debts still cannot be repaid. (Emphasis in original.)

32. "A Mixed Bag: Plunge in Oil Prices Will Bring Benefits but Spur Trouble, Too," Wall Street Journal, 22 January 1986.

33. Michael Bruno and Jeffrey Sachs, "Adjustment and Structural Change in the World Economy" (NBER Working Paper No. 852, 1982).

James Street has also argued that the Latin American debt situation is entirely due to oil shocks. See his paper "The Latin American Debt Problem: Liquidity or Growth Crisis?" (Unpublished manuscript, Rutgers University, 1983).

34. For example, as William Cline points out in International Debt: Systemic Risk and Policy Response (Washington, DC: Institute for International Economics, 1984), p. 8, Mexico's growth in external indebtedness was accompanied by the rise in petroleum prices in the late 1970s. As Cline observes, "Mexico first borrowed heavily to develop oil production, and subsequently the promise of oil exports was the main basis for its ability to borrow large amounts more generally in pursuit of a high-growth strategy."

35. Roman Frydman, "Towards an Understanding of Market Processes: Individual Expectations, Learning and Convergence to Rational Expectations Equilibrium," *American Economic Review* 72 (1982): 652–68. Also see J.M. Keynes, *The General Theory of Employment, Interest, and Money* (London: Macmillan, 1936): 154–56—specifically his beauty contest metaphor.

36. Makin, *The Global Debt Crisis*, p. 752.

37. Stephen P. Magee and William A. Brock, "The Rise in the Third World's External Debt/Equity Ratio As A Redistributive Game and the Political Regressivity of Adverse States of Nature" in Michael P. Claudon, ed., *World Debt Crisis: International Lending on Trial* (Cambridge, MA: Ballinger Publishing Company, 1986), pp. 173–98.

38. Lance Taylor, "The Theory and Practice of Developing Country Debt: An Informal Guide for the Perplexed," *Journal of Development Planning*, no. 16 (1985): 202.

39. Ibid., p. 202.

CHAPTER 5

Irrational Credit?
Institutional Weaknesses and the Crisis in International Finance

At the opposite pole from rational expectations based explanations for the debt crisis are explanations that attribute the situation to poor judgment and banker errors, or more generally, to structural flaws in the commercial banking system. Unlike the rational expectations view—that the bankers were as well informed as possible in making their loans—this other perspective holds that bankers operated without adequate knowledge of available information. Bad loans were made because of carelessness and insufficient investigation of the circumstances of the borrowers. Poor knowledge led to the current "catharsis" in international finance.

The explanation could even be given in generational terms. Arguably, the current wave of bank managers have either forgotten or were never familiar with the troubled history of loans to the nations on the periphery. Fifty-year waves of LDC loans occur precisely because it takes approximately that amount of time for the older group of bankers to be replaced entirely with a new group unversed in the lessons of the past. Recurrent debt crises can be attributed to the training of young bankers that neglects tutoring them in the history of financial crises.[1]

HABITS OF THE TRADE

S.C. Gwynne's revelations on the foreign loan business as an employee of a medium-sized Ohio bank provide some support for this "poor judgment" explanation. He describes his own rise as a twenty-five year old front-line loan officer in the Philippines in 1978—during the Marcos era—after: ". . . one and a half years of banking experience [after joining] the bank as a 'credit analyst' on the strength of an MA in English [and after promotion] eleven months later to loan officer and [assignment] to the French speaking Arab nations [because of my fluency in French]."[2] Gwynne adds further that he was by no means unique:

> I am far from alone in my youth and inexperience. The world of international banking is now full of aggressive, bright, but hopelessly inexperienced lenders in their mid-twenties. They travel the world like itinerant brushmen, filling loan quotas, peddling financial wares, and living high on the hog. Their bosses are often bright but hopelessly inexperienced twenty-nine-year-old vice presidents with wardrobes from Brooks Brothers, MBAs from Wharton or Stanford, and so little credit training they would have trouble with a simple retail installment loan.[3]

As for those still higher above these young, "Whartonized" vice presidents—the senior loan officers—Gwynne describes them as "pragmatic nuts-and-bolts bankers whose grasp of local banking is often profound, the product of twenty or thirty years of experience. [However, they] are fish out of water when it comes to international lending."[4] According to Gwynne, the senior bankers had no desire to move into the foreign loan market "but were forced into it by the internationalization of American commerce; as their local clientele expanded into foreign trade, they had no choice but to follow them or lose the business to money-center banks."[5]

On the face of it, Gwynne's story is one of inadequate information at all levels of the banks' decision-making apparatus—at least among the second tier of banks, if not the money center banks as well. But his story also involves the market-making function of the loans on behalf of the bank's domestic corporate depositors. How do we then interpret the actions of the senior loan officers who approved the loan: were they acting out of ignorance or self-preservation? Presumably they managed to retain their important customers, although eventually they had to write down the loan. To the extent that the customers were able to make some sales to the importer in the Philippines, some of the funds lent abroad may have "returned" to the bank through the depositor's own account, generating a balance sheet puzzle on the liabilities side of the ledger. The conundrums associated with capital flight from the LDCs gives depth to this problem. Ultimately, the line between rational and irrational lending for regional banks like Gwynne's may be drawn by posing the question of whether it is worthwhile to the bank, on net, to keep a good customer by making a bad loan?

Typically, loan negotiations have been conducted between LDC governments and large banks. Negotiations bring together a wide range of public and private sector borrowers in the developing world and numerous second and third line banks in the developed world. The transactions costs associated with "carefully investigating each project to determine its profitability and potential to repay borrowing, assuming they even had the language skills and technical and regional experience required to do so" were bypassed by the bankers by dealing directly with governments, since the governments "guarantee[d] these debts, pledging as collateral their ability to tax their citizens."[6]

The bankers presumably did not need to worry about their individual borrowers' capacity to pay, only the borrowing nation's capacity to pay.[7] These governmental guarantees might have contributed to the impression among the bankers that their loans were immune from repudiation: "The pledged word of a great republic like Brazil is very imposing at the time it is given, and somehow it induced a retroactive belief that governments do not default their debts."[8]

Unreasonably Low Spreads?

David Folkerts-Landau contends that the basis for commercial bankers' beliefs that their developing country loans were beyond default includes other considerations besides guarantees offered by borrower countries' governments. The lenders' home country regulatory institutions also provided explicit or implicit guarantees. Central banks and deposit insurance agencies were expected to come to the lenders' aid when liquidity problems arose. Specific financial and legal innovations that have increased default costs for borrowing nations have presumably raised the costs so high that a borrowing nation would never contemplate outright debt repudiation. These financial innovations are two-fold—large-scale syndication and the inauguration of cross-default clauses in loan contracts; the legal type of innovation, passage of the Foreign Sovereign Immunities Act of 1976.[9]

Large-scale syndication can be viewed solely as a risk-spreading device, but a companion effect exists that could deter default. Syndication of sufficient breadth, coupled with cross-default clauses, would insure that the impact of default from a single borrower would be spread over a wide range of bank lenders. This would make it extremely difficult for individual borrowers to declare default on particular loans and then seek additional credits from another group of borrowers. Syndication plus cross-default clauses were financial innovations introduced in the mid-1970s and designed to assure that a defaulting borrower could not reenter international credit markets.[10]

The Sovereign Immunities Act of 1976 removed the doctrine of "absolute sovereign immunity" from U.S. courts. As Folkerts-Landau observes: ". . . immunity will not be recognized if the relevant borrower is a commercial agent of a foreign state or its agencies." Consequently: "[t]he net effect of these financial and legal innovations [has] been to raise the cost of defaulting on any loan, by efforts to ensure that a borrower in default will be denied access to the international banking markets and have its external economic relations interrupted."[11]

According to Folkerts-Landau, the commercial banks were convinced that the costs of default had been increased to an intolerable threshold for borrowers. Therefore, the banks did not incorporate the risk of default in the spreads over LIBOR on their loan rates in transactions with LDCs. The spreads reflected, instead, prospective losses due to loan reschedulings, specifically the foregone interest and principal agreed upon in the event of a rescheduling. As Folkerts-Landau concludes: ". . . the institutional evolution of the international bank loan market has been a movement away from pricing to offset the expected risk of outright default, to a new system where rates on syndicated international credits reflect only the (lower) expected cost of rescheduling."[12]

Folkerts-Landau provides evidence that interest rates offered by commercial banks to developing country borrowers do not include default risk: (1) despite the emergence of the debt crisis in 1982, the spreads over LIBOR on loans to non-oil developing countries typically remained less than one-half a percentage point above the rates paid by industrial country borrowers between 1974 and 1983; (2) the gap between the typical spread paid by developing country borrowers with a rescheduling and the typical spread paid by industrial country borrowers was under one percentage point until 1981, when it went up to one and one-half percentage points; (3) the typical rate of interest on non-oil developing country loans has been below that for loans to large U.S. corporations; and (4) interest rates in the international bank loan market have consistently been below the rates for international bonds, the latter rates presumably incorporating the risks of outright default.[13]

If his assessment of the scope of risk reflected in the spreads offered to developing country borrowers is correct, Folkerts-Landau's analysis leads us to ask whether such spreads indicate irrationality on the part of the bankers. Have the banks succeeded in protecting themselves altogether from outright debt repudiation by a major borrowing nation, or have they embraced a grand self-deception?

Governments—particularly on bond issues—have been declared in default in the past despite the potential dangers of being ousted from international credit markets. After the defaults of the 1930s, the international bond market steered clear of making loans to governments on the periphery for about three uninterrupted decades.[14] It is less clear whether such governments, based upon their bond default record, were denied access to other sources of credit. They certainly could obtain public sector assistance from the industrial center, particularly during the "development decades" of the 1950s and 1960s.

Plus, there is a peculiar "brinksmanship" involved in large-scale syndication and cross-default clauses. This may spur major debtors to form a cartel and indicate a willingness on their part to default *en masse* that may not have existed in the more diffuse environment that preceded the 1976 innovations. Indeed, will defaulting countries be made to show up for trial—and how will court decisions be enforced? Old fashioned economic imperialism could again resume.

Furthermore, reschedulings and refinancing arrangements plunge borrower and lender into a murky region, where according to some interpretations default occurs automatically. Losses on reschedulings could approach the losses associated with default or repudiation of the debt. Indeed, the following question should be posed: are expected losses associated with prospective rescheduling sufficiently small, relative to the private costs of default, to justify extensive lending to the periphery if "official" default really has been rendered impossible?

Disaster Myopia and Following the Herd

These questions must be addressed if one seeks rationality in the international banks' practices to set interest rates. Guttentag and Herring swallow the rationality "kernel" altogether, opting for a view of banking practice imbued with, at a minimum, nonrationality. International capital markets are quite imperfect, according to Guttentag and Herring. Thus, international lending is beset by "structural weakness" due to the tendency of the bankers to periodically acquire "disaster myopia." The bankers, they say, "have sometimes behaved . . . as if the probability of a major shock affecting their international loan portfolios were zero":[15]

[Disaster myopia] is suggested by [the international banks'] willingness to lend amounts equal to a major portion of their capital to a single foreign country at interest rates that exceed the cost of funds (the "spread") by such small margins that any risk premiums included in the spreads must be extremely modest. It is also suggested by their willingness, except during crisis periods, to lend heavily at very narrow spreads to other international banks, some of which are not regulated, some of which have no assured lender of the last resort, and some of which depend for their creditworthiness on legally ambiguous assurances of parental bank support. Other evidence of disaster myopia is the willingness of these banks to reduce their capacity to withstand major shocks during the 1970s when shock probabilities were rising.[16]

This last point refers to the accelerated growth in external, private LDC debt during the 1970s. In this vein the same authors report elsewhere:

- Between 1960 and 1980, foreign branches of U.S. banks grew almost 800 percent—from 124 to 800.
- By 1980, several LDCs and Eastern European nations had external indebtedness to the commercial banks in excess of their entire obligations to foreign governments, international institutions, and direct investors.
- During some years in the 1970s, over 50 percent of the earnings of the ten largest U.S. banks came from foreign sources.[17]

Guttentag and Herring envision such growth in international finance as harboring dangers for the world economy—invoking the dangers of a global banking collapse and credit contraction. But, they argue, the bankers refuse to behave as if such an outcome is possible until the outcome is manifest.

Guttentag and Herring contend that bankers rely upon revocable commitments and "travelling with the herd" as means of eliminating the economic dangers.[18] But these means are not infallible. If any single bank revokes "a commitment [this] almost always shifts problems onto other banks."[19] Following others means that many banks will concentrate their foreign loan portfolios in the same few countries. But if risk is actually diversifiable—if, in fact, the concept of risk is meaningful at all for the uncertainties in banking—it does not diversify when the entire pack follows the same trail to country exposure.

There is a certain logic in following the herd, however. Given the nature of the regulatory system it seems to be advantageous for one bank to keep its actions in line with those of other banks. In addition, as Guttentag and Herring point out themselves: "This tactic minimizes vulnerability to criticism and increases the probability of government aid in the event of a crisis since the entire banking system will be in jeopardy, not just a single bank."[20]

In a recent empirical study of U.S. commercial bank loans in 1977–82, Jain and Gupta conclude, doubtfully, that "herding" took place in the narrow sense that "small banks *blindly* replicated the international lending decisions of large banks."[21] They report a mixture of evidence suggesting whether the nine largest U.S. banks or the next fifteen largest were leaders or followers in LDC loan activity in the major borrower countries. But it does appear that the remaining 125 to 147 "regional" banks followed *both* sets of larger banks overseas.[22] On the basis of Jain and Gupta's study, there can be little doubt that there was a remarkable clustering of LDC loan activity around a small subset of developing country borrowers. Jain and Gupta report that by the close of 1982:

> The top nine banks had lent 51.6 percent of their developing country loans to the top five borrowing countries, 68.4 percent to the top 10 and 85.1 percent to the top 20 borrowers. The corresponding figures for the [next] fifteen banks are 57.5 percent, 76.5 percent, and 89.9 percent, and for the regional banks, they are 60.5 percent, 76.8 percent, and 90.9 percent.[23]

The difficulty with arguments to explain the debt crisis that impute irrationality or nonrationality to bankers also surfaces in the environment of "bunched" lending (or, syndication). Invariably, bad loans can somehow be made to appear "good." As suggested in the previous chapter, even loans of dubious quality can be positive from the bankers' perspective. For example, Makin suggests that the larger banks had a reasonable pecuniary motive for creating the foreign loan syndications. The banks could receive loan fees at the outset to set up the consortium of lenders. The larger the loan, the greater the winnings for the banks acting as syndicating agents, because of banking's economies of scale:

> Fees for arranging the loans averaged about 1 percent of their value. . . . One percent of a $200 million loan is $2 million, while 2 percent of a $100,000 loan is only $2,000. It does not require anywhere near one thousand times the effort expended on a $100,000 loan to arrange a $200 million loan, and even if syndication costs should be large, they can be covered by additional fees assessed "up front" (before the loan is granted).[24]

Loan fees could ease the pain of any self-deception on the part of the senior loan officers at the largest banks. But loan fees also create incentives to increase the size of the overall loan and to make participation in the syndicate appear as attractive as possible to second and third line banks. Even Gwynne's evidence of a lack of knowledge among second line bank managers can be reinterpreted as bankers trying to keep their major depositors happy. And Makin's discussion of money center banks "securing" their loans with guarantees from the developing country government gives way to a discussion of the concrete financial advantages of receiving loan fees.

Inadequate knowledge on the part of either set of bankers could become secondary to all these other considerations mentioned in the previous paragraph. The case should now be considered where banks rationally pushed loans on the periphery without expecting successful payment by their debtors. Advocates of improved information for the bankers—including access to "special" information possessed by the World Bank or the IMF on the internal conditions of specific LDCs—are simply wrong if the debt crisis is not due to misinformation on the part of the bankers.[25]

The Bankers' Propensity for Suicide

Keynes explained the manic lending of the 1920s as a failure of bankers to sensibly forecast the future. In Keynes' estimation, the bankers were partially the victims of bad advice from other economists who, he continued to argue throughout the 1930s, misled practical men (the bankers) with policy recommendations rooted in unsound theory. In particular, the American economists—or "so-called 'economists' " as Keynes called them—who were often hired by the banks, counselled the necessity of greater deflation "regardless of what should be the obvious fact that their cure, if it could be realised, would be a menace to the solvency of their institutions."[26] The bankers were also, Keynes argued, victims of their own penchant for conventions—conventions that paved a path to ruin: "A sound banker, alas! is not one who foresees danger and avoids it, but one who, when he is ruined is ruined in a conventional way along with his fellows so that no one can blame him."[27] Better to go down doing what everyone believes bankers ought to be doing, rather than stay afloat as a lonely maverick in the world of high finance.

For Keynes, the bankers were prisoners of customary responses to stimuli from an economic world that propelled them onto unwarranted lending sprees from which they eventually recoiled, only to deepen their peril. They "pushed" loans (later proven to be of low quality) because it was conventional to be making such loans at the time. Their penchant for conformity led Keynes to conclude in 1931, with a magnificent sense of drama, that "The present signs suggest that the bankers of the world are bent on suicide."[28]

As for virtually all of Keynes' hypotheses, this one too is intriguing, but it also leaves several important questions unanswered. Who sets the convention of the moment, that is, who is the leader of the banking pack? How is the convention recognized as such so that the herd follows? If, in fact, there are profit advantages in rejecting the convention, why does it remain so attractive to assure that if failure comes, it comes only "in a conventional and orthodox way?" The latter question could be answered with the reasoning that if the profit advantages from unorthodox behavior are uncertain, there is little reason not to follow a convention.

Bankers are blind to an unknowable future and may have sensibly adopted habitual behavior to cope with an irrational world that places an impenetrable shield over tomorrow. This perspective is consistent with much of Keynes' later argument about subjective uncertainty in *The General Theory*. Businessmen adopt a convention when facing the intractable problem of forecasting future events that will impinge upon the profitability of their investments.[29] The bankers' response to an uncertain world is analogous—a convention that leads bankers to follow the herd can also result in loan pushing if the herd, collectively, seeks borrowers on the periphery.

INSTITUTIONAL WEAKNESSES

An alternative approach exists to understand the debt crisis as rooted in the institutional shortcomings of commercial banking. This approach arises from application of the problems confronted in analyzing the relationship between a "principal" and an "agent" in pure contract theory. At stake in this approach is the structure of incentives that the principal offers the agent to induce desired behavior. Here, the principal could be either the senior loan officer or vice president in the commercial bank's home office. The agent would be the junior loan officer working overseas who, first-hand, arranges for the loan.

Principals and Agents

Traditionally, the structure of their contracts has rewarded junior loan officers for their success in meeting and surpassing assigned loan quotas.

They advance by arranging as many loans as possible—with the proviso, of course, that the loans meet with the approval of their superiors. Just as it appears to be advantageous for the money center banks to make large-scale syndicated loans look attractive to the regional banks, it appears to be to the junior loan officer's advantage within a single bank to "doctor" each loan package sufficiently to sell it successfully to superiors. This "doctoring" may include setting up a variety of "guarantees" from sources in the borrowers' country.

Such loan packaging practices would catch up with junior loan officers if they stayed with a single bank long enough for the results of their loans to be realized. But frequently, it is argued, they are likely to have moved on to new employment; they are highly mobile participants in the credit industry.[30] Therefore, the argument continues, junior loan officers receive high points for bringing loan packages to fruition and few demerits when the loan proves to be of poor quality.

The principals—in this case, senior loan officers or bank vice presidents—are pulled along on an overlending wave by those beneath them. The debt crisis thus becomes a product of overzealous junior loan officers who, in maximizing their personal utility, negatively affect the international banking system and the world economy. The root of the problem is the failure of management to construct incentive programs for junior loan officers that will extract greater prudence from them in arranging loans. The debt problem, in summary, if we use the principal–agent approach, is due to a breakdown in the hierarchical operations of lending institutions.

This is a clever, though probably not substantive explanation for the origins of international liquidity and solvency traumas. It does not answer the question of why the failure to rein in junior loan officers would be so widespread and so persistent as to produce a decade-long accumulation of low caliber loans to the developing countries. Coase's theorem implies that sooner or later—presumably sooner—a new scheme of rewards would be designed for the lower strata of bankers who do the majority of work in foreign countries.[31] Sooner or later, mechanisms should be developed so that results of their prior lending records follow junior loan officers to their interviews with new, potential employers. Is the problem that these adjustments only come too much later and if so, why has substantial friction resulted in modification of the incentives for the junior loan officers?

Presumably, the principals have strong incentives themselves to keep the junior loan officers from pushing questionable loans. Penalties for the results of actions taken by inferiors fall heavily on superiors in the banking world. For instance, the Drysdale and Penn Square Bank incidents led to the removal of two high-level officials and five middle-level executives at the Chase Manhattan Bank. In addition, two more bank vice presidents resigned after news reports identified them as accepting loans generated by Penn Square.[32] Citibank reportedly is a bit more benign in its treatment of executives who make or approve loan decisions that later prove unsound. Instead of firing those executives "who show potential," Citibank removes them from decision-making authority (or, puts them in the "penalty box") for twelve to eighteen months; slowing their advancement.[33] In either case, those penalties should have a chilling effect on over-exuberant upper-level bank personnel and make them more carefully examine loan packages brought to them for approval and support.

Of course, the severity of these penalties is contingent on the nature of the severance agreements, or "golden parachutes," guaranteed bank executives upon termination. The matter of incentives, in this case the incentives facing senior bank management, is again at stake. One can speculate that with punitive penalty systems in operation for upper-level bank managers, junior loan officers must be allowed relative freedom in arranging foreign loans because those particular loans do not fail as blatantly as domestic loans.

In fact, there has been no publicized major housecleaning of bank personnel over LDC loans in the 1980s. The banks' aforementioned capacity to roll over foreign loans indefinitely postpones the day of reckoning. For example, Citicorp Vice Chairman Thomas Theobald, whose bank had the largest exposure in the Third World, continued to maintain that Citibank was making a profit on its Latin American loans in early 1984. Skeptics suggested that this profit was due to various steps taken to delay a precipitous markdown of earnings.[34]

In general, it is less likely that the actions of the junior loan officers were as critical as permissiveness towards those actions by senior bank management.

Discipline from the Stock Exchange?

To the extent that it is advantageous to bank management (regardless of their objectives) to maintain high and/or rising prices for the banks' equity, the stock exchange may constitute another source of lending discipline for banks with publicly traded shares. Even if a bank refuses to mark down its earnings on nonperforming loans, well-informed investors can still sell off the bank's stock.

Consider the recent experience of the large U.S. banks with significant exposure to the four Latin American nations with the largest borrowing. (See Table 16.)[35] The case of Continental Illinois obviously comes to mind. Its domestic loans, of an unusually low quality, pushed the bank over the edge into bankruptcy. But there is evidence to suggest that this bank's Latin loans generally were (unofficially) in the nonperforming category.[36] As of late 1982, 11 percent of Continental Illinois's foreign loan portfolio was devoted to Argentina and Mexico, amounting to 3 percent of the bank's total assets of $37.57 billion.[37] Even before the crushing mid-1984 run on Continental by its major institutional depositors, the bank's share prices began a long decline; its common stock eventually dropped from $25 per share to below $4 per share.

The performance of Manufacturers Hanover's common stock shows an even stronger relationship to bad news about its foreign loan portfolio. A bank with significant exposure in Argentina, Manufacturers Hanover stock experienced a moderate decline in mid-1982, falling from about $32 per share to $26.50 per share. It is not clear whether the Falkland Islands crisis played a role in the stock price drop. In 1984, however, three Wall Street Journal reporters directly linked rumors about the shakiness of Manufacturers Hanover's foreign loans to its equity position. They emphasized the impact of these rumors in explaining the one-day $3.375 drop during May 1984 in its share price to $27.625 per share on heavy trading of 1.3 million shares.[38]

Manufacturers Hanover has the largest net exposure to the large Latin American debtors; Citicorp has the largest absolute exposure. (See Table 16.) But Citicorp did not experience as severe a drop in its stock pricing. It has been suggested that this is due to Citibank's strong ability to earn on its domestic operations which are separate from the Latin debt problem.[39] It may also be true that Citicorp was more effective in arranging reschedulings among its foreign borrowers—especially in Brazil—to maintain its ability to record high profitability on its loans.[40] In general, LDC loans in 1984 seemed to have depressed large banks' equity positions.

The weakness in money center banks' share prices was accompanied by weakness in their earnings. Nineteen major banks reported a loss of $5.6 million during the second quarter of 1984—the *only* sector of American business to experience an overall loss during the period. The banks' earnings position was overwhelmed by Continental Illinois's $1.16 billion negative earnings, a record in U.S. banking. But removing

Continental from the picture would still leave the remaining eighteen banks with a 4 percent decline in net income. The foreign loan factor played a role in the decline, particularly "[s]tricter accounting rules adopted by regulators [that] led the banks to put significant amounts of Argentinian loans on nonaccrual status, reducing earnings."[41]

It appears that the stock exchange only penalizes the banks through their (the banks') decision about whether to buy or sell bank stock *after* news surfaces that the loans are in trouble. This news can be "announced" by unofficial sources long before the banks actually put the loans on nonaccrual status. Nevertheless, downward pressure on share prices from LDC loans seems to materialize fairly late in the process. No such declines occurred when the initial loan commitments were made throughout the 1970s—if anything, bank share prices tended to gain throughout the previous decade, and it seems that the stock market's reaction to the development loans was also favorable at that time.

If dominant investors follow the fundamentals in judging whether to buy, sell, or hold a stock, they must have been favorably disposed toward the LDC lending boom when it first began. They changed their minds in the 1980s when incoming news suggested that all was not well with loans to the developing world. But evidently, the market did not forecast that the Latin loans would have an adverse effect on bank earnings in the 1970s, or the market was so enthused by other bank operations that this entirely offset the negative impact of the Latin loans.

If the dominant investors are speculators, in Keynes' sense, they utilize the news to anticipate the actions of other investors rather than to forecast the earnings performance of the banks issuing the securities. In this case, bullishness and bearishness will depend upon the various speculative strategies pursued by stock exchange participants.

Regardless of which theory of stock exchange pricing one adopts, it is unclear how much discipline this pricing provides for bankers. Conditions in 1984 did not favor bank share prices, but the consequences of the liquidity crisis of 1982 on bank share prices remain ambiguous. Kofi Amoateng, who undertook a statistical analysis of 24 large U.S. banks using cumulative stock market returns from the period 1980–83, found that banks' returns were not related to their Third World lending.[42] The unresolved empirical question is whether or not the net effect of developing country loans over the course of an entire fifteen year period has been advantageous or disadvantageous for bank stock.

Suppose further study indicates that *all* the news about the loans—despite the recent news that identifies problems with them—has had a positive effect on bank stock. Also suppose that bank managers want to raise the value of their enterprise's equity, and they could have anticipated that on balance, the stock exchange would favorably assess their LDC loans. Then it can be reasonably argued that the existence of a stock exchange facilitated rather than impeded loans to the periphery. To the extent that maintenance of high share prices matter to bank management, it would have been perfectly rational for senior loan officers to let their employees push loans. Of course, it is still unknown what additional news about the LDC loans will be forthcoming and the stock market's future reactions to such news.

True Insurance?

There may be still another reason, entirely rational and calculatedly political, that bankers believed debt repudiation to be unlikely. At worst, bankers could rest assured that in the event of debt servicing difficulties, leaders of the borrowing, developing countries would seek reschedulings rather than declare default. Consider the banks' own liability structures—the fact that the banks hold vast amounts of deposits from members of wealthy Third World elites. In the event of default, the bankers could impound large portions of the wealth of the richest citizens of the debtor nations. Mutual recognition of such a possibility may lead to a semi-invisible handshake between the commercial banks and the Third World's aristocracy—the banks agree to maintain the desired degree of liquidity for their depositors' funds; the wealthy citizens agree to pressure their respective governments either directly or indirectly to renegotiate in good faith if debt repayment becomes problematic.

The magnitude of the multinational banks' liabilities owed to the richest citizens of the LDCs is potentially staggering. In an insightful commentary on the international circulation of finance, James Henry recently argued that the international debt crisis cannot be understood independent of the phenomenon of capital flight. Henry even claims that: "In some cases, the wealthiest class of poor countries have actually sent more money out of their countries than foreign borrowing has brought in—and it's often the same money."[43] Henry contends that over fifty percent of the funds lent to Mexico, Venezuela, and Argentina have gone back to the lenders, soon after they flowed in to each country. He writes:

> Indeed, there are already enough private foreign assets owed by the citizens of major debtor nations to go a long way toward servicing their countries' foreign

debts. The most aggressive banks such as Citibank, have probably accumulated almost as much in assets from poor countries as they have loaned to them.[44]

The wealthy individuals in the Third World who are responsible for this large-scale capital flight sometimes are astonishingly close to the authority figures in their countries. Former Mexican president Lopez Portillo, Henry reports, ". . . who moved to Rome after leaving office is widely rumored to have absconded with over one billion dollars." His successor, Miguel de la Madrid, was found in May 1984 to have "been accumulating substantial deposits in a Swiss bank account—at least $162 million during 1983 alone."[45] In general, Henry finds that 1979 through 1981, the period of most rapid capital flight from Mexico, coincided with the period of the most rapid buildup in foreign debt. When the debt boom slowed down after 1981, capital flight decelerated as well.[46] Regardless, Henry estimates (albeit crudely) "Mexicans have at least $30 billion more socked away in U.S. banks than Mexico owes to U.S. banks."[47]

To the extent that the same multinational banks are holding both assets and liabilities with the same LDCs, this may be the bankers' "trump card" in the debt crisis. If the banks refuse to acknowledge the possibility of disaster, it could only mean that they assign too low a probability to revolutions that would remove their "friends" from power and replace them with leaders without a personal stake in avoiding default. Banker irrationality would amount to an excessive sense of confidence, on the bankers' part, in the stability of the existing class structure in the borrower nations.

The Secondary Market: A Viable Escape Hatch?

Bankers riding the herd momentum into large–scale lending to the periphery in the late 1970s and early 1980s may have felt reassured by prospects for eventual conversion of bank loans into primary securities. By mid-1985 evidence had surfaced that banks with large Latin American loans had become participants in "a multibillion-dollar secondary market that makes it easy for them to swap the loans or sell them outright."[48] In effect, bankers could find a potential cure by reverting to a type of underwriting function they performed in the 1920s with respect to developing country bond issues. The objective in underwriting is to spread the risk by selling off participation in Latin loans.

The sales apparently began in earnest in early 1982 during "La Guerra de Las Malvinas," when banks sought to release Argentinian debt.[49]

But the rise of the secondary market in commercial bank loans may be more indicative of banker desperation than a well reasoned, calculated ploy, held in abeyance when loans were first contracted until circumstances dictated such a step. The discount rates on loan sales to the secondary market carry implicit losses for the banks' portfolios. In mid-1985, for example, investors could purchase ". . . a Nicaraguan loan for about 10 cents for each dollar of face value or a Mexican loan for about 85 cents on the dollar."[50] At the same time:

> Loans to Bolivia, which [was] more than a year behind in interest payments and which suffers from possibly the most chaotic economy in the world [sold] for about 20 cents on the dollar. Peruvian debt, under the burden of that country's economic woes and a guerilla war, trade[d] for half of its face value. Argentine debt trade[d] for about 70 cents on the dollar, while loans of Venezuela, probably the least troubled Latin debtor, [sold] for about 90 percent of face value.[51]

Discount rates on the secondary market suggest the collective assessment investors made on the quality of loans to different Latin American borrowers. Investor confidence was apparently greatest with respect to the Venezuelan debt and weakest with respect to the Nicaraguan debt. But the broadest generalization is the reluctance of investors to dip heavily into the market for bank loans. One estimate put the volume of the market at $3 billion in 1984, comprised largely of swaps between banks rather than outright sales, while the outstanding commercial bank debt of Latin nations was about $360 billion.[52] Furthermore, the secondary market has been devoted almost exclusively to transfers of initial loans; the secondary market for rescheduled loans is close to nonexistent.[53]

Even the debtors, who can buy back their loans at a discount and avoid paying full value, have not surged into the secondary loan market. The bankers themselves are wary and somewhat secretive participants as the suppliers on the secondary market. They fear acknowledging loan losses explicitly and thereby face higher loan-loss reserve requirements as the sales reveal a market valuation of their credits that is below face value.[54] Plainly, the stampede of the herd does not find a comforting cushion in the secondary market for bank loans. If the bankers actually believed the secondary loan market was a potential safeguard, they have been proven wrong.

NOTES

1. Perhaps the new entrants into the upper echelons of today's banking houses simply need to be compelled to read any number of Charles Kindleberger's studies. For example, they could be urged to read his article "Historical Perspective on Today's Third-World Debt Problem," *Economies et Societies* (1985): 109–34.

2. S.C. Gwynne, "Adventures in the Loan Trade," *Harper's* 267 (September 1983): 23.

3. Ibid.

4. Ibid.

5. Ibid.

6. John H. Makin, *The Global Debt Crisis: America's Growing Involvement* (New York: Basic Books, Inc., 1984), p. 139. Even private sector "guarantees" appeared to enhance the appearance of a loan. Gwynne, "Adventures," p. 26, describes how he put the finishing touch on his Philippine loan by arranging a guarantee on the loan from a Philippine bank that was "handing them out . . . like free samples."

7. This would suggest that LDCs with more diverse tax systems, more efficient revenue collection agencies, and larger tax bases would receive larger loans and/or softer terms. The evidence remains ambiguous about whether or not this is true. Forthcoming research by Kofi Amoanteng, Stephen Magee, and William Brock is intended to tackle certain aspects of this issue.

8. Makin, *Global Debt Crisis*, p. 139.

9. David Folkerts-Landau, "The Changing Role of International Bank Lending in Development Finance," *International Monetary Fund Staff Papers* 32 (June 1985): 323–27.

10. Ibid., pp. 327, 330.

11. Ibid., p. 327.

12. Ibid., p. 332.

13. Ibid., pp. 332–35.

14. Kindleberger, "Historical Perspective," p. 124. Kindleberger contends that the thirty year delay has been replicated in approximate fashion over the course of two centuries: ". . . default in most cases delayed for about thirty years a country's access to borrowing from abroad. The measure is rough, but Third World borrowing rose and fell in the middle 1820s, the 1850s, the late 1880s, and, with interruptions for world wars, in the 1920s and 1970s."

15. Jack M. Guttentag and Richard J. Herring, *The Current Crisis in International Lending* (Washington, D.C.: The Brookings Institution, 1985), p. 2.

16. Ibid.

17. Jack Guttentag and Richard Herring, *The Lender-of-Last Resort Function in an International Context* (Essays in International Finance No. 151, Princeton University, May 1983, p. 2).

18. Guttentag and Herring, *The Current Crisis,* p. 2. Ronald McKinnon also refers to "the great herd instinct among international bankers" and the myopia of investors in LDCs after liberalizations in "The International Capital Market and Economic Liberalization in LDCs," *The Developing Economies* 22 (September 1984): 477–78.

19. Ibid., p. 2–3.

20. Ibid., p. 3. Indeed, following the herd could be interpreted as entirely *rational* behavior. Jain and Gupta indicate that if such behavior occurs, the motives could be quite reasonable for similar reasons:

   > Individual banks could feel safer participating in a syndicated deal to a country because syndication involves banks of different sizes and of different national origins in a single issue. There is some security in the knowledge that any country that would default on a loan would face legal opposition from a large number of banks from many countries and might get cut off from the market for the foreseeable future. . . . Looking like everyone else also protected banks against possible actions by the regulatory authorities. . . . Furthermore, a bank assuming a share of a syndicated loan could rely on the analysis performed by the lead managers who themselves had a stake in their own analysis. In view of the high costs of collecting information, banks may have accepted the ability of the lead bank to evaluate loans. . . .

   See Arvind K. Jain and Satyadev Gupta, "Some Evidence on 'Herding' Behavior of U.S. Banks," *Journal of Money, Credit, and Banking* 19 (February 1987): 80.

21. Jain and Gupta, "Herding Behavior," p. 78, emphasis added. Also see p. 87.

22. Ibid., pp. 83–87.

23. Ibid., p. 83n.12.

24. Makin, *Global Debt Crisis,* p. 139.

25. For a representative statement of the position that bankers need access to better information see Robert Slighton, "Improving Country-Risk Judgments," *The Chase Economic Observer* 3 (July/August 1983): 3–4. Slighton argues that improved information would enhance the quality of bank lending decisions to borrowers in foreign countries.

26. J.M. Keynes, "The Consequences to the Banks of the Collapse of Money Values (Aug. 1931)," in *Essays in Persuasion* (New York: W.W. Norton & Company, Inc., 1963), p. 176.

27. Ibid.

28. Ibid., p. 178.

29. J.M. Keynes, *The General Theory of Employment, Interest, and Money* (London: MacMillan, 1936). See especially Chapter 12.

30. For example, S.C. Gwynne, "Adventures," was long gone from his midwestern bank when his Philippine loan went bad.

31. For the general discussion see Ronald H. Coase, "The Problem of Social Cost," *Journal of Law and Economics* 3 (October 1960): 1–44.

32. "Chase Reports Operating Loss for 2nd Quarter," *Wall Street Journal,* 21 July 1982. For a thorough autopsy on the demise and subsequent repercussions of the collapse of Penn Square Bank in Oklahoma City see Mark Singer, "Annals of Finance: Funny Money (1)," *The New Yorker* 61 (22 April 1985): 51–52t; Mark Singer, "Annals of Finance: Funny Money (2)," *The New Yorker* 61 (29 April 1985): 41–42t; and Mark Singer, "Annals of Finance: Funny Money (3)," *The New Yorker* 61 (6 May 1985): 49–50t.

33. Daniel Hertzberg, "Banking Behemoth: Citicorp Leads Field in Its Size and Power—and Its Arrogance," *Wall Street Journal,* 11 May 1984.

34. Ibid., p. 16.

35. The Latin American debt far exceeds the indebtedness of any other region of the Third World. For example, by mid-1984 the total debt of the Latin nations was estimated to be greater than $230 billion when compared with the estimated debt of about $50 billion for all of Africa's nations. This does not mean that the situation in terms of debt management is any easier for the African countries. The smaller magnitude of the African debt removes the leverage the Latin nations possess to threaten the formation of a debtor's cartel. For several African nations, debt service ratios exceed those of Mexico and Brazil plus, virtually all African nations have severe problems with balance of payments. See "Africa's Debts Appear More Troublesome Than Others," *New York Times,* 1 July 1984.

36. Lee Berton, "Early Warnings: Long Before the 'Run' at Continental Illinois Bank Hinted of Its Ills," *Wall Street Journal,* 12 July 1984 reports:

> ". . . Continental's loans—the main assets at the Chicago institution are of poorer quality than its competitors', the banks' most recent financial reports show. At the end of the 1984 first quarter, for instance, Continental's nonperforming loans—those 90 days or more past due on interest and principal—were 7.7% of its total loans, compared with 2.7% for the 14 money-center banks." Berton also quotes bank accountants as describing Continental as being "notorious in the industry for 'shooting craps' by lending to companies that other banks avoided." The bank's customers had included "once-ailing Chrysler Corp., International Harvester, and Braniff." Between 1975 and 1981 it lowered its loan-loss reserve from 1.34% to 0.87% while other money-center banks typically maintained a 1% figure. Continental also had a remarkable record in lagged writeoffs. *After* the 1982 shut down of Oklahoma City's Penn Square Bank "by Federal regulators, Continental charged off only 4.5% and classified only 15.1% of its Penn Square loans as nonperforming [while] Chase Manhattan Corp. had by then charged off 21.2% and classified 35.4% as nonperforming, and Seafirst Corp. had charged 4.4% and classified 27.3% as nonperformers."

37. "Troubled Nations Hold 11% of Foreign Loans by Continental Illinois," *Wall Street Journal,* 29 November 1982.

38. Daniel Hertzberg, Tim Carrington, and John Andrew, "Confidence Game: Large Banks Are Hit By New Set of Rumors and Stock Prices Fall," *Wall Street Journal*, 25 May 1984.

By the end of 1983, Manufacturers Hanover had $6.5 billion in loans to the four largest Latin borrowers which amounted to 284 percent of its shareholders equity. In addition, Hertzberg, Carrington, and Andrew report that there were rumors in the London money market that Manufacturers Hanover "was selling off a large position in British government bonds."

39. Ibid., p. 6.

Citicorp was first in line among U.S. banks in entering the Latin American loan market in the late 1960s. See "Citibank's Pervasive Influence on International Lending," *Business Week*, 16 May 1983. It also led U.S. banks into Latin America in the 1920s as well. See Anthony Sampson, *The Money Lenders* (Harmondsworth: Penguin Books, 1984), pp. 69–70.

40. "Citibank's Pervasive Influence," p. 126.

41. "Corporate Profits Advanced 31% for Second Quarter; Rises Are Expected to Extend into '85 at Slower Pace," *Wall Street Journal*, 6 August 1984.

Banks registering earnings declines included Citicorp, Bank America, Chase Manhattan, Manufacturers Hanover, and J.P. Morgan—all with significant Latin American loan exposure.

42. Kofi Amoateng, *Essays on International Debt: Theory and Evidence* (unpublished dissertation, University of Texas at Austin, 1986, Chapter 2). Published studies on this subject include Bradford Cornell and Alan Shapiro, "The Reaction of Bank Stock Prices to the International Debt Crisis," *Journal of Banking and Finance* 10 (1986): 55–73 and Robert F. Bruner and John M. Simms, Jr., "The International Debt Crisis and Bank Security Returns in 1982," *Journal of Money, Credit, and Banking* 19 (February 1987): 46–55. Both of these latter papers report results of "event" studies and find strong adverse effects on commercial bank share prices from their LDC loans. Unlike Amoateng's study, however, the Cornell-Shapiro and Bruner-Simms window of analysis is confined to the events of 1982, when reports of problems with developing country loans were widely published. The latter studies, therefore, do not assess the net effect on commercial bnak share prices of LDC loans from their inception—precisely the task that Amoateng undertakes. In addition, unpublished work by Sule Ozler finds that the stock market penalized the banks for their LDC loans, using a rational expectations approach. See his "Valuation of Rescheduled Loans, 1978–1983" (Working Paper #414, UCLA, August 1986). Ozler, however, also finds evidence of a decline in bank stock prices linked to LDC loans for 1981–83. Ozler does not assess the net effect of the loans over the entire course of their existence, either.

43. James S. Henry, "Where the Money Went: Third World Debt Hoax," *The New Republic*, 14 April 1986.

44. Ibid. Paul Krugman, in "International Debt Strategies in an Uncertain World" in Gordon W. Smith and John T. Cuddington, eds., *International Debt and the Developing Countries* (Washington, DC: The World Bank, 1985), p. 80, contends that the threat of seizure of assets by creditors may not deter default since, "[f]or heavily indebted nations . . . the seizable assets are generally small relative to their debt." This overlooks the political significance of whom claims possession of the seizable assets. Plus, in the Mexican case, the seizable assets are quite large relative to the nation's external debt if Henry's estimates are credible.

45. Ibid., p. 20. Darrell Delamaide, in *Debt Shock: The Full Story of the World Debt Crisis* (Garden City, NJ: Doubleday, 1985), p. 104, adds the following anecdote on Lopez Portillo's personal finances:

> Lopez Portillo himself followed the traditional route of retiring presidents. He built four mansions for his family on a hill outside the capital. Satirists quickly dubbed the location "Dog Hill," from Lopez Portillo's 1981 statement that he would "defend the peso like a dog." Corruption accentuated the gross discrepancy in incomes in Mexican society.

46. Ibid., p. 21.
47. Ibid.
48. Nicholas D. Kristoff, "The Market for Latin Debt," *New York Times* 17 July 1985.
49. Ibid., p. C2.
50. Ibid., p. C1.
51. Ibid., p. C2.
52. Ibid.
53. William Cline, *International Debt: Systematic Risk and Policy Response* (Washington, DC: Institute for International Economics, 1984), p. 207.
54. Kristoff, "Latin Debt," p. C2.

CHAPTER 6

The Debt Pullers: Overborrowing by the Developing Countries

G uttentag and Herring unabashedly commit themselves to the stance that the debt crisis is due to structural weaknesses in the ongoing scheme of international finance. Such weaknesses predispose bankers toward episodes of overlending, and unless the weaknesses are correctable and corrected, recurrences of overlending are all but inevitable.

Before advancing their hypothesis, however, Guttentag and Herring mention two standard explanations for the crisis which they dismiss without significant discussion. The two explanations are "bad luck" and "imprudent borrowing" on the part of the developing countries.[1] The former is consistent with the general "rational expectations" style of explaining debt problems (See Chapter 4) that attributes the crisis to outright surprises. It also is consistent with William Cline's specific emphasis on the primacy of "external shocks" in driving LDCs into debt-service difficulties.[2]

The second argument—"imprudent borrowing" by the developing countries—shifts the onus for financial crisis onto the shoulders of decisionmakers in LDCs. Authorities in the developing countries are characterized as the aggressive agents in international financial markets, pursuing and acquiring amounts of external credit far beyond their optimal norms.

Extensive technical literature in economics seeks to establish criteria for optimal borrowing by nations.[3] The literature is premised on maximization of some objective or set of objectives dictated by national welfare. Often, economists choose maximization of consumption per head as the objective over an indefinite time period. Finance ministers in LDCs who have engaged in debt pulling have either been (1) unaware of this literature, (2) have misunderstood it, or (3) have ignored it, anxious to pursue other goals besides those utilized in the economists' optimal borrowing exercises. In any event, overborrowing is non-optimal borrowing for economists. However, virtually any pattern of borrowing can be proclaimed optimal since the literature gives no guidance about how the future is to be discounted relative to the present.

Imprudent borrowing is potentially but not necessarily the antithesis of loan pushing. It is possible for the two to coincide, producing a lively "conflagration" of overborrowing-cum-overlending. Typically, though, proponents who use the loan pulling explanation for debt crisis do so to refute claims that the commercial banks bear central responsibility for the destabilization of the international financial system.

SALEM'S LOT

The rhetoric of blame for developing country debt-service problems—banks as loan pushers or finance ministers as debt pullers—has become so heated on occasion that participants on both sides of the debate have been attacked. Mario Simonsen, a finance minister himself during a recent phase of Brazil's accumulation of external debt (and by no means a disinterested observer), has issued the following lengthy reproach directed at both sets of disputants:

> Who is to be held responsible for the debt crisis . . . commercial banks that behaved as imprudent lenders, or debtor developing countries that misused the borrowed external funds? This is the fashionable debate in witch-hunting circles, where every crisis provides [a] unique opportunity to practice their favorite sport.
>
> The debate reflects nothing but poor logic, since it does not even meet elementary probability tests. Until late 1982, commercial banks never behaved as a collective, but rather as independent decision units. Similarly, debtor countries never coordinated their economic policies. The chances of widespread crises being precipitated by the errors of a large number of *independent* actors are minute. A plausible explanation for the debt crisis must rely on either some external factor or the inadequacy of the recycling system, or both. Hence, the witch-hunting investigation might well be left aside, were it not for the insistent charges by conservative-populist politicians and by poorly informed observers.[4]

But accepting Simonsen's injunction to call off the "witch hunt" is tantamount to relinquishing a large set of provocative and challenging insights into the origins of the debt crisis. Plus, Simonsen's charge that "[t]he chances of widespread crises being precipitated by the errors of a large number of *independent* actors are minute" is ill-founded. There is nothing implausible or improbable about large numbers of economic actors (in this instance bank managers), forming quite similar forecasts about future prospects, given a common information pool, without significant consultation and cooperation between them. If bankers proceed to act in a similar manner on the basis of similar forecasts, then a clustering of loan commitments would be observed. If all those commitments fail concurrently, one would conclude in retrospect that the banks were the "wicked witches" who overlent.

In actual experience, plunging and clustering behavior is quite commonplace among banks. This has proven to be true whether their activities are self-serving or altruistic. Penny Lernoux's remarkable expose, *In Banks We Trust*, provides disturbing examples of banks moving *en masse*, directly or indirectly, to invest in the eventually ill-fated oil and gas industries, government securities speculation, illegal drug trafficking, and finance for international terrorists as well as, of course, economic development projects in LDCs.[5]

When bankers cluster, their institutions simultaneously become vulnerable when loan commitments go bad. But why should all the bankers' apparent forecasts prove to be wrong at the same time? Aren't the chances of this "minute?" Once again, rational expectationists might argue that bankers were buffeted by a shock—the absolutely unavoidable element of their ignorance, the purely random aspects of the world in which they make decisions. This might be the "external factor" that Simonsen mentions, but it is not the inherent "external factor" that produces the crisis. The crisis is produced by actions of the lender—dare we say prudence of the lender—in recognizing the possibility of such random events in making a loan commitment. It is the good sense of the borrower—prudence again—in being alert to the damage a random shock might exercise on ability to pay.

A Keynes disciple would go further, arguing that it is natural to be generally ignorant of salient facts about the future relevant to investment decisions. Subjective uncertainty is an immutable and fundamental condition of existence it could be argued. Forecasting is mere shadow play. Bankers only issue forecasts to legitimize commitments made on far less systematic grounds; with the Keynesian view it is impossible for bankers to make commitments on systematic grounds—they adopt rules of thumb to cope with the situation.

Guttentag and Herring carry all this a step further (Chapter 5) to specify the bankers' contemporary rules of thumb, such as following the herd. Following the herd assures that each banker does not stray too far from the crowd and in the event that decisions go bad, no banker will be left standing alone. Jeffrey Sachs is even willing to impute a certain rationality to sticking with the crowd, contending that in making their decisions, bankers must anticipate actions of other bankers. This became especially evident during the recent round of debt reschedulings and rollovers for the major Latin debtors:

> . . . each bank's loan decision is properly affected by the loan decisions of other banks. Since no bank alone can extend all the credit that Mexico or Brazil needs to stay afloat, it is prudent for each bank to lend new money only if other banks are making new loans as well. Because of this interdependence of the banks' decisions, aggregate bank lending may stop not because the country's position has changed, but because each individual bank believes that all of the other banks have decided to stop lending. . . .[6]

Thus it is not only uniformity of forecasts about future prospects—however such forecasts are concocted—that causes problems. Uniformity of anticipations of other bankers' decisions also leads, in Sachs's words, "[t]he prophecy of a loan cutoff [to] become self-fulfilling."[7]

Guttentag and Herring's claims of herd behavior suggest that commercial banks acted collectively or at least with uniformity well before 1982. For these two experts, syndicated lending and sticking with the crowd *produced* the crisis that became manifest in 1982—and they make the argument without necessarily impugning the bankers' actions as conspiratorial.

Simonsen's willingness to acknowledge that "inadequacy of the recycling system" may also be a root of the debt crisis allows reentry of those predisposed toward witch hunters. After all, precisely *why* was the system inadequate? Guttentag and Herring's indictment of banker psychology is especially well-suited to support systemic flaws. Similarly, if borrowing nations' leaders were able to pursue and contract prohibitively large sums of credit—as debt pull proponents would have it—that is also a potential source of weakness in the recycling system.

Therefore, the authors of this text remain inveterate witch hunters. Whether we should be classified among Simonsen's "conservative-populist politicians" or among his "poorly informed observers" is not altogether clear, but since neither one of us have any conscious political ambitions, the latter unfortunate category seems to be the only option. Unlike Simonsen, though, we are convinced that serious analysis of the causes of the debt crisis requires serious consideration of arguments to locate blame. In this chapter we address arguments that place the blame for the crisis on leaders of the debtor nations.

The Nigerian Case: A Willing Addict?

Nigerian journalist Chinweizu, in a discussion of his nation's external debt situation, presents an interesting bridge from loan pushing to debt pulling. He describes Nigeria as having sunk into "debt trap peonage."[8] Cheryl Payer, a radical critic of International Monetary Fund activities, had applied the same term to the experiences of developing countries that received loans from official Western-based sources from the 1950s through the early 1970s, well before the current turmoil in international finance.[9] Payer used Chinweizu's term to describe a circumstance of various developing countries virtually abdicating their national sovereignty to the United States' strategic interests (ideologically construed as anti-Communism), conceived by American public officials in leadership at the time. Subordinate status for these Third World nations was induced by their perpetual financial indebtedness to the U.S. government. Payer, in examining the period between the early 1950s and early 1970s, found that the Philippines, Chile, Indonesia, Brazil, Cambodia, Mexico, and Laos were among the nations whose sovereignty was jeopardized or contravened by U.S. government lending and IMF mediation.

Debt bondage translated into financial crisis for the countries in question, but during the period Payer studied, individual country-by-country crises did not constitute danger for global financial arrangements. This situation does not prevail now. Payer's book was written on the basis of events that largely antedated full development of the Eurocurrency markets and the first oil price boom. Unofficial, private sector lending by the commercial banks had yet to begin its explosive climb.

The international financial system was not at risk in the 1960s. Only individual debtor nations were faced with economic problems in 1970, due to their acquisition of borrowed funds.

Today, the indebtedness of the "Big Four" Latin American borrowers (Brazil, Mexico, Argentina, and Venezuela) is viewed as an imminent threat to the world economy. But similar to the situation of developing country borrowers of the 1950–70 era, the indebtedness of subsaharan

African nations is not considered cause for international alarm. There has been no fear expressed that the African debt today, if sharply underpaid, could bring about global financial collapse. Consequently, the African debt problem is considered a crisis only for African nations, not an international crisis. Their people must bear the repercussions alone. The bankers, on the other hand, devote deep attention to the debt-service problems of Brazil, Mexico, Argentina, and Venezuela—recognizing that they themselves are at stake. In the bankers' eyes, the aggregate subsaharan African debt is a pittance compared with the external debt of the four Latin American nations. The total subsaharan African debt is no more than 20 percent of the total for the four Latin borrowers. Of course, in principle, bankers would like to see steady payment on all their debts; although they do not feel the same compulsion to develop endless stretchout schemes for the African versus the Latin borrowers.

Among subsaharan African nations, however, Nigeria's external debt is the largest, amounting to about $17 billion in 1984. Debt service charges alone—if paid in full—would have required $5 billion in external payments, or close to 40 percent of Nigeria's 1984 export earnings.[10] Conventional wisdom had it that Nigeria's petroleum resources would permit ready financing of large amounts of external debt.[11] Borrowed funds could then be devoted to rapid economic development, thereby generating additional revenues to augment the petroleum funds and facilitate debt payment.

What went wrong? Nigeria's income from oil dropped considerably after 1982 as world petroleum prices plunged downward. According to Chinweizu, the borrowed funds were not devoted assiduously to investment in worthwhile projects but were used instead to maintain consumption levels. Chinweizu hints that the extravagant consumption levels of Nigeria's elite were upheld in particular.[12]

Of course, the same conventional wisdom that continued to predict an unequivocally bright future for oil producing nations also heralded the commodity prices boom of the early and mid-1970s as a foundation for borrowing in other LDCs. Food and metals prices went on an upward spiral, reversing trends that had lasted for half a century. But by the close of the 1970s, that boom's temporary nature was also apparent.[13]

The Company Store

In Chinweizu's discussion, Nigeria's descent into "debt trap peonage" occurred with a strong external push. In 1979, he contends, the seduction of Nigeria began; the nation was "lured into unnecessary borrowing by lenders eager to recycle petrodollars."[14] In applying the concept of debt peonage to Third World countries in general and to Nigeria in particular, Chinweizu describes Western authorities as anxious to enmesh the developing countries in a debt trap. He holds there were two major reasons for this—first, the loans extend markets for Western producers—the market-making function of lending. Second, the loans help preserve an international pattern of specialization that keeps the Third World confined to raw materials and mineral production—rather than manufacturing—frequently at disadvantageous trade terms.[15]

Multinational banks, in the peonage concept, resemble the company store in the old coal miner's folk song "Sixteen Tons." The LDCs "owe their souls to the company store" in perpetuity—much like the debt peon who cannot escape to a new town or master. Such a vision depicts Nigeria, as it witnesses the evaporation of its expected oil revenues, as "turning into a loan addict"[16]—and a grievously wasteful addict at that:

> Our urge is to grab loans and ever more loans, like a drug addict who must have more and more heroin to keep going. And like the heroin addict, we are craving these loans, not for sound purposes, but simply to finance our spend-thrift consumer habits and our ambitious maldevelopment programs.[17]

The analogy with the heroin addict seems particularly appropriate to Chinweizu for three reasons:

> First, both [Nigeria's and the heroin addict's] debts are unsecured consumer debts, made up of subsistence and spending-spree expenses, and with future income only as collateral.
> Second, both loans are pure peonage loans, that is, loans made not because of the potential of the project the loan is to be used for, but simply in order to secure legal control over the economic and political behavior of the debtor. Third, the only way made available for getting *out* of both debts is by getting *into* more debt. . . .[18]

Thus far it would seem that Chinweizu simply has made another case for loan pushing. The commercial banks, in conjunction with and at the behest of Western governments, pressed credit on Third World countries to entice them into debt trap peonage. The time was ripe for this in the 1970s because commodity and petroleum price increases made it plausible for LDC authorities to believe they could repay large external debts. Chinweizu's argument for loan pushing is predicated largely on the basis of Western economic domination of the Third World.

But Chinweizu's discussion demonstrates precisely that in some cases it is a matter of emphasis whether an argument lies on the loan push or the debt pull side of the ledger. Chinweizu contends that although the West was eager to create debt peons among the developing countries, Nigeria's authorities were anxious to embrace the very conditions that eventually would put their nation into this position! Chinweizu observes: ". . . I must stress that Nigeria was not captured and forced into this situation, *but volunteered itself into it.*"[19] Nigeria was faced with no necessity to incur debt. Peering through the window of 1978, Nigeria, in Chinweizu's words, "had more income from oil than it could sensibly spend."[20] Nevertheless: "Though it did not need the debt, it allowed itself to be persuaded to sample the pleasures of debtorship."[21]

Maintaining his "drug addict" analogy, he views his government's complicity in producing its own debt crisis as evidenced by its willingness to take the first "hit" of billions of dollars of external debt:

> . . . Nigeria is more like the person who was persuaded to take a first shot of heroin, got to like the thrill, and took more and more, soon becoming an addict. Indeed Nigeria did enjoy the thrills of being a spendthrift, and took more and more, soon becoming an addict. Nigeria has become not just a debt trap peon, but a squander-addicted debt trap peon. . . .[22]

Why exactly is the condition of a "squander-addicted debt trap peon" such a hazardous state of affairs? Chinweizu argues that it bears psychological dangers, subjecting Nigerian financial affairs to neocolonial supervision under the auspices of the IMF.[23] In this condition, the IMF has the propensity to gear the debt adjustment process in a way that precludes Nigeria becoming "a powerful, prosperous, modern industrial nation."[24] The IMF, Chinweizu argues, as an agent of the Western nations, seeks to deflect all Third World countries from turning into commercial and industrial rivals for the West. Therefore, IMF programs are intended to keep Nigeria on the receiving end of even greater sums of debt. Loan addiction will undermine Nigerian efforts to pursue economic development by placing a prior, indefinite claim on export earnings.

Not only will IMF policies prove counter to Nigerian interests with respect to substantive economic development, but conventional IMF austerity measures will also fuel social discontent. Chinweizu expects infamous IMF strikes and riots to occur soon in the streets of Lagos and Ibadan, Nigeria. He even notes that a Nigerian newspaper has recently given close coverage to the Brazilian experience, an experience revealing in Chinweizu's estimation, the face of the future for his country.[25]

Cold Turkey

The debt peon may desire and seek to avoid his creditor. A nation locked in debt peonage may eventually opt to repudiate its debt. Chinweizu says the latter action requires power—military power. A potential response of creditor nations—whether loans were issued by public or private sources—is to engage in overt economic imperialism when debt repudiation is imminent or declared:

> If you examine the history of the Caribbean, you will find that, earlier in this century, debts owed to European and U.S. interests served as occasions for the takeover of nations by the U.S. marines, and for the takeover of their finances for the purpose of collecting payments. One remarkable example was that of the Dominican Republic. In 1905 the United States took over its finances and used the proceeds from its customs to pay off its foreign debt. The exercise lasted until 1924, when the U.S. military finally left. . . .[26]

Debt repudiation could lead to Nigeria's reduction to the status of an early twentieth century "banana republic." Chinweizu concludes that debt repudiation is not a viable option since Nigeria lacks the military strength to resist an imperialist show of force from the West. Nor could it do much to prevent less brutal measures—such as the seizure of Nigerian citizens' assets located abroad. So, Chinweizu states, repudiation is out and Nigeria must pay off its external debt. But Nigeria must also discontinue its borrowing. To pay without incurring additional debt means an abrupt retreat from a pattern of "profligacy" on the part of Nigeria's elite—foregoing the "daily Chivas or Remy;" acceptance of driving "a dented Mercedes Benz."[27]

Chinweizu selects a "cold turkey" strategy for Nigeria: stop borrowing immediately and accept a reduction in the standard of living, at least until the debt is paid. Once the debt is paid, Nigeria can proceed at last with economic development on its own terms. Chinweizu advocates a sharp break with external financial dependency and proposes a new, relatively autonomous direction for his nation after a period of self-imposed austerity.

Somehow, Chinweizu believes that self-imposed austerity will fare better with the Nigerian populace than IMF-imposed austerity. Nigeria's citizenry will make the necessary sacrifices in their standard of living, he says, if the cause is just—the promise of escape from debt trap peonage—unlike the IMF programs, which he views as structured to maintain debt dependency.[28] After all, IMF programs typically establish preconditions for additional external borrowing to be extended or renewed. Of course, regardless of whether Nigeria's elite would come to embrace Chinweizu's solution and the associated goals, it is also questionable whether the non-elite, the largely poor mass of Nigerians, prefer austerity imposed from within to austerity imposed from without (particularly since the Nigerian masses had nothing to do with obtaining the loan).

Chinweizu wants the addict to break free from his own addiction. In his causal explanation, the addict bears responsibility for getting "hooked" in the first place—the funds were available, and Nigeria pulled them in excessive amounts.

The excessiveness, of course, remains such in retrospect in the sense that excessiveness has been revealed by debt-service difficulties, i.e., Nigeria did not borrow "reasonably." But borrowing still may have been "optimal" in the following sense: even in the economic literature on optimal borrowing, a sufficiently high rate-of-time preference on the part of a nation's citizens or their leaders could lead them to heavily discount the future, and gorge themselves with present consumption financed by debt accumulation. A heavily discounted future could mean that the long-term consequences for economic development or future financial health are ignored altogether. Extreme present orientation could lead to the observed pattern of a country borrowing an unpayable debt.

This simply throws the responsibility back into the lender's court. The lenders have the last word, and the last word always can be "credit denied." Lenders did, indeed, make the funds available. Even if borrowers were eager to respond, presumably the lenders should separate out those borrowers eager to absorb a volume of debt they have no concern about paying, or those borrowers who are liable to be profligate spenders even if sincere in their desire to meet their obligations. Regardless of the borrowers' enthusiasm, if lenders turn off the tap, their borrowing thirst must remain unquenched.

DEBT AND DISTORTION: A CAULDRON OF *LAISSEZ FAIRE* AT THE WORLD BANK

Chinweizu sees Nigeria as a nation that voluntarily—even eagerly—plunged into the quicksand of external debt. Its overborrowing accompanies its misdirection of the funds obtained, due to the preference of Nigeria's leadership to raise present consumption rather than long-term investment and hence, presumably future consumption. Different preferences would have led to different decisions about mobilization of the borrowed funds. Different choices could have been made; simply, they were not.

But a somewhat different position is evident in policy literature emanating from the World Bank. The Bank holds that many Third World nations were already constrained in their use of funds by a legacy of inappropriate past policies—specifically those policies that block the full operation of market forces to set relative prices.

Policy "Errors"

The World Bank, once a policy center that placed great emphasis on the government's role in directing and promoting economic growth in the poorer nations, the Bank has today gravitated increasingly toward the position that unhampered market activity will develop the under-developed world. This stance perhaps is symptomatic of an institutional response to maintain good relations with its official funding sources in an era when those sources also espouse a *laissez faire* ideology. The ideological swing may account for Anne Krueger's recent tenure as head of World Bank economic researchers, a tenure characterized by a new predominance of analyses and policy recommendations focused on removing impediments to market determination of prices in develop-ing countries.[29]

The clearest signal of change at the Bank came in the form of a pamphlet prepared for the right-leaning Institute for Economic Affairs in London by one of Krueger's lieutenants, Deepak Lal, entitled *The Poverty of Development Economics.*[30]

Lal denounced development economists for endorsing state direction as the centerpiece of strategies to raise Third World per capita incomes. Their errors are abundant for Lal, stemming from their misguided belief that conventional economic theory is inappropriate for Third World economies. Therefore, according to Lal, development economists are prone to (1) doubt the efficacy of free trade for the LDCs, (2) question the significance of efficiency gains from "freeing up" the price mechan-ism, (3) support nations running up large *fiscal* deficits, and (4) endorse continued state management of a variety of prices such as exchange rates, grain or bread prices, and wage rates. There are bleak consequences for the developing countries to the extent that Third World leaders have listened to the development economists or used the economists' advice to support their own predisposition toward such policies. Such policies doom the countries to slow or negative growth (or no growth), stifling the entrepreneurial initiative that otherwise would bloom in the poorest of nations. Interventionism is, for Lal, anti-development and bad economics. The Third World is a victim of the affinity for *dirigiste* policies of the development economists.

The relationship of this line of reasoning to the debt crisis is two-fold: (1) bad policies led these countries to need to borrow to maintain a balance of payments and (2) bad policies now make it difficult for these countries to manage debt service. Both arguments appear in one of the World Bank's most self-consciously balanced documents, its annual *World Development Report*. "Policy failings" in the report, are not isolated as "the *only* cause of recent debt-servicing problems."[31] But policy mistakes, that is, excessive interventionism, are certainly given pride of place as an important source of LDC difficulties. Not only were the inappropriate policies a spur to overborrowing, but the inflow of foreign finance into ostensibly "distorted" economies was bound to be misallocated. The waste is not due merely to elite profligacy (as Chinweizu would have it) or due to elite corruption—in the Bank view, it is due to incorrect price signals that serve as a guide to investment.

On the surface, the Bank solution appears to follow naturally from Lal's argument. Economies beset by bad policies should mend their ways. Remove obstacles to market forces and private initiative; liberalize and privatize.

In practice, the process of change is undoubtedly more complicated. If it is impracticable to remove all of a country's distortions simultaneously, economic theory offers no unambiguous guidance about how to ensure efficiency gains. Neoclassical welfare economics informs us that the "first best world" is one free of all price distortions. But if we are not already in such a world and cannot reach it in one motion, the sequence or order of liberalization then becomes a serious problem. Is there a priority list to remove distortions to guarantee an efficiency gain? What is the optimal path if we are in a "second" or "third best" world?[32] There are no general guidelines independent of the particular circumstances of each country. Effective, piecemeal removal of distortions must be contingent on the characteristics of particular economies.

Krueger herself suggests a political basis for resistance to liberalization in LDCs, resistance that will not be swept aside by mere proselytizing by the World Bank. She has been instrumental in the development of neoclassical political economy, that postulates the emergence over time of interest groups who reap "rents" from various government interventions.[33] An obvious example of this theory are domestic manufacturers who might be shielded from foreign competition by import controls. But a case can be made that any distortion possesses a supportive rent-seeking lobby. If so, getting from the status quo of bad decisions to the good old land of *laissez faire* might prove to be a tricky circumnavigation.

"Dirigisme" and Debt?

But did countries run into debt-service problems because they have been pursuing bad policies? William Cline, for one, is skeptical, pointing out many countries had so-called *dirigiste* policies long before there was a debt crisis.[34] It might be argued that those policies eventually led the countries into a period of inadequate growth and balance-of-payments deficit, driving them to borrow excessively. The reasons why bankers would accommodate countries in poor shape policy-wise and performance-wise is not obvious, but the argument can be made. In fact, however, the largest volume of loans of the 1970s were to countries that were growing rapidly and had solid balance-of-payments positions. The loans were primarily for development, not adjustment purposes. It was only after debt-service difficulties emerged around 1982 that lending went to low growth countries with payments difficulties. They were the same countries.

Even if the countries' debt burdens were not caused by their policies, was their inability to pay policy-related? Ironically, several countries— particularly those in the southern cone of Latin America (Argentina, Chile, and Uruguay)—underwent major liberalizations that coincided with their absorption of immense external debt.[35] Empirically, a wide range of Third World countries, regardless of their policy orientation, are encountering debt-service problems. A case might be made on behalf of "the Asian tigers," defining them as relatively non-*dirigiste* nations with few debt-service problems.[36] But the southern cone stands in direct contrast to nations that liberalized and found themselves in the debt trap.

Again it might be argued that the Southern Cone nations did not go far enough or chose an incorrect order of liberalization.[37] But the real issue is more elemental. The Krueger-Lal axis of economists imply that a world of pure *laissez faire* will be crisis-free. But credit and finance can wreak havoc quite readily in a world of negligible or zero market obstructions (See Chapter 9) in either developed or developing countries.[38] Commercial banks are really not present in the rarefied world of pure trade and welfare theory models from which Krueger and Lal make their descent to save development economists from themselves. If banks are present in this "world," they are indistinguishable from other enterprises—their special ability to turn on the tap of investment, even in the absence of new acts of personal savings, is not recognized.[39] Their potential for destabilizing economies is largely ignored. As noted in Chapter 3, the late Carlos Diaz-Alejandro, however, was intensely sensitive to the special properties of banks. The suggestive title of his final published paper, "Good-Bye Financial Repression, Hello Financial Crash," implies that lifting all restraints on commercial banks—anywhere—is a recipe for disaster.[40] After all, as we have suggested throughout this volume, the origins of the debt crisis must find their true roots in the unregulated Eurodollar market. We continue to return to the banks as our "witch hunt" continues.

NOTES

1. Jack M. Guttentag and Richard Herring, "Commercial Bank Lending to Developing Countries: From Overlending to Underlending to Structural Reform," in Gordon Smith and John Cuddington, eds., *International Debt and the Developing Countries* (Washington, DC: The World Bank, 1985), p. 129.

2. See William Cline, *International Debt: Systemic Risk and Policy Response* (Washington, DC: Institute for International Economics, 1984) and William Cline, "International Debt: Analysis, Experience and Prospects," *Journal of Development Planning*, no. 16 (1985): 25–56.

3. The principles derived from this literature are summarized in non-technical fashion in Yves Maroni, "How to Borrow Reasonably" (International Finance Discussion Paper No. 203, Washington, DC: Federal Reserve Board of Governors, February 1982).

4. Mario Henrique Simonsen, "The Developing-Country Debt Problem" in Gordon Smith and John Cuddington, eds., *International Debt, Developing Countries*, pp. 117–18 (emphasis in original).

5. Penny Lernoux, *In Banks We Trust* (New York: Viking Penguin, 1986).

6. Jeffrey Sachs, "Comment," (*Brookings Papers on Economy Activity 2*, 1984).

7. Ibid.

8. Chinweizu, "Debt Trap Peonage," *Monthly Review* 37 (November 1985): 21–37.

9. Cheryl Payer, *The Debt Trap: The International Monetary Fund and the Third World* (New York: Monthly Review Press, 1974) pp. 48–49.

10. Chinweizu, "Debt Trap Peonage," pp. 21–22.

11. Ibid., p. 22.

12. Ibid., p. 23.
13. Alfred J. Watkins, *Till Debt Do Us Part* (Washington, DC: Roosevelt Center for American Policy Studies, 1986) pp. 19–21.
14. Chinweizu, "Debt Trap Peonage," p. 21.
15. Ibid., pp. 22–23.
16. Ibid., p. 22.
17. Ibid.
18. Ibid., p. 23.
19. Ibid. (emphasis added).
20. Ibid.
21. Ibid.
22. Ibid.
23. Ibid., p. 23–24.
24. Ibid., p. 25.
25. Ibid., pp. 25–26.
26. Ibid., p. 27.
27. Ibid., p. 29.
28. Ibid., p. 26.
29. See Krueger's own research such as "Analyzing Disequilibrium Exchange Rate Systems in Developing Countries," *World Development* 10 (1982): 1059–1068.
30. Deepak Lal, *The Poverty of Development Economics* (Hobart Paperback No. 16, London: Institute of Economic Affairs, 1983).
31. The World Bank, *World Development Report 1985* (New York: Oxford University Press, 1975), pp. 43–45 (emphasis in original).
32. See R.G. Lipsey and Kelvin Lancaster, "The General Theory of Second Best," *Review of Economic Studies* 25 (1956–57): 11–32.
33. Anne Krueger, "The Political Economy of the Rent-Seeking Society," *American Economic Review* 64 (June 1974): 291–303.
34. Cline, *International Debt, Risk and Policy.*
35. Persio Arida even argues there is a correlation between liberalization and debt–service difficulties. (See Chapter 3.)
36. Most of the East Asian countries appear to have done better in terms of economic growth. Whether this has been due to anti-*dirigiste* policies or aggressive export promotion or other reasons remains a topic of hot debate. Chile was, however, a Latin country that liberalized and pursued outward looking policies that got it into trouble. Korea appears to have barely brushed back from the edge of debt-service troubles. See Jeffrey Sachs, "External Debt and Macroeconomic Performance in Latin America and East Asia," (*Brooking Papers on Economic Activity*, 1985 pp. 523–64) and the comment by John Williamson in the same issue, pp. 565–70.
37. See Larry Sjaastaad, "Failure of Economic Liberalism in the Cone of Latin America," *World Economy* 6 (1983): pp. 5–26.

38. A similar point is made by John Toye in "*Dirigisme* and Development Economics," *Cambridge Journal of Economics* 9 (1985): 1–14.
39. On investment's independence from saving due to the existence of bank credit see J. Snippe, "Finance, Saving and Investment in Keynes's Economics," *Cambridge Journal of Economics* 9 (1985): 257–69.
40. Carlos Diaz-Alejandro, "Good-Bye Financial Repression, Hello Financial Crash," *Journal of Development Economics* 19 (1985): 1–24.

CHAPTER 7

Minsky Cycles and the Global Debt Crisis: Financial Instability

I f any theory is a tailor made explanation for the current international debt crisis, it is Hyman Minsky's financial instability hypothesis. Minsky often attributes the spiritual origins of this hypothesis to Keynes' *Treatise on Money* and *The General Theory*.[1] It appears, however, that the strongest intellectual antecedent for Minsky's vision is the work of his former professor at Chicago, the late Henry Simons.[2]

FROM HENRY SIMONS TO HYMAN MINSKY

Simons was a passionate advocate of *laissez faire* economics. Nevertheless, he feared two aspects of unregulated capitalist economies. First, he perceived that free competition and inter-enterprise rivalry would lead to some businesses staking out monopoly positions. To prohibit this, a state agency would be needed to regulate industry, performing an antitrust function that would sustain atomistic competition. Second, Simons believed that there were inherent dangers in the commercial banks' ability to simultaneously accept deposits and make loans. The banking system was vulnerable to collapse. Again the state would be needed to regulate deposit-taking institutions, by imposing 100 percent reserve requirements on them. Institutions that required loans could only obtain funds through the sale of their own securities.[3] The connection between deposit-taking and lending was to be severed, to remove the inherent fragility of the financial system and curb fluctuations in the money supply associated with swings in bank credit.

It is Simons' insight about the inherent vulnerability of the banking system that carries directly into Minsky's work. Although Minsky lacks Simons' unabashed enthusiasm for *laissez faire* and although Minsky is not a proponent of 100 percent reserves (he seems to feel that proper central bank management of credit-creation and countercyclical fiscal policy can generally avert crises), he embraces the core of Simons' analysis of why crises come about.[4]

Minsky has usually applied the financial instability hypothesis exclusively to the propagation of economic depression in a closed economy. Specifically, the U.S. serves as his illustrative example, with negligible attention devoted to international linkages. It is only recently that Minsky has begun extending the financial instability hypothesis to the foreign lending waves of the 1970s; this overture has not been explicit.[5] To fully convert the financial instability hypothesis into a theory of the global debt crisis will require filling in gaps at certain stages of Minsky's standard analysis of the periodic breakdown of capitalist economies.

Long Waves and Capitalist Breakdowns

The financial instability hypothesis mandates that the credit mechanism of capitalist economies is inherently prone to malfunction, contributing directly to recurrent cyclical downturns.[6] Cast in the context of a long wave analysis, Minsky contends that long periods of prosperity propel lending institutions to extend credit to borrowers with increasingly weaker financial positions. The long wave in Minsky's sense is truly long in a chronological sense, extending forty to fifty years. An extended economic upswing will feature minor recessions; an extended downswing will feature minor recoveries.[7] Whether the long wave is a period of expansion or contraction is defined by the secular trend in real income or output over several decades. Minsky's long wave of prosperity breeds the conditions for the destruction of prosperity.

Profit-seeking enterprises that receive new credit are more leveraged in borrowing than their predecessors and more exposed to an inability to repay their debts when a decline occurs in after tax profits. Older borrowers who take on additional credit (often in part to refinance previous obligations) acquire less sturdy financial postures. Eventually, a drop off in after tax profits occurs and businesses fail to meet their payments. The lenders subsequently retreat from extending additional credit.[8] The credit crunch that supplants the credit boom propagates a generalized fall in investment, income, and employment.

Minsky's upturn is characterized by: "changes in the structure of financial assets and liabilities [occurring] during a period in which only mild depression cycles take place . . . such as to make the financial system less stable."[9] Minsky highlights three of these structural changes: (1) a general rise in debt-to-income ratios in the economy's productive sectors, (2) a general upward movement in stock market and real estate asset prices, and (3) a decline "in the relative size of ultimate liquidity."[10] By "ultimate liquidity," Minsky means strictly "outside" money—government liabilities to the public and, when countries are on the gold standard, the stock of gold.[11] Simultaneously, the depth of "financial layering"—the interdependence of financial institutions—becomes more intricate.[12]

As these changes occur, the overall performance of the economy becomes more susceptible to a sharp downturn if any disturbance occurs that causes a fall in income or a default on a financial contract. In effect, a momentum builds over the long wave making the economy more imperiled by negative income shocks that have adverse repercussions on the financial system. The capacity of the system to absorb the shock without producing widespread depression softens, as the period of relatively sustained growth continues.

Ponzi Schemes Everywhere?

Minsky has found it fruitful to identify enterprises as possessing "three types of financial postures"—hedge finance, speculative finance, and Ponzi finance positions.[13] In the first case, the inflow of cash is expected to exceed the outflow of cash in every period, so financial enterprises, or units in such a position expect to cover their immediate debt obligations with current gross receipts. Speculative finance units can be expected to run shortfalls in the near term but "in the longer term are expected to [have cash inflows that] exceed cash payments commitments that are outstanding." In the short term, the speculative finance unit will have "to roll over or refinance debt." Finally, the Ponzi finance unit can only cover its debt obligations by reaping "a 'bonanza' in the future which makes the present value positive for low enough interest rates." In the meantime, it must continually raise "its outstanding debt to meet financial obligations."[14]

The argument about cumulative system instability still applies concerning Ponzi units. As the economic upswing continues, proportionately more and more businesses take on speculative and Ponzi types of financial postures. The banks, as we shall see below, make the financing available to borrowers who adopt riskier and riskier positions. Such units are especially unguarded in the event of major disadvantageous swings in prices. Minsky emphasized the extensive impact of short-term interest rate increases in a 1978 paper,[15] but it would be even easier in 1986 to highlight the somewhat narrower significance of sharp declines in oil and gas prices. Regardless, an economy featuring a substantial proportion of businesses in speculative and Ponzi positions will be an economy that is closer to the edge of a crash. Financial panics are endogenously generated over time, through the normal long cycle performance of capitalist economies.

FINANCIAL INSTABILITY AND GLOBAL DEBT

There are at least two distinct routes to pursue in taking the financial instability hypothesis from an analysis of purely domestic crises to an analysis of international crises. One route is simply to graft onto the basic Minsky model a new set of borrowers, specifically foreign borrowers (both public and private sector) in developing countries. These borrowers may be viewed as generally liable to possess speculative finance postures, at a minimum, from the standpoint of their expected cash flow position. They may even possess Ponzi finance postures from the outset. These positions are of course the most dangerous to sustain in a Minsky world. This additional set of borrowers becomes the object of lenders' attention to a greater and greater degree as long as the upswing advances. The longer the duration of the worldwide cyclical upturn, the larger the proportion of foreign businesses and governments, alongside domestic businesses, that come to hold these more perilous positions. Now the international financial system becomes decreasingly shock-proof; a sufficiently large foreign borrower's default or debt repudiation could set off a ripple effect through the layers that would provoke a deep, global depression. The potential for depression is internationalized because lending has been internationalized.

An alternate route would have the commercial banks reaching externally to foreign borrowers as the downturn sets in at home or throughout the developed countries. As overextended domestic borrowers contract their operations or file for bankruptcy, the banks may look toward an entirely new set of borrowers who have seemingly brighter prospects. Bankers' retreat from domestic lending may constitute a switch toward LDC borrowers rather than a complete contraction in worldwide credit provision.

To the Periphery on the Upswing or the Downswing?

Whether the banks' push toward LDC borrowers occurs on the upswing or downswing of a Minsky long wave is both a conceptual and an empirical issue. Should the long waves be defined purely in terms of the performance of the more developed countries, or on a global basis? How should the recession of 1974–75 be interpreted: as the conclusion of the long wave of prosperity dating from the end of the Great Depression, or as a relatively severe but minor recession on a long wave of prosperity that has yet to culminate in a major crash? This definition is important with respect to the route one chooses with the Minsky thesis, since the growth in bank loans to LDCs starts in the late 1960s but does not reach explosive proportions until the late 1970s.[16]

Of course, it is reasonable to suggest that these two routes are not mutually exclusive. Over the long upswing, banks may seek to broaden the sweep of their net to catch borrowers, including developing country borrowers. But if problems first become manifest with domestic borrowers due to the conclusion of four decades of growth, the banks may also switch overseas *en masse*.

U.S. banking in the 1920s suggests such a pattern of borrower switches. Commercial banks initially concentrated their lending efforts in the domestic manufacturing sector. They moved into lending to developing countries in Latin America and to Germany, as the latter sought to recover from the devastation of World War I. Since there were no prohibitions on such practices at the time—the Glass-Steagall Act was a product of the later financial panic—banks then turned toward funding speculative activities on the New York Stock Exchange. But this pattern does not immediately resolve the questions of timing and precision in the application of the Minsky theory to LDC lending. The U.S. was in a phase of prosperity throughout the entire period of borrower switching, although the depression that was to reach the U.S. had already become evident in various countries in Europe by the mid-1920s. These ambiguities do not seem to undercut the basic insight that the financial system routinely grows more fragile over a long period of growth.

Competitive Pressure

Minsky's theory is not fully a theory, insofar as it is weak in providing the causal basis for the repetition of the pattern he has discerned. At times the financial instability hypothesis slips into no more than a mere description of a long wave, with an emphasis on the idea that the financial sector can have a pronounced effect on the real side of the economy both when it lends and when it refuses to lend. Long waves of growth culminate in near-manic lending booms that open up the prospect of deep depression. These are repetitious events, even if they require forty to fifty years to complete a full turn.

But if Minsky has detected the periodicity of these events, why have the bankers failed to do so themselves? Why do they repeat the overlending practices that contributed to depression in the past? Why have they not learned from the mistakes of the 1920s, for instance? Why will they make the additional loans to businesses that will tip into speculative or Ponzi financial postures?

We simply have circled back to one of our basic themes—the rationality or irrationality of the bankers. If the Minsky model provides an accurate picture of the structural properties of the financial system, bankers ought to acknowledge its accuracy and lend with far greater circumspection, or so it would seem.

Minsky tends to argue that the bankers believe their loans would perform, but they cannot individually manage the performance of the world economy. Policy makers such as the Federal Reserve could avert the credit crunch, but to do so would require reinflation of the economy. Furthermore, bankers and Federal Reserve officials alike are prisoners of the false doctrines of monetarism which argue that if the Fed maintains steady money growth, the economy will be self-adjusting or self-correcting.[17]

The bankers have been seduced by the siren call of the monetarists. Instead, Minsky would contend, they should heed the financial-monetary theory of Minsky, Simons, and Keynes, realizing the dangers of their normal practices. Minsky asserts that monetarism misleads the bankers by leading them to believe it is intervention by the monetary authorities that destabilizes the financial mechanism, rather than the normal, unfettered practices of private banks themselves. If the Federal Reserve had continued an easy money policy, by this theory the debt crisis may never have materialized. For Minsky, cyclical fluctuations are characteristic of the unregulated capitalistic economy; *appropriate* regulation will eliminate the cyclical swings.

We prefer to go beyond Minsky's identification of monetarist ideology as the source of the repetitiveness of financial instability. Monetarism was not extant in the 1920s—although of course, there were plenty of *laissez faire*-minded economists to be found who, perhaps, had the bankers' ears. But even under *laissez faire*, it can be argued that competitive pressure among the banks could lead them to extend loans to less and less well secured borrowers. Although there may be lessons to be learned from past lending booms, the profit wars of today place an insurmountable impetus on the commercial banks to increase their assets through new lending. If it fails to "keep up," a bank must accept a lower rate of return than its competitors during the long economic upswings, paying the price for greater stability in its performance.

Competition does not come merely from other banks, but also from non-bank financial intermediaries such as investment houses. Coupled with the elimination of Regulation Q which set ceilings on interest rates banks can pay to depositors, the competitive floodgates have been opened for U.S. banks.[18] Banks are compelled to seek riskier lenders or cut profit margins under the force of a relatively unregulated environment of free competition.[19] Guttentag and Herring even suggest that "prudent decisionmakers" may be driven out of the market when competition is raging: "A bank that attempts to charge an appropriate default premium for low-probability hazards is likely to lose business to banks that are willing to disregard the hazard."[20] Bogdanowicz-Bindert, a senior vice president in the International Banking Division of Shearson Lehman/American Express; and Sacks, a managing partner of Multinational Strategies, Inc., have argued that the country information available to the banks in the 1970s was not particularly good. However, even if this information had been high quality, under "the pressures of excess liquidity and increased competition" it would have been ignored or biased in favor of lending.[21]

Competitive pressure among banks points to another tender spot in conventional economic theory—the concept of competition itself. Our description of the process that might be best viewed as engendering recurrent destabilization of the financial system and thereby the world economy, bears no resemblance to neoclassical economics' benchmark of "perfect competition." The competitive pressure described above involves rivalry, conflict, price cutting, etc.—all absent from perfect competition, a world in which businesses are price takers and have no effect on the demand for their products. For the neoclassicist, what has been described as competitive pressure is some variant of "imperfect competition." But we prefer to view the warfare between businesses as (1) the relevant benchmark for the empirically relevant and theoretically important concept of competition, and (2) as suggesting fundamental weaknesses in the way offered by conventional economics for thinking about competition.[22]

Moral Hazard

Finally, it is worth noting that certain regulatory policies might aggravate overlending. If, for example, the Federal Reserve performs its function as lender of last resort without any major *quid pro quo* from the rescued financial institution, this would only serve to encourage others to continue making injudicious loans. Minsky succinctly pinpoints the moral hazard problem—the problem that arises when lenders who perceive that there are institutions willing to "insure" their operations become more willing to pursue loan options they might otherwise avoid:

> If lender-of-last-resort interactions are not accompanied by regulations and reforms that restrict financial market practices, then the intervention sets the stage for the financing of an inflationary expansion, once the "animal spirits" of business people and bankers have recovered from the transitory shock of the crisis that forced the lender-of-the-last-resort activities in the first place.[23]

For Minsky this is the serious danger with central bank monetary management policies—the problem that such policies may aggravate the very behavior the central bank seeks to prevent. Simons would have stopped the music altogether; his preference would have been to keep deposit-taking institutions out of lending altogether.

Minsky's worries about the moral hazard problem suggest that Simons is perhaps closer to the truth with his extreme advocacy of 100 percent reserve requirements. Moderate regulations may persuade economic participants that a deep depression is no longer possible, although they fully recognize the cyclical nature of a capitalist economy. Minsky himself observed:

> There are forgetting as well as learning relations in economic decision processes. Within a capitalist framework, an essential element in the felt uncertainty is the realization by all decisionmakers that the economy's experience is cyclical. As past cyclical experience that was associated with, for example, financial difficulties recedes in time, the willingness to experiment with novel financial instruments and financial positions increases. This tendency to experiment is reinforced by the fact that financial and government usages change over time; the belief grows as past troubles recede in time that new institutions make difficulties similar to those experienced in the past virtually unlikely. . . .[24]

Those worried about excessive regulation fear that renewed, extensive banking system regulation will hinder the efficiency of credit allocation. But as we have previously noted, in much the same spirit as Minsky, the late Carlos Diaz-Alejandro offered a stinging rebuttal in the title of his final paper, "Good-Bye Financial Repression, Hello Financial Crash."[25] Diaz-Alejandro suggested that the lending practices of unregulated banks everywhere, including banks in the Third World, propel their economies toward periodic disasters. After all, prior reputed and efficient allocation of credit becomes meaningless after the crash.

NOTES

1. See Hyman Minsky, *John Maynard Keynes* (New York: Columbia University Press, 1975).
2. Minsky counts Oskar Lange and Henry Simons as his most important mentors when he studied at Chicago. On his intellectual relationship with Simons see Hyman P. Minsky, "Beginnings," *Banca Nazionale Del Lavoro Quarterly Review* 38 (September 1985): 218–21.
3. The clearest statement of Simons's theoretical posture is in an unsigned memorandum entitled "Banking and Currency Reform," a memorandum that Aaron Director has said was written primarily by Simons. See Milton Friedman, "The Monetary Theory and Policy of Henry Simons," *Journal of Law and Economics* 10 (October 1967): 2n.1. Simons's memorandum contains an analysis obviously based upon the chain of events associated with the fall of U.S. banks during the Great Depression. Also see J. Bradford De Long, "In Defense of Henry Simons' Standing As A Classical Liberal," unpublished manuscript, Harvard University, 24 February 1986.
4. Simons, ibid., however, did not feel confident in the ability of a central bank to "fully control or prevent unhealthy expansion of credit." He expressed the following reservations while "[a]dmitting . . . that effective control is quite possible, in principle . . ." "(a) No body like the Reserve Board is likely to restrain expansion adequately, unless it proceeds under an unambiguous mandate from Congress in the form of a mechanical rule of action;" and "(b) Even with such a rule, moreover, the scheme is inelegant, in that the superior authority must always exercise its control, as it were, against the 'nature' of the system which it is controlling." Concluded Simons, pessimistically: ". . . a considerable expansion of bank loans and, thereby, of the community's effective money is likely to occur before any automatic checks become operative."
5. Hyman Minsky, "Financial Interrelations, the Balance of Payments, and the Dollar Crisis," in Jonathan D. Aronson, ed., *Debt and the Less Developed Countries* (Boulder, CO: Westview Press, 1979), pp. 103–22.
6. The financial instability hypothesis has been elaborated by Minsky in a number of places. Of particular note are his essays "Can 'It' Happen Again?" reprinted in Hyman Minsky, *Can 'It' Happen Again?: Essays on Instability and Finance* (Armonk, NY: M.E. Sharpe, Inc., 1982), pp. 3–13, originally published in 1963; "Longer Waves in Financial Relations: Financial Factors

in the More Severe Depressions," *American Economic Review: AEA Papers and Proceedings* 54 (May 1964): 324–35; "The Financial Instability Hypothesis: A Restatement," in Philip Arestis and Thanos Skouras, eds., *Post Keynesian Economic Theory: A Challenge to Neoclassical Economics* (Sussex, England: Wheatsheaf Books, 1985), pp. 24–55, originally published in 1978 as a Thames Paper in Political Economy; and his book *John Maynard Keynes*; and his essay "The Financial-Instability Hypothesis: Capitalist Processes and the Behavior of the Economy," in Charles P. Kindleberger and Jean-Pierre Laffarque, eds., *Financial Crisis: Theory, History, and Policy* (Cambridge, MA: Cambridge University Press, 1982).

7. Minsky, "Longer Waves," pp. 324–25.

8. Given his stylized characterization of lending waves, it should be evident that Minsky's work would have appealed to Charles Kindleberger. See Charles P. Kindleberger, *Manias, Panics, and Crashes: A History of Financial Crises* (New York: Basic Books, 1978). Kindleberger's enthusiasm for Minsky's financial instability hypothesis seems to be more muted lately, although the reason is not entirely clear.

9. Minsky, "Longer Waves," p. 326.

10. Ibid., pp. 326–27.

11. Ibid., p. 325, n.3.

12. Ibid., p. 325.

13. Minsky, "Financial Instability: Restatement," pp. 43–44.

14. Ibid.

15. Ibid., p. 44.

16. Christina A. Bogdanowicz-Bindert and Paul M. Sacks, in their article, "The Role of Information: Closing the Barn Door?" in Richard Feinberg and Valeriana Kallab, eds., *Uncertain Future: Commercial Banks and the Third World* (New Brunswick, NJ: Transaction Books, 1984), p. 72, point out that: ". . . non-oil developing countries and the Eastern bloc countries increased their indebtedness to banks sevenfold between 1971 and 1982." The bulk of the growth in indebtedness occurred in the latter half of the decade.

17. This is precisely the policy stance that Henry Simons felt was insufficient to guard against system instability. (See Note 4.) Of course, Minsky also rejects the efficacy of a monetary growth rule. See especially Hyman Minsky, "The Federal Reserve: Between A Rock and a Hard Place," *Challenge* (May/June 1980): 30–36. In personal correspondence dated 11 July 1984 Minsky wrote the following to the authors:

> No banker and businessman—not even Continental Illinois and its clients—entered upon contracts with the expectation that loans would not perform. But the individual decision makers—even at the scale of Citicorp—do not have command over system performance. Furthermore, the prevailing conventional wisdom is that the economy is capable of sustained expansion at stable prices and of course the Captains of Industry (and Finance) believe in the virtues of Capitalism and

consider anyone pointing out the flaws of Capitalism as such as being subversive or worst. Past crises and depressions are imputed to institutional weaknesses or policy errors—not any inherent characteristics of our economy. The "alibis" for preceding performance shortfalls are believable: for example if you read Friedman and Schwartz's Great Contraction would you believe that the contraction reflected deep flaws in our economy or that it was due to avoidable policy errors by the Federal Reserve in managing *The Money Supply?* (emphasis in original).

18. James Glassman, "The Money Culture: Lust to Lend," *The New Republic,* 9 June 1986.

19. T.H. Donaldson has focused on falling margins under competitive pressure in *International Lending by Commercial Banks* (New York: John Wiley and Sons, 1974), pp. 158–61.

20. Jack M. Guttentag and Richard Herring, "Commercial Bank Lending to Developing Countries: From Overlending to Underlending to Structural Reform," in Gordon W. Smith and John T. Cuddington, eds., *International Debt and the Developing Countries* (Washington, DC: The World Bank, 1985), p. 133.

21. Bogdanowicz-Bindert and Sacks, "Role of Information," p. 72. Lawrence Brainard, senior vice president at Bankers Trust Company, in his essay "More Lending to the Third World?: A Banker's View," in Richard E. Feinberg and Valeriana Kallab, eds., *Uncertain Future: Commercial Banks and the Third World* (New Brunswick, NJ: Transaction Books, 1984), p. 31 (emphasis added) offers the following revealing anecdote about bank competition in sovereign lending in the 1970s:

> A vivid recollection from my early career in banking is a meeting that took place in early 1974, after the first oil price shock. I joined a small group of senior bankers discussing the request of Denmark for a balance-of-payments credit. The key issue before us was whether private commercial banks had any business making unsecured loans to sovereign borrowers. After much soul searching the request was turned down. Within a day, another bank had stepped in to underwrite the loan at rate even lower than we had been considering. Within several months, the initial resistance of my banking colleagues to sovereign balance-of-payments lending gave way *under the influence of competitive pressures.* The large-scale expansion of bank lending to developing countries that followed is now history.

22. After all, neoclassical perfect competition is not robust with respect to assumptions about returns to scale. For example, if businesses producing a common product experience decreasing costs over the relevant range of output, they cannot all be price takers and earn positive profits. If businesses experience increasing costs over the relevant range they cannot be viewed as price takers in the input markets. Under constant costs, their individual output decisions become indeterminate.

23. Minsky, "The Federal Reserve," p. 35.

24. Hyman Minsky, "*Money and the Real World:* A Review Article," *Quarterly Review of Economics and Business* 14 (Summer 1974): 12.
25. Carlos Diaz-Alejandro, "Good-Bye Financial Repression, Hello Financial Crash," *Journal of Development Economics* 19 (1985): 1–24.

CHAPTER 8

Marxist Theory and the Global Debt Crisis

M arxist thought typically holds that international capitalism is necessarily predisposed toward crisis. Marxist theorists would hardly be surprised by the phenomenon of overlending to the developing countries; for them, it would simply be another item on the menu of disastrous courses taken by the path of evolving capitalism. However, the diversity of mechanisms Marxists are likely to identify to explain the generation of a worldwide financial crisis may surprise those outside the Marxist tradition of scholarship.

To limit the scope of our own inquiry, we shall restrict our attention to three potential approaches within Marxism: (1) the Austro-Marxist explanation following Rudolf Hilferding, (2) the Trotskyist explanation expressed by Ernest Mandel, and (3) a "fundamentalist" approach that we extrapolate from David Harvey's superb work, coupled with current research on the rise of a "new class," the managerial class. There are, indeed, many more Marxist approaches that could be adapted to the analysis of developing country indebtedness, but we find these three to be particularly challenging. In each case the application of each approach to the debt crisis requires a fairly detailed exposition of the crisis theory.

FINANCE CAPITAL AND
THE GLOBAL DEBT CRISIS

Rudolf Hilferding, widely considered a leading theoretician of the Austro-Marxist school, placed the financial aspect of capitalism at the center of propagation of fluctuations in capitalist economies. Concomitantly, Hilferding advanced a theory of capitalist imperialism that is rooted in the movement of investment from the more to the less developed regions. Virtually his entire extension of Marxist theory to account for the emergence of corporate enterprises and external finance at the close of the 19th century can be found in his monumental work, *Finance Capital,* originally published in German in 1910.[1]

Austro-Marxism

The perspective of *Finance Capital* reveals a peculiar blend of Austrian economics and Marxist influence unique to Hilferding's generation of intellectuals, who were located throughout the Prussian principalities. While still a student, he constructed a well-crafted defense of Marx against Bohm-Bawerk's complaints over the transformation problem.[2] Nevertheless, Hilferding's own theoretical framework was deeply infected by the Austrian economists' vision of the operation of the economic system, despite his steadfast rejection of subjective brands of economics.

Specifically, in Hilferding's hands, Austro-Marxism came to share (with Austrian economics) an emphasis on the configuration of prices, the time structure of production, and the destabilizing effects of distortions of relative prices. Austrian economics attributed the distortions primarily to the intrusion of the state in the marketplace. In more recent iterations, special emphasis is given to the adverse impact of central bank policy in aligning the rate of interest. In turn, the interest rate distortion is alleged to disrupt the proper division of production between consumption and investment goods.[3]

In contrast, Hilferding argued on behalf of Austro-Marxism, that price distortions arise from the normal, unimpeded operations of the pricing system. Distortions have endogenous causes that exist independently of interventionist activity by the state.[4] In *Finance Capital,* Hilferding isolates at least four reasons why he believes the price system will produce, under "natural" conditions, what he terms "disproportions in prices." These reasons are: (1) the diversity across the economy of the "organic compositions of capital" (the ratio of constant to variable capital); (2) an inherent propulsion toward *overaccumulation* in sectors with high organic compositions of capital; (3) imbalances in the availability of money credit by sectors; and (4) the propensity for consumption to lag behind production as a prosperous wave proceeds, due to the entrepreneur's increasing share in total income.[5]

All of these factors, said Hilferding, tend to drive a wedge between market prices (or actual prices) and their potential centers of gravitation—prices of production, the latter dictated primarily by labor costs. These "deviations" between market prices and production prices occur regularly and persist sufficiently to lead to "disruptions in the regulation of production."[6] Unlike Austrian economics, Hilferding's theory posits an environment of untrammeled private enterprise; there is free banking and no stabilization policy pursued by the government. The departures of market prices from production prices occur routinely in Hilferding's world, with negative repercussions on the economy's performance. Distortions in Hilferding's sense are self-generated by capitalist economies, rather than merely induced by "external" forces.

Falling Interest Rates and Disproportions

Linked to his view that the price system normally sets the wrong prices is Hilferding's argument about two related sources of capitalist crisis. He invokes both the law of the tendency of the rate of profit to fall and the problem of disproportionality in production as essential precipitants of system-wide fluctuations.

Marx developed the law of the tendency of the rate of profit to fall to demonstrate why capitalist society sows the seeds of its own doom.[7] In Marx's analysis, the source of profit is surplus labor time, which is the amount of time the laborer works beyond the time required to produce goods sufficient to reproduce himself and his family. But the nature and direction of technical change progressively lowers the socially necessary labor time, thereby reducing the necessity of labor's presence in the capitalist work process. This weakens the chain that links the laborer, whose work creates profit, to that same capitalist work process. The secular tendency for the profit rate to fall brings countertendencies into existence that retard the decline but cannot altogether arrest it.[8]

On the other hand, Hilferding rejected what he labelled "the dogma of the falling interest rate."[9] Instead of maintaining an interpretation of the law as a direct statement of the inevitability of capitalism's demise, Hilferding treated it as a basis for a theory of the capitalist business cycle. The rate of profit does not drop secularly for Hilferding, but instead, swings up and down periodically, carrying the economy up and down with its movements.

Although Hilferding uses Marx's language of constant and variable capital and adopts the definition of the ratio of the two as "the organic

composition of capital," he treats the ratio as equivalent to more orthodox economists' notion of a capital-labor ratio. This conceptually
separates his notion of the rate of profit from Marx's, for Hilferding
virtually treats what he terms as the rate of profit as being inversely related to the capital-labor ratio. His cycle theory follows in a straightforward fashion.

On a prosperous economic upswing, the capital-labor ratio deepens,
putting downward pressure on the rate of profit. The fall in the rate
of profit leads to a slowdown of the economy as entrepreneurs lose their
incentive to make the economic commitments that would preserve
growth. A recession/depression ensues and the capital stock undergoes
an erosion, since it is not subject to renewal due to the braking of investment. This means in turn an eventual decline in the capital-labor
ratio, which restores the rate of profit and provides a renewed stimulus
to investment and growth. In a sense, growth is self-defeating and the
recession/depression is self-correcting, due to the effects on the rate of
profit of the accompanying changes in the capital-labor ratio.[10]

For Hilferding, a capitalist "crisis" occurs at the point when the rate
of profit begins to fall after a "long period of prosperity, in which prices
and profits are high."[11] The renewal of prosperity after the downturn
is facilitated by factors associated with a new demand stimulus:
(1) opening of new markets, (2) establishment of new branches of production, (3) introduction of new technology, or (4) expanding needs
due to population growth.[12] The new markets obviously could be
abroad, a point we shall return to shortly.

Indeed, Hilferding saw capitalism as also doomed, but not primarily due to an ongoing fall in the rate of profit. Capitalism's demise, for
him, was to come from the increasing concentration and centralization
of production—a growing "socialization" of production that would progressively improve the feasibility of socialist organization of the economy.
Capital's increased concentration and centralization were symptoms of
monopolization of the means of production by finance capital, a consequence of the ferocious rivalry that in Marxist theory is characteristic
of capitalistic competition.[13] On this basis, somewhat ironically,
Hilferding may have been reluctant in practice to restrict capitalist
development. Such limitations would have reduced prospects for the
socialist takeover.

In addition to the cyclical fluctuations produced by swings in the
rate of profit, Hilferding saw capitalism's pricing mechanism, as noted,
as consistently giving the wrong signals to producers. Imbalances or

"disproportions" would arise between consumption and investment goods production, since enterprise managers are unable to receive reliable messages from the prevailing array of relative prices. Hilferding even argued that the periodic collapse of the profit rate might coincide with "the disruption of these proportional relations."[14]

A Hilferding Crisis and Developing Country Loans

Downturns in the profit rate were triggered repeatedly by three events: (1) Over the course of the upswing, turnover time—the time that elapses between commitment to production and receipt of return from profit—is extended. Competition forces extension of turnover time, since it becomes more difficult to use old machines without replacement for wear and tear, and it becomes necessary to introduce additional workers who lack previous training specific to the enterprise. (2) Economic growth during the upswing leads to upward pressure on wages, hence higher labor costs. (3) Interest costs rise above normal levels, adversely affecting both borrowing costs for external finance and profitability.

Hilferding does not take the position that the crisis *must* occur. If banks would continue to maintain liquidity, in his view, crisis could be averted. But the banks do not remain steadfast. They are faced with a rapidly expanding credit demand while they are inclined to retreat. Speculation in commodities and securities grows and pressures credit facilities. The "fictitious capital"—claims to future profit not yet created—is growing at an exaggerated pace, particularly on an exploding stock exchange. Producers who have relied in part on circulation credit—the implicit or explicit loans they make available to one another—turn toward the banks, especially as production turnover time lengthens. Moreover, the enterprises' profit rates are falling anyway. The banks do not continue to make sufficient credit available to counter the forces pushing the economy into a slump.[15] The crisis of capitalism, although finding its origin outside the financial sector, is confirmed in the decisions made by the bankers.

Paradoxically, the fall in the profit rate at the center of the capitalist world stimulates the banks to accelerate lending abroad. Their refusal to continue to extend more domestic credit consolidates the crisis in the developed centers of capitalism. But their refusal is based on the drop in the rate of profit at home. The banks turn outward toward the periphery of capitalism, where profit rates are higher. The lower level of capitalist development on the periphery means, in Hilferding's use of Marx's language, that "the organic composition of capital" is lower. Hilferding can be interpreted to mean that the capital-labor ratio is lower on the periphery—hence the rate of profit is higher.

Finance capital's search for the highest rate of return—adjusted for the greater "risks" involved in lending to the underdeveloped countries—leads to a movement of credit to the "backward" locations. This movement accelerates with the cyclical fall in the profit rate at the center (or the "more developed" countries), and it can be part of the stimulus to recovery. The export of finance opens new markets abroad for the products of the center—both consumer goods as well as intermediate goods—that serve infrastructural building purposes.[16]

Finance capital's accelerated lending to countries on the periphery should be associated with the economic downturn in the established centers of capitalism in Hilferding's theory. It helps lead the way toward the economic upswing and also becomes the cutting edge of imperialism. The financial interests in capitalism's centers are linked closely with the military power of the state that is called upon to secure the foreign markets that will become the new outlets for exports. But in addition, if countries on the periphery are seen as a source of raw materials for a center that is relatively specialized in manufacturing, then some segment of the population of the nations on periphery must be transformed into a working class. Again, the coercive power of the state will be called upon.[17] Hilferding's theory of capitalism, in the phase where the bankers' activities (and external finance in general) can play a decisive role at times of crisis, lays the foundation for a theory of capitalist imperialism.[18] The bankers lead the way into the virgin regions, accompanied by the military. Industry will follow after the "field" appears to have been fixed securely.

The crisis worsens at the center as finance goes overseas, but eventually "the export of capital" becomes instrumental in prompting recovery at the center. Finance capital sparks the development of new markets abroad for producers of the lender nations, helping to restore their rate of profit. The movement of finance abroad also pushes down the rate of profit in the nations on periphery, leading toward a levelling of international profit rates, reducing the incentive for a greater net outflow of credit abroad. "Loan pushing" in the nations on the periphery would be associated with a fall in the profit rate at the center, or lending nations.

A Hilferding Crisis and Big Banks

The staggering of credit sites that is evident in Hilferding's theory seems to have been a feature of lending by U.S. banks in the 1920s, as noted in the previous chapter. Initially, bank loans were directed toward domestic producers, then shifted progressively toward the "developing" countries (Latin America and post World War I Germany), and increasingly moved toward speculation on the New York Stock Exchange. At each stage, the previously preferred lending site suffered a deceleration in the rate of growth and an eventual net decline in its access to credit.

Another feature of Hilferding's theory merits special note. The periodic downturns would involve shakeouts that would extinguish smaller businesses and produce greater concentration in both the financial and industrial spheres. Of course, the stage of finance capital—the stage Hilferding locates chronologically in the late 1800s—was one in which the tendency toward concentration under capitalist competition became visible.

It is notable that in the 1930s, when thousands of U.S. banks permanently closed their doors during the Depression, survivors included Citicorp, J.P. Morgan, Chase Manhattan, and Bank of America.[19] It also is of interest that with the exception of Continental Illinois, the current wave of bank failures has left the giant money center banks untouched. The large continue to be the survivors even to this day.

Where Hilferding developed his theory of the evolution toward greater concentration in an analytical environment of pure *laissez faire* capitalism, there are reasons to believe that the contemporary regulatory apparatus strengthens the position of larger banks. Even when help is forthcoming for smaller banks, "help" means a transfer of ownership that will frequently translate into absorption by a larger banking institution.[20]

To the extent that big banks can expect a degree of help not given to smaller banks, the big banks could have a further advantage in attracting depositors over the smaller banks and other depositing-accepting financial institutions.[21] Even if small bank depositors do not withdraw their funds entirely and instead diversify by placing their funds with several banks, this still could hurt the banks that previously held entire deposits. A shift has already occurred toward transfer of deposits from smaller to larger banks.[22] Although the Federal Deposit Insurance Corp. (FDIC) rescue operation for a large bank can lead to dismissal of bank officials, the effect can have great benefits for the large banks that are still solvent. The policy can induce a shift in depositors toward remaining large banks, enhancing concentration of bank resources.

Regulatory proposals under consideration to increase disclosure of bank loan portfolio performance may have a differential effect on banks of different sizes. In terms of domestic loans, the "large banks whose shares are publicly traded already disclose considerable information through the Securities and Exchange Commission's reporting system" while the smaller banks would have to surrender new information that, they fear, could subject them to runs by an already panicky public.[23] The larger banks, with a larger proportion of their portfolio in foreign loans, have the potential to preserve the illusory quality of those loans more easily than can the smaller banks with their problem domestic loans.

Large money center banks have a clear gain in the foreign loan business from the large fees they obtain for arranging a syndicate. When nervousness about LDC loans sets in, smaller banks tend to be the first to pull back from continued lending.[24] The larger banks have an incentive to keep the second line banks involved in new lending efforts to extract the loan fees.[25] But if the larger banks cannot keep them involved they can still take over some of the smaller banks' claims when the latter pull out from providing funds to a country with payments difficulties.[26] Presumably, the larger banks absorb the claims from the fleeing banks at a reduced price, and the smaller banks must correspondingly write down their asset positions.

A general principle may emerge here: periods of broad liquidity crises permit the larger banks to gain at the expense of the smaller, weak banks. Although the larger banks are rivals among themselves, in general, economic crises serve them collectively versus other banks by producing the conditions under which the large banks can consolidate their position. If they are at least partially conscious actors in this process, they may push LDC loans to advance such concentration. Ironically, Hilferding could claim that the capitalist bankers are also advancing the cause of socialism.

Finally, Hilferding's position suggests the debt crisis can be averted altogether by state action. If the commercial banks refuse to lend sufficiently to block the downturn, a central bank could do what the commercial banks will not.[27] But this opens up the Pandora's box of difficulties associated with the lender of last resort function of the central bank. We shall take up this issue again in the final chapter of this book.

MANDELIAN LONG WAVES AND WAVES
OF LENDING

Ernest Mandel's development of a Marxist theory of long waves in his 1978 Marshall lectures provides another intriguing theory of the debt crisis.[28] Mandel's tabulation partitions the long history of capitalism as follows: 1789–1848 was the period of the Industrial Revolution, the era of what Mandel terms "the great bourgeois revolution." The world market was consolidated. In this first phase, Mandel dates the upswing over the interval 1781–1815 (or 25), while the downturn dates over the interval 1826–48. The second long swing occurred during the latter half of the nineteenth century, 1848–93. This was the period of "free competition" and the crowning ascension of industrial capitalism. Mandel identifies the upswing with the segment of the half century, 1848–73, while the downswing, the "long depression of free-competition capitalism," exhausted the remainder of the long swing.

The third long swing dated from 1893 through 1940. The upswing of the third wave encompasses the period 1893–1913, effectively from the partition of Africa to the first World War; Mandel's third upswing coincides with the "[h]eyday of classic imperialism and finance capital." The downturn of this phase of capitalist history is the period of the Great Depression, "the epoch of the decline of capitalism, of the epoch of imperialist wars, revolutions, and counter-revolutions." The fourth and most recent long wave dates from World War II to the present. Mandel locates the upswing from 1940(48) to 1967, the period he characterizes as "late capitalism"—a period "born out of the historical delay of world revolution and the great defeats of the working class in the 1930s and 1940s, but accompanied by further phenomena of decline and decomposition of the system." For Mandel, the downswing dates from 1968 into the present.[29]

Of Booms and Slumps and the Profit Rate

Although Mandel does not make the connection explicit in the Marshall lectures, these long waves also feature lending booms, as credit flows from the nations at the capitalist center to the nations on the periphery. Aside from the financial movements associated with the period of classical imperialism, the lending booms typically overlap with the downswings. The lending period to Latin America and European nations after World War I via bond finance straddled the turning point of the third long swing. Borrower default and lender revulsion coincided with worldwide depression. Initial expressions of alarm about overlending to the developing countries in the most recent period occur in the late 1960s, Mandel's turning point in the fourth long swing. Extreme overlending becomes apparent in the late 1970s and early 1980s, as the secular downturn deepens. Periods of relative decline in the capitalist centers seem to produce waves of lending to the nations on the periphery. The exceptional period of imperial finance may prove to be the rule, insofar as the imperial impulse can be viewed as an escape route from a stagnant phase in capitalist history.

Given such a long view, it really is quibbling to point out that there may have been shorter cyclical movements in capitalist economies concerning output, employment, and credit flows within the epochs identified by Mandel. The key point is the over-arching rhythm that he detects—similar to Minsky—of the fifty year swing.

But what causes these periodic up and down movements of capitalism every half century? The cause is "the inner logic of the capitalist laws of motion," in particular, the law of the tendency of the rate of profit to fall.[30] Mandel displays equanimity about whether the fall in the rate of profit constitutes the basis for a cycle theory—as Hilferding would have it, although the Mandel cycle is much longer—or constitutes a basis for a theory of the permanent decline of capitalism. Mandel effectively chooses to have it both ways, by affirmatively answering the following rhetorical question:

> Is it possible, with the conceptual tools of Marxist economic analysis, to explain long-term upsurges in the average rate of profit at certain historical turning points, in spite of the cyclic downturn of that same rate of profit at the end of each industrial cycle, and in spite of the secular decline pointing to the historical limit of the capitalist mode of production?[31]

For Mandel, there is a persistent secular decline in the rate of profit that signals "the historical limit of the capitalist mode of production," but there is also the overlay of (long) cyclical swings in the rate around its downward trend. The source of the secular decline finds its origins in the conventional Marxist analysis of technical change that reduces necessary labor time under mature capitalism. The relative recovery of the profit rate on the upswing is determined by countertendencies to the law of the tendency of the rate of profit to fall, countertendencies that Marx indicated would "hamper, retard, and partly paralyze this fall [in the profit rate but would not] do away with the law."[32]

The precise timing of the turning points of the upturn and downturn of each long wave—in effect, the timing of the shift in the direction of movement of the profit rate—is more or less external for Mandel. There is an *a priori* indeterminacy to the turning points, although there is a routine periodicity to the long cycles. Mandel is explicit in rejecting the view "that the long waves can be explained by purely endogenous mechanisms of the capitalist economy."[33] He refers to "exogenous extraeconomic factors" that trigger the turning points: the recovery from 1940(48) was borne by "the historic defeat suffered by the international working class in the 1930s and 1940s (fascism, war, plus the cold war and McCarthyism period in North America) that enabled the capitalist class to impose a significant increase in the rate of surplus value."[34] For Mandel, in 1848 the long waves were explained by social revolution, in 1893 by imperialist conquest.[35]

Although Mandel describes social revolution and imperialist conquest as "exogenous extraeconomic factors," he presumably does not view them as random occurrences or events that arise independent of the pulse of capitalist development. But the outcomes of these critical events are uncertain, lending a randomness to the exact timing of the turns in the long cycles.[36]

Mandel on Developing Country Indebtedness

Mandel locates the recent wave of lending to LDCs in the context of a major, long-term cyclical downturn of the world economy. The current downswing is, for Mandel, "a long depressive wave which started in the late 1960s and early 1970s, and which will certainly continue through the 1980s."[37] The flow of funds to the LDCs via the commercial banks is seen as the mechanism that has prevented the global downturn from being more severe than it might have been otherwise; the performance of the world capitalist economy has been propped up in the midst of depressive pressures by nothing less than "a large credit inflation."[38]

At the core of the depressed state of the capitalist world economy is, once again, a secular decline in profitability which of necessity must be accompanied by *"overproduction of capital"* and *"overproduction of commodities."*[39] Lending to the nations on the periphery is only one aspect of a general pattern of bank loans-cum-government aid to faltering corporations that has been intended to prevent outright collapse of the world capitalist economy. Mandel refers to the "very impressive list [that can] be made of top multinational corporations which run huge annual losses but which continue to operate obviously with the help of bank credit and government subsidies: Chrysler, International Harvester, Massey Ferguson, AEG, Peugeot, Cockerill, Dome Petroleum, etc."[40] Mandel points out that despite the attention drawn to LDC debts, their external indebtedness is not unique; several "industrialized countries such as Denmark, Belgium, Italy [and] France" are all plagued by "huge debts."[41]

In Mandel's hands the global debt crisis is merely a symptom of a general periodic crisis of capitalism precipitated by a fundamental cause—a general decline in profitability dating from the late 1960s as the postwar long boom dissipated. In response to the fall in general profitability, the multinational banks have lent large loans wherever they could find borrowers with some semblance of creditworthiness. They have done so with the encouragement and support of governments in the centers of world capitalism. This encourgement and support could take the form of implicit or explicit loan guarantees, or legislative initiatives to deregulate or liberalize the banking sector.

To compound matters, bank credit—as a device to mitigate the impact of depression—carries with it another set of contradictions for policymakers. Commercial bank loans used as a "finger in the dike" of deep, unrelenting economic depression is after all, a fragile "finger" indeed. This fragility has led policymakers down paths that appear quite inconsistent with their ideological leanings and rhetoric:

> The general movement of huge debt and bank money expansion continue under the new conservative administrations in the West. This is undoubtedly a factor which has so far limited the depth of the depression; at the same time, however, it increases the threat of collapse of the bank system and the credit system. It is not accidental that President Reagan, of all people, came to the help of the Jaruzelski government in Poland when it was in danger of being declared insolvent. He was afraid this would cause a run on the banks as the result of the collapse of several large Western banks. He took over a guarantee of some of the debts of the Polish government. This is indicative of the fear that exists today in the highest circle, i.e., an important bank failure must be prevented because it could create an avalanche throughout the Western economy.[42]

Of course, the issue for Mandel is always whether capitalism can weather each of its self-imposed storms. Will the depressive wave be so harsh and severe as to produce a political opposition to capitalism that overturns the social system?[43] Will the credit inflation that has prevented the depression from deepening further give way to financial collapse and thence, capitalism's collapse? Or will capitalism maintain itself long enough for profitability to recover and ride on a renewed upswing? Mandel, however, leaves us with no answers to these questions.

THE END OF CAPITALISM?

In Mandel's analysis, the debt crisis opens the door to the possibility of the collapse of international capitalism. The end of capitalism could, in principle, be brought about by the activities of the banks—the same institutions that have been mobilized to facilitate survival of the system during its most recent long depressive wave. But an alternative analysis suggests that the debt crisis is a surface manifestation of capitalism's death throes. In short, capitalism's heyday is already over; this particular wave of lending to the developing countries is simply another indicator of its demise.

"The Law as Such"

Marx's critical law of motion for capitalism—the law of the tendency of the rate of profit to fall—contained the analytical justification for his expectation that capitalism, as a mode of production, could not last forever. In Marx's analysis there are two essential phases in the history of capitalism. The first phase is the period in which capital, as a class, can continue to extract additional surplus value from the working class in *absolute* form, that is, by lengthening the working day. The second phase occurs when capital must accept reduction of the length of the working day due to political opposition to its hegemony over the conditions of labor. This opposition comes from both the working class and perhaps other classes, for example, the landed aristocracy in Britain, surviving from earlier historical modes of production. Capital then seeks to maintain the rate of profit by cheapening the cost of producing the requirements of subsistence for labor, in short, reducing the necessary portion of the working day by introducing machinery. Capital, in Marx's view, extracts surplus value in *relative* rather than absolute form.

Wage-goods production will be first to experience mechanization, but the process must spread over time to production of capital-goods, since all sectors must experience the adverse impact on profitability of the progressive secular reduction in the length of the working day. If the total working day is shorter, then the unpaid portion of the working day—the ultimate source of capitalist profit—will also be shorter unless labor power can be "devalued," that is, unless the labor time required to produce the worker's means of subsistence can be reduced. But mechanization creates a tension for capital. Not only does it effectively lower the socially necessary portion of the working day—capital's desired objective—but it also discharges labor power from the capitalist labor process. And labor power happens to be the only commodity that produces surplus value or profit in pure form.

Countertendencies

Marx depicted this tension with his tendential law. Defining the pure rate of profit as the ratio of surplus value to the sum of variable capital and constant capital (where surplus value is unpaid labor time, variable capital is paid labor time, and constant capital is "dead" or non-living labor embodied in machinery), Marx projected an explosive growth in constant capital relative to the other components of the rate of profit. The ratio of constant to variable capital—what Marx termed the organic composition of capital—would rise progressively with mechanization, pushing the rate of profit toward zero. The rate of exploitation, that is, the ratio of surplus value to variable capital or unpaid to paid labor time, could stay unchanged or even rise while the rate of profit falls. It is the movement of the rate of profit which is the fundamental driving force underlying capitalism. If the rate of profit approaches zero, the *raison d'etre* for capitalism is over. The end of capitalism thus becomes a possibility only in the second phase of capitalism's history, when capital introduces machinery in what proves, collectively and secularly, to be a futile maneuver to maintain the rate of profit. Of course, individual capitalists could experience lucrative returns from being first in line with the new technologies.

Moreover, Marx did identify a variety of counteracting tendencies to "the law as such." These included the following: (1) attempts to intensify the exploitation of labor within a working day of given length; (2) reduction of wages below the value of labor power, that is, below the customary subsistence standard; (3) cheapening the elements of constant capital, that is, more extensive mechanization of the production of machinery; (4) utilizing capitalism's reserve army of the unemployed to open up new lines of production with low organic compositions of capital; (5) foreign trade to obtain cheaper "elements of constant capital" and cheaper "necessities of life for which the variable capital is exchanged;" and (6) exclusion of interest bearing capital from the industrial capitalists' general rate of profit calculation.[44] But Marx perceived that these counteracting tendencies would only deflect "the law as such" temporarily—albeit the temporary deflection could span a decade or more:

> . . . the same influences which produce a tendency in the general rate of profit to fall, also call forth counter-effects, which hamper, retard, and partly paralyze this fall. The latter do not do away with the law, but impair its effect. Otherwise, it would not be the fall of the general rate of profit, but rather its relative slowness, that would be incomprehensible.[45]

Thus, the rate of profit *must* fall, over the long history of capitalism, heralding its termination as a historical mode of production.

The remaining puzzle for a Marxist historian is the characterization of the end of capitalism. Many interpreters of Marx have concluded that Marx himself had in mind a final all-consuming conflagration associated with a final capitalist crisis, whereupon a revolution conducted by the working class would empower the proletariat. There is indeed a basis for such an interpretation, particularly in Marx's political writings in the 1840s.[46]

The Coming of the Managerial Class

However, some Marxist theorists such as Alvin Gouldner have criticized Marx for slippage into uncharacteristic idealism.[47] Precapitalist modes of production had fallen in large measure due to the eventual mounting resistance to the system by exploited classes, but the fall of an older social system had not empowered the exploited class. The end of the slave mode of production had not led to rule by the slaves, but instead to the regime of dominance by feudal lords. The end of feudalism had not uplifted the serfs to social leadership, but instead had given way to the era of the capitalists. Why then should one expect that at the end of capitalism the working class would seize the reins of power?

Marx's own analysis of social history suggested that more likely claimants to social authority would be another social class that emerged in the bowels of the older society—as a sometime collaborator, sometime competitor, and eventual successor to the older ruling elite. Merchant capitalists and nascent industrialists grew along the crevices of feudal society with main arteries filled with lords and serfs.

Capitalism in its mature phase also produced a third great social class—professional intellectuals, intelligentsia, and social workers in the broadest terms. A managerial class evolved, in the sense of *social* managers, between capital and labor. This "new" class is predicated on its control over knowledge, information, and expertise rather than wealth, finance, and enterprise in the manner of the older capitalist ruling elite. The "new" class has ushered in the age of science and technology, potentially unfettered by the restraints set by capital's interest in profitability.

The rise of the managerial class to dominance can be dated from the 1930s. The crisis of the Great Depression produced the foundation for the managerial class to gain a base for action, with a new found degree of independence from capital through the expanding welfare state:

> The New Deal did, indeed, bring the managerial class into power in the United States. This was a change that amounted to much more than making "concessions" to the working class. It catapulted the intellectual-administrative strata into a position of social authority. The working class should be seen more as incidental "beneficiaries" of these "reforms," rather than as a primary recipient. For these were authentically revolutionary reforms from the standpoint of the middle class; that is, they were empowering reforms for the managerial elite.[48]

The 1930s produced an end of capitalism's age not with a proletarian revolution, but with the managerial revolution.[49]

Ironically, even in Mandel's work, which is predicated so intently on the assumption that the world is still predominantly capitalist, we find hints that there is something new under the sun. Failing to recognize these phenomena as indicators of an evolution toward a post-capitalist society, Mandel refers to "the direct link between scientific progress and the emergence of new technology [appearing] relatively late in the development of the capitalist mode of production" and "[t]he formal reunification of 'abstract science' and 'concrete technological innovations' [occurring] with the appearance of 'applied science.' "[50] Mandel even argues that to produce "a long-term sharp increase in the rate of profit . . . would empty a new qualitative leap forward in automation" toward extensive robotism.[51] But this would mean, in turn, "a radical increase in permanent unemployment," greater difficulties in realization of surplus value, and a temporary improvement in the rate of profit that still would not match the magnitude of the outlays required to finance robotism.[52]

Global Debt and the End of an Era

So how could the international debt crisis be a manifestation of the end of capitalism? There are at least two potential lines of argument. First, there may be a critical, spatial aspect to capitalism's decline. Decline is more pronounced in the older centers of capitalist development, centers that already have given way to dominance by the managerial class. This may be the inner meaning of the outward phenomenon of "de-industrialization"—the ongoing transition from a capitalist to managerial society. Capital moves instead toward the developing countries as sites for renewed capitalist development, with lending to the nations on the periphery as the financial wedge to start the process. This would conform, at a much different level of abstraction, to Beenstock's vision of international financial flows from MDCs to LDCs, in search of the higher rate of return. Unlike the lending wave of the 1920s, which may be interpreted as an act of confidence by capital as a class, the lending wave of the 1970s can be interpreted as an act of fear by capital as a class.

Second, one might recognize the special, historical function of finance within capitalism. According to Marx, capital's earliest forms were linked to finance—"as moneyed wealth, as the capital of the merchant and of the usurer."[53] Capital in mercantile and interest bearing forms could be content to allow surplus labor time to be extracted by the labor exploitation processes in noncapitalist societies, but realized as capitalist profit through exchange. Capital in those forms could continue to function indefinitely on the outskirts of a world where production was conducted largely on a noncapitalistic basis. Therefore, if late in its history capital is driven from the sphere of production as a new social order evolves, it would most likely retreat to finance, its original home in the sphere of exchange or circulation of commodities.

Fictitious Capital Once Again

As David Harvey points out in a brilliant dissection of interest bearing capital and the credit system: ". . . the claim upon future labour which fixed capital defines is converted via the credit system into a claim exercised by money capital over a share of future surplus value production. Money capital is invested in future appropriation."[54] But the social system under which future appropriation takes place need not be capitalistic, that is, loans to Poland need not be less attractive because Poland does not practice capitalist production. Furthermore, the date of ultimate appropriation to make good on the debts can be deferred, since as Harvey points out: "producers [can] re-finance their debt on an annual basis or . . . market titles to shares of future surplus value production directly [equity shares]."[55] Capital as finance thus trades on claims to surplus labor time that do not yet exist at the time the debt is incurred. This is, once again, the ambit of "fictitious capital."[56]

Although Harvey himself does not propose that capital is now retreating to its roots in finance, his analysis of the nature of money capital is quite consistent with such a vision. Consider the following passage:

> In all such cases, money capital is invested in appropriation. The money capitalist is indifferent (presumably) to the ultimate source of revenue and invests in government debt, mortgages, stocks and shares, commodity futures or whatever, according to rate of return, the security of investment, its liquidity and so on. All connection with the actual expansion of capital is thus completely lost, and the conception of capital as something with automatic self-expansion properties is thereby strengthened. The result, Marx holds is that interest-bearing "is the fountainhead of all manner of insane forms" in which "even an accumulation of debts" can "appear as an accumulation of capital." Everything, he says "is doubled and trebled and transformed into a mere phantom of the imagination." The credit system registers the "height of distortion" to the degree that the accumulation of claims far outruns real production. . . .[57]

One might add that the accumulation of claims can be disconnected as well from the social conditions under which real production takes place. There is a sense in which the bankers/financiers operate with a certain independence from capitalist production.[58] They can live on, beyond the social system their progenitors spawned, in the realm of circulation. Perhaps they might even live to promote a counter-revolution to restore old fashioned capitalism worldwide from a new industrial base in the Third World. The accumulation of debt by developing countries, from this perspective, represents something quite different from the effects of the Hilferding or Mandel capitalist cycles. Here, LDC debt represents the decline of capitalism and the rise of the managerial estate, particularly in the former centers of capitalism. Modern banking is no more than merchant banking in disguise. The capitalists have come full circle to their starting point: awash in money claims but without their "natural" social order. The feudal lords, of course, were left with some land—but without their serfs.

NOTES

1. Rudolf Hilferding, Tom Bottomore, trans., *Finance Capital: A Study in the Latest Phase of Capitalist Development* (London: Routledge and Kegan Paul, 1981).

2. See Paul Sweezy, ed., *Karl Marx and the Close of His System by Eugen von Bohm–Bawerk and Bohm–Bawerk's Criticism of Marx by Rudolf Hilferding* (New York: Augustus M. Kelley, 1949).

3. See Friedrich A. Hayek, *Prices and Production* (London: George Routledge and Sons, 1931).

4. For more on this theme also see Hilferding's final published essay, "State Capitalism or Totalitarian State Economy," in C. Wright Mills, ed., *The Marxists* (New York: Dell Publishing, 1963).

5. Hilferding, *Finance Capital*, pp. 264–66.

6. Ibid., p. 266. Hilferding's theoretical vision was never filtered through neoclassical economics. Austrian economics was distinctive and, while sharing the ideological commitment of much of neoclassicism to *laissez faire,* it did not embrace the conventional supply and demand theory of relative prices. Austrian economics had instead its process view. In some respects, Hilferding's price theory harks back even further than Marx to the first Classical economist, Adam Smith, and his concern for departures of market price from average or natural price, the latter finding its basis in labor costs. See Adam Smith, *The Wealth of Nations* (New York: Modern Library, 1937), pp. 55–63.

7. Karl Marx, *Capital, Volume 3* (New York: Vintage Books, 1981), pp. 317–75.

8. Ibid., p. 346.

9. Hilferding, *Finance Capital*, p. 104.

10. Ibid., pp. 257–58. This, incidentally, closely resembles Kalecki's algebraic business cycle theory. See Michael Kalecki, "Outline of a Theory of the Business Cycle (1933)," *Selected Essays on the Dynamics of the Capitalist Economy 1933–1970* (Cambridge, MA: Cambridge University Press, 1971), pp. 1–14.

11. Hilferding, p. 257.

12. Ibid., pp. 257–58.

13. Ibid., p. 264 and pp. 367–68.

14. Ibid., pp. 239–66.

15. Ibid., p. 260.

16. Ibid., see especially pp. 314–19.

17. Ibid., p. 319.

18. Ibid., pp. 364–70. Hilferding believed that the principal agent of resistance to capitalist imperialism would be the working classes. Lenin dissented. In

his 1916 pamphlet, *Imperialism, the Highest Stage of Capitalism: A Popular Outline* (Peking: Foreign Languages Press, 1975), p. 131, Lenin wrote: " 'General' enthusiasm over the prospects of imperialism, furious defense of it and painting it in the brightest colors—such are the signs of the times. The imperialist ideology also penetrates the working class. No Chinese Wall separates it from the other classes."

19. Anthony Sampson, *The Money Lenders: The People and Politics of the World Banking Crisis* (Harmondsworth: Penguin Books, 1983), pp. 94–109.

20. Journalist Jack Anderson recently applauded the new FDIC chairman, William Seidman, for his sense of equanimity toward banks of all sizes. However, Anderson describes Seidman's strategy with respect to the smaller banks as one in which, rather than let them fail, "the FDIC will try to keep a failing small bank open until new owners are found." Of course, that does not preclude the new owners being owners of another bank. See Jack Anderson, "Feds to Give Economic Transfusions to Keep American Banks Solvent," *Durham Sun* 1 September 1986. As of September 1986, ninety–nine banks had failed since the start of the year in the United States. See "Two Southwest Banks Fail, Bringing the Total to 99 in the U.S. in '86," *Wall Street Journal,* 5 September 1986.

21. Dennis Jacobe, research director of the U.S. League of Savings Institutions, made just such a point while complaining about inequity of the FDIC's rescue policies in 1984. See Daniel Hertzberg, Tim Carrington, and John Andrew, "Confidence Game: Large Banks Are Hit by New Set of Rumors and Stock Prices Fall," *Wall Street Journal* 25 May 1984.

22. Such a shift was described in G. Christian Hill and Edward A. Finn, "Condence Crisis: Big Depositors' Runs on Beleaguered Banks Speed the Failure Rate," *Wall Street Journal,* 23 August 1984. On p. 6 the authors reported, for example, that "Jean Campbell who runs a tax service in Sun Valley, California, took out $420,000 of uninsured deposits held at American Pacific by a client. She is placing most of the money at Bank of America, the nation's second-biggest bank, and Home Savings of America, the second largest thrift."

23. Tim Carrington, "U.S. Agencies Want Nation's Banks to Disclose More Data on Problems," *Wall Street Journal,* 22 August 1984.

24. See Willene A. Johnson, "Bank Size and U.S. Bank Lending to Latin America," *FRBNY Quarterly Review,* 8 (Autumn 1983): 20–21 and Willene A. Johnson, "U.S. Bank Lending to Latin America: The Implications of Bank Size," (Federal Reserve Bank of New York Research Paper No. 8320, January 1984, p. 33). Johnson suggests that the smaller banks can pull back more easily because they hold a larger proportion of short rather than long term claims on LDCs. Her work is the most detailed on variations in lending to Latin borrowers by banks of different sizes.

25. Jane D'Arista, "Private Overseas Lending: Too Far, Too Fast?" in Jonathan D. Aronson, ed., *Debt and the Less Developed Countries* (Boulder, CO: Westview Press, 1979), p. 63.

26. See Johnson, "U.S. Bank Lending."

27. Hilferding, *Finance Capital*, p. 66.

28. Ernest Mandel, *Long Waves of Capitalist Development: The Marxist Interpretation* (Cambridge, MA: Cambridge University Press, 1980).

29. Ibid., p. 105–6.

30. Ibid., p. 24.

31. Ibid., p. 12 (emphasis in original).

32. Karl Marx, *Capital Vol. 3* (New York: International Publishers, 1967), p. 239.

33. Mandel, *Long Waves*, p. viii.

34. Ibid., pp. 23–4.

35. Ibid., p. 23.

36. Oddly enough, there is some resemblance to the business cycle theory of the New Classical economists who trace the source of economic fluctuations exclusively to unanticipated events (shocks). See Robert E. Lucas, Jr., *Studies in Business-Cycle Theory* (Cambridge, MA: Massachusetts Institute of Technology Press, 1981).

37. Ernest Mandel, "World Crisis and the Monetarist Answer," in Karel Jansen, ed., *Monetarism, Economic Crisis and the Third World* (London: Frank Cass and Company, 1983), p. 79.

38. Ibid., p. 80.

39. Ibid., p. 90 (emphasis in original).

40. Ibid., p. 81.

41. Ibid.

42. Ibid.

43. This was an aspect of Joseph Schumpeter's expectations that capitalism would come to an end—the political resistance to capitalism would grow to fatal dimensions in response to its periodic cyclical downswings. See Joseph Schumpeter, *Can Capitalism Survive?* (New York: Harper-Colophon, 1978).

44. Karl Marx, *Capital: Volume 3*, pp. 232–40.

45. Ibid., p. 239.

46. Karl Marx, *The Revolutions of 1848*, ed. David Fernbuch (New York: Vintage Books, 1974).

47. Alvin Gouldner, *The Future of the Intellectuals and the Rise of the New Class* (New York: Seabury, 1979).

48. William Darity, Jr., "The Managerial Class and Industrial Policy," *Industrial Relations* 25 (Spring 1986): 214–15.

49. See James Burnham, *The Managerial Revolution: What Is Happening in the World* (New York: John Day, 1941).
50. Ernest Mandel, *Long Waves*, p. 38.
51. Ibid., pp. 197–8.
52. Ibid., pp. 108–10.
53. Karl Marx, *Capital: Volume 1* (New York: International Publishers, 1967), p. 146.
54. David Harvey, *The Limits to Capital* (Chicago: The University of Chicago Press, 1982), p. 266.
55. Ibid., pp. 267–68.
56. Ibid., p. 268.
57. Ibid., p. 269.
58. Ibid., p. 286.

CHAPTER 9

Why Nothing Will Work (Perfectly): Solutions to the Debt Crisis

S olutions to the LDC debt overhang are as abundant as the credit flows that produced the crisis. They fall into two broad categories: (1) solutions geared toward management or containment of the current crisis and (2) policies that should be inaugurated to prevent a recurrence of the crisis in the future. Stanley Fischer has suggested that the first category—those solutions aimed at handling the present situation—can be further characterized by four main features: whether or not proposals seek to lengthen "the effective maturity of debt;" whether or not proposals seek to change the "nature of claims on the LDCs;" "whether [or not proposals] offer genuine debt relief;" and the type of conditionality that will be imposed in proposals for altering (that is, relaxing) the terms of the loans.[1] The second category of proposals follow from the particular causal theory one accepts as an explanation for the emergence of the developing country debt crisis. But neither category of solutions—neither the short-term nor the long-term proposals—offer answers that are devoid of serious dangers and unsettling implications of their own.

THE STATUS QUO: CASE BY CASE

There is, *de facto,* a *status quo* plan of action to cope with LDC indebtedness: it is to treat each debtor nation on a case-by-case basis, arriving at separate rescheduling agreements with each through separate negotiations between each LDC and the banks. Where necessary, the bankers' governments are expected to facilitate the negotiations. The International Monetary Fund (IMF) establishes a set of policies that the debtor nation must consent to pursue before the banks will engage in serious negotiations. The Fund's "carrot" is its ability to provide some monies of its own to assist the debtor nation in restoring the timeliness of payments.

Expanding the IMF's Role?

Some marginal variations on this strategy involve (1) expanding the resources available to the International Monetary Fund, (2) giving the Fund more fully the character of a global lender of last resort, and (3) getting the World Bank to devote more of its efforts to lending for "structural adjustment" rather than projects, its customary emphasis. For example, a contingent of West German economists have recommended a major increase in the Fund's Compensatory Financing Facility, to be obtained "by skimming off part of the surplus of countries with positive balance of payments."[2] U.S. government officials, the United States being the major contributor to both the IMF and the World Bank, have been pressuring the Bank in recent years to take a growing part in designing its lending policies to aid in the debt crisis. Rimmer de Vries, chief international economist for Morgan Guaranty Bank, explicitly recommended that the Bank adopt loan policies far more similar to those of the IMF, complaining that "the bank's role in the debt crisis since 1982 [has been] 'rather disappointing' and that "[the bank] 'has continued to concentrate on project lending even though this has proven inadequate,' without changes in underlying economic conditions."[3]

But the foregoing steps are mere modifications to the outlines of the current course. The IMF, *de facto,* provides the creditors' governments in the Paris Club with a multinational club to wield vis-à-vis each debtor government.[4] Debt reschedulings came in abundance from 1978 onwards. Whereas the Paris Club arranged $5 billion worth of rescheduled debt for nine countries between 1956 and 1978, between 1978 and 1981 almost twice as much debt was rescheduled for fifteen countries. In the cases of Peru and Poland, however, "where the IMF was not present to enforce 'conditionality,' the only sanction was to declare the debtor Government to be in default" but such a ". . . sanction . . . could only be used once, and if it was used then the banks concerned could forget about regaining the money they had lent."[5] The extreme sanction was not utilized, although in the case of Poland the threat appears to have been sufficiently adequate in the fall of 1981 to get that country's government to agree to rescheduling terms.[6]

"Special" Treatment?

The central feature of the *status quo* approach is to treat each country encountering debt payments problems as a more or less unique case, requiring individualized treatment. Each country is expected to arrive independently at an agreement with the IMF and then enter independently into formal debt rescheduling negotiations with the Paris Club.

It a "pulse-reading" had been taken in early 1985, optimism appeared to be growing; a critical corner apparently had been turned in the debt crisis. Brazil, Mexico, and Argentina through the combination of an export boom and an export compression, had all succeeded in achieving substantial trade surpluses. The combative rhetoric of officials of the major debtor nations had become more muted, so there appeared to be less likelihood that any major debtor or group of debtors would refuse to engage in Paris Club negotiations. In early 1985 two major business weeklies virtually pronounced the crisis at an end.[7]

But the ostensible successes of the case-by-case strategy—largely intended to block formation of a debtors' cartel—rested on a global economic climate that permitted the recovery of 1984. Both sources recognized the fragility of that environment. One of the pair observed:

> A feeling of hard times . . . still pervades the major Latin American countries. Their economic feats, mainly in international trade, haven't brought similar gains throughout their economies. These countries are plagued by excess capacity in industries that produce for domestic markets, as well as high unemployment and declining real wages. . . . Clouding all these countries' future is the still stupendous task of servicing their foreign debt—a total of some $520 billion for the 16 largest Third World debtors, with interest payments amounting to about $55 billion. A spike in interest rates, a drop in commodity prices, or a sudden slowdown in the world economy could bring fresh setbacks on the long journey back to creditworthiness.[8]

The second source also expressed concern about the adverse consequences of a new round of tight monetary policy in the United States.[9] Sufficient re-inflation of the U.S. economy would certainly ease the debt burden for the borrowers. A renewed commitment to disinflation, however, could lead to "a spike in interest rates" that could prove to be a devastating antidote for those who believed the current course sound.

Austerity and Indebtedness

The *status quo* strategy is thus premised on the view that there is not a fundamental problem of insolvency on the part of debtor nations, nor is there a relatively long time horizon over which they will be unable to fully service their debt. The problems are seen as temporary illiquidity difficulties (à la William Cline) that can be corrected by sensibly rescheduling the debt. Moreover, if countries adopt the IMF policy package—the austerity package—the presumption of the *status quo* strategy is that they will be placed on a sound footing and then better able to service the debt over the long term.

By no means is there unanimity of opinion about the efficacy of the IMF policy package—including (in *all* cases) exchange rate devaluation, restraints on government expenditure, increased taxation, etc.—in restoring economic growth. Even staunch defenders of the IMF's practices typically concede near-term contractionary effects if the policy package is adopted. Critics wonder if there is any impetus whatsoever to growth from IMF "adjustment" measures.[10]

A "pariah" of privatization such as Jamaica's current Prime Minister Edward Seaga, would seem to be the ideal leader to implement an IMF package and tout its benefits. By late 1985, after following suit on IMF-styled "restructuring" of the Jamaican economy, even Seaga could be found espousing a certain sentimentality with respect to the perceived consequences of the measures:

> It is as if the prevailing wisdom dictates that since there is no path of painless change, it matters not how painful the process may be. . . . But it does matter. It matters to the human element which in the final analysis is in fact the target of the adjustment program. We do not adjust economic systems. We adjust the lives of people who make these systems work.[11]

Jamaica, in late 1985, had a 25 percent unemployment rate, a 25 percent inflation rate, a current account deficit of more than $100 million, and a negative real growth rate—all *after* following the IMF's recommendations.[12]

More recently, Zambia's President Kenneth Kaunda has discontinued compliance with IMF prescriptions, refusing to meet debt payments—in this instance payments primarily owed to the IMF and the World Bank. He has knowingly jeopardized Zambia's access to foreign credit. But Kaunda's attitude indicates that he believes it is necessary to gut Zambia's IMF-designed "economic recovery plan in order to save Zambia."[13] IMF officials will not concede that their recommendations have contributed to a further decline in Zambia's economy, but they will admit "that [they] made serious miscalculations in determining Zambia's ability to repay the loans . . . by anticipating unrealistically high prices for copper, Zambia's major export."[14]

The political history of the IMF also makes it a somewhat unwieldy agency to manage the international debt crisis since it has been implicated in too many episodes as a direct instrument of U.S. government foreign policy efforts. From Chile to the Philippines, to Indonesia to Indochina, the timing and the nature of IMF involvement was plainly linked to U.S. government attempts to destabilize undesirable regimes and install preferred regimes.[15] It means, in turn, that the IMF stakes out two unattractive options for existing regimes, those lacking radical leanings: (1) to deal with the IMF and suppress the political opposition that arises from the hostility invoked by compliance with the IMF, as well as the depressant effects of IMF policies on the economy or (2) to refuse to deal with the IMF, accept loss of access to foreign credit, and spur a general radicalization of domestic politics that may reach well beyond the IMF.[16]

It also is worth noting that recent actions by the banks themselves suggest that the assessments of early 1985 were not accurate. Individual debt reschedulings have not restored confidence in loan quality. The banks now are moving to raise loan-loss reserves. This effectively means "that some existing [loans] are seen by banks themselves as worth less than full face value."[17] A further contraction in lending to LDCs seems likely—a deepening of the revulsion phase. But there has been no formal reduction in the debt burden of the LDCs, nor do the banks subject the debt to open revaluation in the marketplace via raising their reserves.

FROM BAKER TO BRADLEY

Prominent among the alternatives to the IMF-sponsored case-by-case approach is the plan advocated by U.S. Treasury Secretary James Baker. Now dubbed "the Baker Plan," the Secretary's proposal calls for additional lending from the commercial banks, coupled with an extension of the maturity dates of the loans and financial support to the LDC borrowers from the U.S. Treasury. The *quid pro quo* for Treasury is that the debtor nations must pursue trade liberalization, financial liberalization, eliminate government subsidies, and turn public sector enterprises over to private ownership.[18] Baker proposes, in effect, to extend the premises of the Caribbean Basin Initiative to the resolution of the international debt problem. In a sense, the debt problem becomes a Trojan Horse for the Reagan administration to promote "free market economics" in LDCs.

An implacable commitment toward the premises of *laissez faire, laissez aller* on the part of the Reagan administration may be coming at the wrong time. Albert Hirschman has used the phrase "out of phase" to describe the all too frequent situation where "[i]ntellectual fashions in thinking on development . . . [tend] to go through changes in the United States . . . matched only in the opposite direction, shifts occurring at about the same time in the mood of Latin America."[19] Hirschman contends that throughout Latin America skepticism is now pervasive about either *laissez faire* or planning-oriented policies to guarantee a period of sustained economic growth. Simultaneously, United States officials are expressing an intensely radical posture with respect to the alleged efficacy of liberalization-cum-privatization:

> Just as many influential Latin Americans are in a post-ideological mood, with considerable mistrust toward any system of thought that pretends to have all the answers to the complex problems faced by their societies, they are confronted, particularly in the area of economic policy, with relentlessly ideological positions taken up by the current government of their principal trading partner, foreign investor, and creditor.[20]

Being "out of phase" does not, of course, encourage smooth negotiations between the relevant parties. The Baker Plan simply is another among "relentlessly ideological positions" taken by the Reagan administration.

Limits to Baker's Plan

Bankers, although generally sympathetic to the Baker vision, have expressed doubts that the Latin nations—especially Mexico—will actually follow through on such reforms, even if they consent to the plan. In the fall of 1986, the bankers were insisting that the World Bank guarantee a portion of new loans they might make to Mexico before they agreed to contribute $6 billion in credit out of a $12 billion loan package.[21]

Critics such as economist Patrick Conway advance several reservations about the potential effectiveness of the Baker Plan. Conway complains that the presumed connection between market reforms and structural adjustment is not straightforward. The classic efficiency gains ascribed to removal of distortions are guaranteed theoretically only if no other distortions remain.[22] Conway reminds us that "As long as externalities, either policy-induced or natural, continue in place, removal of distortions leaves the economy in a second-best equilibrium with uncertain effects on efficiency."[23] Therefore, on purely theoretical grounds, no general forecast can be made about the consequences of market reforms. Past experience suggests genuine dangers of instability associated with extreme liberalization of the financial sphere. A thoroughly "free" domestic banking sector may be a fertile incubator for economic collapse.[24]

Conway also complains that at a practical level Baker-style reforms "[do] not directly generate funds needed for repayment."[25] Appraisal and monitoring of the adoption of reforms is also problematic. The Baker Plan also pushes for a shift in World Bank actions from project lending to general purpose lending, and Conway argues that this is inappropriate and ignores the special expertise possessed by the World Bank.[26] Fischer concludes that ". . . further lending promises little in the way of a lasting solution to the debt problem. So long as real interest rates remain around 6 percent, debtor countries will have great difficulty growing out of their debt problem"[27]

Interest Rate Relief

While the Baker Plan emphasizes maturity extension and conditionality —conditions that go beyond the typical liberalization and fiscal restraint measures imposed by the IMF—a plan advanced by U.S. Senator Bradley emphasizes debt relief. Bradley presumes that IMF austerity measures are disadvantageous for the U.S. economy since by inducing economic contraction in the LDCs, they also lead to a contraction in U.S. export markets. The Baker Plan is dismissed by Bradley on the grounds that it merely piles new debt on top of old.[28]

Bradley proposes instead that commercial banks cut interest rates annually by up to three percentage points. Simultaneously, they would also write off a maximum of three percent of loan principal. The industrial countries' governments, presumably led by the United States, would lend up to $3 billion a year to assist. Conditionality would not be absent, but its scope would be narrower than that of the Baker Plan and linked more to performance than to specific policies. Debt relief would be forthcoming for nations if borrowers raise their economic growth rates. Some specific liberalization measures are still part of the

Bradley package of conditions—steps ought to be taken to reduce capital flight, subsidies, and restrictions on investment and trade.[29] But Bradley pays negligible attention to liberalization of the domestic financial sector in LDCs or privatization of public sector enterprises.

It appears that the major opponents of the Bradley plan are the bankers themselves.[30] Obviously, they are not enthused about being locked into a commitment to progressively write off the principal due on their loans or to reduce interest rates. They certainly do not like agreeing to substantial debt relief under weaker conditionality than that advanced by either the IMF or Secretary Baker. Nor is it evident that the bankers should be pleased with a proposal that seeks to stifle capital flight from the developing countries.

CONVERTING THE DEBT

Another set of proposals to resolve the current crisis involve changing the form of the debt itself. Problems with debt payment are seen as arising from the fact that the debt is in the form of direct commercial bank loans. Recommendations have been made instead to change the form and liquidity of the developing country obligations by utilizing the secondary market for LDC debt, setting up debt-equity swaps, and creating a new debt instrument to replace commercial bank loans, for example, shares in LDCs export earnings.

Secondary Markets and Debt-Equity Swaps

The secondary market in LDC debt remains quite thin. Again, it is not an approach that is warmly supported by the bankers—it means institutionalizing a direct market assessment of the book value of the debt. The stock market's daily valuation of the banks is not a specific assessment of the worth of their loans to nations on the periphery. There is little doubt that the secondary market would revalue the loans downward, as it already has on a limited scale. As Kanatos notes: ". . . the consequent reductions in the banks' level of book equity that would result from such cash transactions has thus far made this obvious approach politically unacceptable."[31]

Debt-equity swaps constitute an *ex post* collateralization of the loans. It means that developing country governments would have to consent to surrender large chunks of their national property to the banks. This strategy has been pursued in a limited way, but would have to be widened considerably in scope for the debt to be considered paid in full. It carries with it all the difficulties that probably lay behind the absence of collateral in the original loan contracts—the borrowers' fears of foreign debt used as an instrument of open imperialistic control over a nation's resources. Would the Mexican government seriously contemplate turning over ownership of Pemex, the state-run oil industry, to a syndicate of North American banks in exchange for cancellation of a large proportion of its external debt? If so, debt-equity swaps of this type can then be viewed as a feasible alternative to the status quo; if not, then debt-equity swaps of this type are irrelevant as a major solution to the debt crisis.

A New Debt Instrument?

A third means of converting the debt is for debtor nations' governments to create a new debt instrument that promises the holder of the note a perpetual share in the country's annual export and/or foreign exchange earnings. The debtor nation would agree to turn over a percentage of its exchange earnings each year to holders of the new debt instrument. The shares would then be traded for existing debt.[32] In the Conway version of the plan, the shares would be distributed among the banks depending upon their shares in the existing debt: "For example, if Citibank held one-fifth of the country's international debt, it would receive one-fifth of the export shares."[33]

Again, this would collateralize the debt. Conway suggests that the percentage of exports that would go toward financing the shares "would be determined in consultation with the commercial banks, the IMF, and the MDFI's [multinational development financial institutions, e.g., the World Bank], but it would be large enough to ensure that the debt-burdened country contributes to the costs of retiring the debt with the commercial banks."[34] He points out that if an official decision was made for substantial debt relief, shares simply could be returned to the debtor.[35]

With an eye toward a long-term resolution of the problems created by bank finance to LDCs, Conway proposes that once these shares have been issued a country would forego additional access to direct commercial bank loans. Instead, he says:

> [A country] could, however, obtain additional international funding through dedicating a larger percentage of export receipts to export shares. It could then issue new shares and sell them at the market price. Negotiations of such larger

percentages would occur with commercial banks, the IMF, and the MDFIs and could be made conditional on reforms.[36]

This is an ingenious proposal, but it is not clear whether it can please both the banks and the countries. The market value of the export shares is not linked to the current book value of the existing debt. The market, in principle, will simply set share prices by constructing a collective estimate of the discounted present value of the fixed percentage of export earnings. The level of fixed percentage that would be necessary to make the bankers feel content that they could sell their shares at prices sufficient to preclude debt losses is bound to be a matter of conflict and controversy. Certainly, the future trajectory of export or exchange earnings for any nation is far more a matter of mystery and miracle than authority.

Peru's leaders recently decided to limit interest payments to 10 percent of their export revenues. Such a percentage has yet to prove adequate to cover interest obligations in full.[37] What *permanent* percentage—tantamount to garnishment of wages—will be sufficient to insure that the market value of the shares will approximate the book value of the debt? Will it be high enough for the bankers and low enough for the countries?

Even if an agreement is reached today, a later regime could argue that no nation can indefinitely barter its future income from trade to foreigners and could simply refuse to honor the claims. This risk presumably would be taken into account by the marketplace, perhaps placing upward pressure on the percentage that the banks would require in negotiations.

Forgiving the Debts

A variant of the secondary market strategy has been advocated by Canadian economist Lorie Tarshis as a route toward complete debt forgiveness.[38] Tarshis is unequivocal in his belief that the creditor nations (vis-à-vis the LDCs) will not maintain policies that will permit the developing countries to obtain sufficient foreign exchange to finance the debt. Authorities in the MDCs do not like trade deficits:

> The emphasis on maintaining high prosperity, reasonably rapid growth, and easy access for imports in the creditor countries can be justified because it is likely to push the balance of their current accounts into *deficits*—as is needed. And one reason why they have failed to grow fast enough and to conquer unemployment is that they are frightened of deficits; and that means they are really frightened of the repayment of debt.[39]

A continual piling of new debt on top of old could keep things going—"[so] long as outside investors continue to lend to LDCs in distress because they want the debt to be serviced, this process can continue indefinitely. . ."[40]—but this "natural solution" merely aggravates the burden of the borrowers: "Even if the banks are able to trick others—for example, the IMF and the Federal Reserve—into increasing their exposure, the position of the debtors would grow more and more hopeless."[41]

Tarshis proposes instead that the U.S. Federal Reserve Board ought to buy up *all* the LDC debt certificates held by commercial banks. Because these certificates already sell at a discount ranging from 20 to 80 percent of book value, the Fed certainly should not pay 100 percent. However, since the Fed will demand to buy up all the debt ". . . it might be well advised to pay a *small* premium over the basic rate—say, 72 percent instead of the 70 percent discounted value."[42]

Tarshis advocates a uniform discount rate on all the debt because in his estimation, the prevailing discount rates do not merely reflect careful calculation of prospective repayment. In some instances the political "dice" are loaded:

> If I did not believe that the reason for Peruvian paper's very high discount was that the IMF had blacklisted Peru for making public its refusal to accept the conditions the IMF had set for further loans, I would favor individual market-set discounts. But the IMF's intervention seems to me to have been vengeful and discriminatory. . . ."[43]

An appeals procedure permitting a higher discount rate could be made available to accommodate banks that may have been prudent in lending. After the Fed has bought the debt it stamps "cancelled" on each certificate and returns it to the country of origin.[44]

There are multiple benefits of such a plan of action, according to Tarshis. The creditor countries can now go back to enjoying an expanding market for their products in nations on the periphery without fear that such growth jeopardizes management of the debt crisis. If the banks, newly released from the restraints imposed by holding bad debt, begin to lend aggressively again at home, the Fed can conduct an offsetting open market operation. The banks would at least have received partial compensation for their credits and the situation would be resolved once and for all. The LDCs, free of the debt burden, could get on with economic development.[45] Tarshis has designed an indirect route to thorough debt relief.

Obviously, the political acceptability of such a proposal from the banks' standpoint will depend on the magnitude of the discount rate. Too low a discount rate and they will refuse the plan, unless it is forced upon them. Too high a discount rate, and the Fed will have, in effect, bailed the banks out completely, with forbidding implications for future commercial bank decisions. Tarshis does not make it entirely clear where the Fed will obtain the dollars to buy all the debt. Seventy percent of $500 billion is no small sum. This purchase would have to exercise effects on U.S. public indebtedness and interest rates. But indeed, if such a policy were implemented it could end the present international debt crisis, even if it precipitated a U.S. liquidity crisis!

Tarshis is not specific about how the LDCs would finance future development efforts. But in a companion article in the same issue of *Challenge* magazine, Eliana Cardoso endorses a fairly hard line: all development investment should be financed out of domestic savings, accessed through taxation.[46] LDCs certainly could not immediately turn back to the commercial banks, although who knows if the banks would not immediately turn back to them.

DEFAULT OR REPUDIATION?

The Tarshis proposal represents an extreme of debt relief. It is, effectively, an *unconditional* forgiving of developing country debts. Fischer worries that any proposal that forgives debt without imposing conditions on developing country policymakers will fail "to ensure that the relief is not wasted" and will not establish any penalties for the borrowers' failure to pay, that is, it will make debt relief "an entirely pleasant experience."[47]

In Tarshis' proposal, the initiative for lifting the debt burden would come from authorities in the bankers' home nations, especially the United States. But the initiative could come in several forms from the borrowers themselves. One form is for officials of debtor nations—as the Peruvians already have done—to set explicit limits on the amount of their external obligations they will meet on an annual basis. Peru will pay back no more than 10 percent of its export revenues, regardless of whether it meets or fails to meet the full amount of interest and principal owed. Anatole Kaletsky has suggested a similar hypothetical scenario that is a realistic possibility for any debtor nation to undertake on its own ". . . a debtor country [could] unilaterally [declare] that it will in the future pay interest of only 3 percent on all its medium-term bank debts and will pay no principal for thirty years."[48] Efforts to set moratoria on debt payments such as Brazil's gravitation toward a temporary suspension of debt payments in early 1987, have a similar flavor.[49]

"Conciliatory" Default

A debt moratorium is default, says Kaletsky, although it is "a *conciliatory* default."[50] The countries in question are not refusing to continue servicing their debt forever, nor are they altering its terms until it is unrecognizable from the initial contractual conditions. Kaletsky feels that such "conciliatory defaults" are manageable within the existing scheme of international finance. The creditors need not declare a debtor nation taking such steps as technically in default; they can make the penalties for such action relatively mild, while easing the debt burden for the particular nation. The tone of the debtor's action is still cast in cooperative terms, with an openness toward further negotiations.[51] Kaletsky concludes that default in this sense is the most likely method borrowing nations would take to reduce their obligations:

> Much more likely than a flagrant repudiation or a debtors' cartel is some form of conciliatory default by one or more borrowers, acting independently in a formal sense, but perhaps with a degree of coordination behind the scenes.[52]

Less likely, in Kaletsky's estimation, is non-conciliatory default, although he says some countries—like Argentina—may engage in " 'tacit default'—failure to fulfill their obligations without actually announcing this policy."[53] Only Brazil may default openly, according to Kaletsky.[54] Kaletsky contends that due to the magnitude of their debt, their political climates, and their geopolitical importance, Argentina and Brazil have the leverage to minimize the scope of economic retaliation that would follow non-conciliatory default.[55] Non-conciliatory default by a large borrower, however, is the flashpoint that could endanger the entire existing system of international finance.

Non-Conciliatory Repudiation

For those who are openly hostile toward that system, non-conciliatory default should tilt toward collective, rather than unilateral, repudiation of the debt. The most forceful presentation of this viewpoint has come from Cuban Prime Minister Fidel Castro.[56] Castro's position is straightforward: (1) Mathematically it is impossible for the Latin debt to be paid.[57] (2) It certainly is impossible for countries to develop when Argentina is using 52 percent of its exports, Bolivia is using 57 percent, Mexico using 36.5 percent, Brazil using 36.5 percent, Chile using 45.5 percent, and Peru using 35.5 percent to pay interest on their external debt.[58] (3) The involvement of the IMF in the rescheduling process has devastating effects on the economies of debtor nations and destabilizes them politically.[59] (4) These facts lead to the conclusion that Latin nations should display the unity they showed in supporting Argentina during the war over the Malvinas and join with other Third World debtors to repudiate the debt.[60]

Castro is unhesitating in embracing the position that the loans were pushed: ". . . the moneylenders, the banks went running after debtors, offering them loans."[61] Castro proposes to push the loans back onto the creditors. He acknowledges that debt cancellation will be insufficient to solve problems in several Latin countries, especially Bolivia, but no movement toward social improvement is feasible with the debt overhang.[62] Castro seems largely unconcerned about a collapse of Western and Japanese commercial banks that would be triggered by massive debt repudiation, for his articulated priorities reside with the impoverished citizens of the developing countries.

SOLUTIONS IN THE LONG-TERM?

Beyond a variety of proposals to solve the immediate crisis, a longer view would advance schemes to prevent repetition of future debt crises. The particular scheme advanced would depend upon the particular theory one holds about the causes of the debt crisis.

Rational Expectations and Long-Term Answers

For those like Beenstock, who deny the crisis is a crisis, no major policy change is needed. At most, steps might be taken to mute the worst effects of the period of disturbance that materialized in the early 1980s. But on this view, the historical trends should reassure us that credit flows have gone in exactly the right direction.

For the random-shock school, a "ride it out" strategy might be deemed appropriate, or a policy might be pursued to improve the potential cushions that smooth the journey. Since shocks cannot be anticipated, *ad hoc* adaptations to particular shocks might be needed from time to time. Shocks can cut in both directions, and there may be an unexpected favorable change in the world economy that would redeem the quality of the loans. In the meantime, since present difficulties are due to un-foreseeable events (and presumably uninsured or uninsurable events), the *status quo* case-by-case approach seems an appropriate strategy in the future—with sufficient flexibility to accommodate the particular form future shocks might take. This might mean larger or somewhat modified roles for the IMF or the World Bank. The Fed could always stand ready to reflate the U.S. economy to ease the debt burden.

Overcoming Institutional Weaknesses

On the other hand, theories that identify institutional weaknesses as sources of overlending imply institutional reforms. For example, some economists such as George Kanatos believe that the presence of public-sector deposit insurance is the key factor that induces banks to acquire risky portfolios: ". . . banks were induced by the existence of federal guarantees to behave imprudently in the extent of their total LDC ex-posure, as well as, in many cases, its nondiversifiability."[63] The obvious policy conclusion embraced by Austro-libertarians such as O'Driscoll and Short is turning over the bank insurance function exclusively to the private sector. For O'Driscoll and Short, Federal deposit insurance has lowered the price of risk too much. Competitive pricing of deposit insurance is needed, they say, and steps should be taken (first via co-insurance), to privatize the provision of deposit insurance to banks and/or their customers.[64]

O'Driscoll and Short never address the reason that the private pro-vision of deposit insurance was perceived as inadequate in the 1930s when federal guarantees were introduced. Moreover, the *quid pro quo* for public-sector provision of deposit insurance has been an accep-tance of prudential regulation by the commercial banks. Of course, O'Driscoll and Short may want such a regulatory apparatus to be re-laxed considerably.

Certainly the bankers want deregulation. In the courts, they have won recent successes in expanding their activities more closely toward in-vestment activities.[65] There is also a quiet movement gathering to repeal the Glass-Steagall Act that separates commercial from investment banking.[66] Of course, J.P. Morgan's official position virtually inverts the O'Driscoll-Short stance; Morgan's view is Glass-Steagall should be repealed, letting commercial banks deal directly in securities markets, while retaining public-sector deposit insurance![67]

If deregulation was coupled with the removal of public-sector deposit insurance, an environment akin to the era of wildcat banking—free enterprise at its "best"—would be restored. Deregulation coupled with retention of public-sector deposit insurance would magnify the imprudential lending effects of concern to Kanatos, O'Driscoll, and Short. Elimination of public-sector deposit insurance coupled with prudential regulation places the burden of confidence in the banks entirely upon public confidence in the regulators. The regulators may feel the need to minimize disclosure of information to avoid bank runs, and the regulators may not be able to maintain independence from the regulatees.[68]

With banks' efforts to satisfy customers leading them to lend abroad, or with a symbiotic relationship between banks and their governments, the regulatory apparatus may be the only possible source of mild salvation—at least as long as finance remains on a capitalistic basis. One of Walter Wriston's most memorable anecdotes was his attribution to Friedrich Hayek the observation "that, without the moneylender capitalism wouldn't be possible."[69] The moneylenders are the premier exponents of the spirit of capitalism, and when they have sufficient discretion ("freedom") will find borrowers when they want to find them. As Victoria Chick has commented, "The banks have shown that if they want to lend, they will find outlets *even in a slump.*"[70]

The radical proposal emanating from the Chicago School's economic conservatives is to make institutions accepting deposits hold 100 percent reserves. If they wish to lend they have to turn to the equity markets, or offer different classes of assets of varying degrees of riskiness. Low risk and low return accounts would be supported in full by 100 percent reserves. The link between liabilities and assets would be severed. But if a bank's valuation on equity markets is plunging, would even holders of low-risk accounts keep their funds there? In the absence of insurance the accounts could be extinguished if the bank failed.[71]

Final Thoughts

But if one takes the view that debt pulling took place, that overborrowing is the source of the crisis, then altering the behavior of the borrowers is the indicated policy. In particular, proponents of liberalization such as Anne Krueger can predictably use the overborrowing view as a basis for prompting LDCs to alter their own policies.[72].

The more interesting financial instability hypothesis has it that debt crises occur in long cyclical waves. Prudential regulation might be one route to help contain crises, but since it possesses a certain inevitability, it is best to have a lender of last resort standing ready to preserve liquidity. This is Charles Kindleberger's standard prescription, with all the attendant difficulties of which he is fully aware.[73] Who should the lender be? Who should get help, that is, all banks, only those that were most prudent, only those of a particular size? Should assistance be random to cope with the moral hazard problem? Who should pay? As early as the 1907 Italian bank crisis, the Italian treasury served as the ultimate lender of last resort; hence, the Italian taxpayer financed the maintenance of the banking system in the face of imprudential lending.[74] No doubt national treasuries and their taxpayers are generally the ultimate lenders of last resort, standing behind central banks, multinational development finance institutions, and public-sector deposit insurance funds.

Next, we consider Marxist analyses of the debt crisis. The critical feature of Hilferding's analysis was the connection between capitalist crises and greater concentration, particularly in the financial sphere. Historical evidence on merchant banking in particular supports Hilferding's perception of such a correlation.[75] Hilferding actually favored increased concentration, because he believed that a more sophisticated capitalistic social infrastructure would make the transition to socialism easier.[76] In a sense, on grounds of pure theory, Hilferding would have preferred to let the capitalist crises run their course, pushing humankind ever closer to the socialist millennium. In contrast, Mandel appears to favor having the crises unfold, to spur the collapse of the infrastructure of capitalism rather than its takeover and appropriation by socialists.

Finally, there is our own modification of David Harvey's analysis. Our analysis views the current international debt crisis as a consequence of capital's retreat into the financial sphere, in the combative transition from capitalism to the managerial estate. Finance provides capitalism its greatest fluidity and power, and through linkages with the state, a broad and often invisible apparatus of ammunition. An understanding of fundamental trends and developments, not policy, is at stake here. The challenge posed for the future is not only avoidance of the dangers of capitalism's instability and penchant for economic traumas, but also avoidance of the dangers of post-capitalist society—where the financial waters are not yet charted clearly. It seems that the fulcrum stands poised between the extreme limits of free banking and thoroughly nationalized banks. Both have charms and seductions as well as entrapments.

Where, then, to go from here? The answers are not clear. But it is always useful to first understand the sources of our problems. The private actions of commercial banks and public-sector responses ratchet society between economic flux and economic restriction. The question remains: will the loan pushers chart a renewed course of pushing in the future or will they be prohibited from doing so? The demise of commercial banks will presumably signal the demise of capitalism, but it need not signal the end to a role for finance. The consequences under a new social order remain uncertain, but we note that there are many roads to social disaster produced both by those who favor freedom for the bankers and those who would circumscribe their penchant for imprudence. If, ironically, the renewed importance of the bankers foreshadows the end of capitalism, will capitalism end in a bang of financial collapse or with a whimper of financial regulation?

NOTES

1. Stanley Fischer, "Sharing the Burden of the International Debt Crisis," *American Economic Review: Papers and Proceedings* 77 (May 1987): 167.
2. Peter Korner, Gero Maass, Thomas Siebold, and Ranier Tetzlaff, *The IMF and the Debt Crisis: A Guide to the Third World's Dilemma* (London: Zed Books Ltd., 1986), p. 168.
3. Art Pine, "World Bank Is Under Pressure from U.S. to Expand Its Role in Global Debt Crisis," *Wall Street Journal*, 1 October 1985. At a conference of bankers and economists in 1985 held in Seoul, Korea, it was proposed that the World Bank shift from project lending to structural adjustment loans. The IMF also was urged to moderate the austerity features of its conditionality arrangements. The "Changed World Bank" and the "reformed IMF" were supposed to help the "debtor nations . . . produce more, meet the debt service on their loans, and steadily move toward 'development.' " See also Roy L. Prosterman and Jeffrey M. Riedinger, "Seoul Offered No Solution to the LDC Riddle," *Wall Street Journal*, 15 October 1985.
4. Marko Milivojevic, *The Debt Rescheduling Process* (New York: St. Martin's Press, 1985), p. 43:

   > Most of the post-war debt reschedulings were . . . reschedulings of official debt, which took place at meetings of creditor Governments, the debtor Government concerned, and multilateral institutions such as the World Bank in the so-called "Paris Club." Since its creation in 1956, this creditor's club has chosen always to meet in Paris, and its meetings have always been chaired by a high ranking official of the French Treasury. Although commercial banks cannot attend such meetings, their interests have been protected. This was because a large proportion of "official debt" was, in fact, credit made available to debtor countries

by commercial banks, but such credit was insured by Western Governments's export credit agencies.

5. Ibid., p. 49.

6. Ibid. Milivojevic observes ". . . in September 1981, after months of lies, inexplicable delays, brinksmanship from the Government in its dealings with its commercial bank creditors . . . [t]he day after [the threat] was made the Polish Government signed a preliminary agreement."

7. Gary Hector, "Third World Debt: The Bomb Defused," *Fortune,* 18 February 1985, and G. David Wallace, Sarah Bartlett, Blanca Riemer, and John N. Frank, "Against All Odds, the Banking Industry Is Looking Healthier," *Business Week,* 25 February 1986.

8. Hector, "Third World Debt," p. 36.

9. Wallace et al., "Against All Odds," p. 83.

10. Ricardo Ffrench-Davis and Sergio Molina, "Prospects for Bank Lending to Developing Countries in the Remainder of the 1980s," *Journal of Development Planning,* no. 16 (1985): 242–43. Eliana Cardoso says IMF policies do not contribute to development in the medium-term. See "Latin America's Debts: Which Way Now?," *Challenge* 30 (May/June 1987): 14.

11. Robert Reno, "Jamaica Follows Painful Advice," *The Charlotte Observer,* 18 October 1985.

12. Ibid.

13. Blaine Harden, "Zambia Applies the Debt Hammer," *Washington Post,* 29 June 1987.

14. Ibid.

15. Cheryl Payer, *The Debt Trap* (New York: Monthly Review Press, 1974). Bahram Nowzad, in *The IMF and Its Critics* (Essays in International Finance, No. 146, Princeton: Princeton University, December 1981), without mentioning Payer by name, seems to be trying to refute her critique of the IMF. He never addresses the IMF's role in cases of specific countries, and his essay appears to be largely the work of a sycophant. He was, after all, at the time he prepared the essay, an employee of the IMF.

16. On the latter point see Rudiger Dornbusch, "Dealing with Debt in the 1980s," *Third World Quarterly* 7 (1985): 550.

17. Peter Truell, "Banking Trouble: Banks' Reserve Action May Make Debt Crisis Even More Vexatious," *Wall Street Journal,* 2 July 1987. Also see David Warsh, "Economic Principals: A New Realism Infects Bankers," *The Boston Globe,* 24 May 1987.

18. Blanca Riemer, Sarah Bartlett, and James B. Treece, "Facing Reality on Latin Debt," *Business Week,* 21 October 1985 and S. Karene Witcher, "Baker Debt Plan Is Alive, but Is It Well?" *Wall Street Journal,* 26 September 1986.

19. Albert O. Hirschman, "The Political Economy of Latin American Development: Seven Exercises In Retrospection" *Latin American Research Review,* (forthcoming).

20. Ibid.

21. Witcher, "Baker Debt Plan."
22. Patrick Conway, "The Baker Plan and International Indebtedness," *World Economy* 10 (June 1987): 193–204.
23. Ibid., p. 204n.13.
24. Carlos Diaz-Alejandro, "Goodby Financial Repression, Hello Financial Crash," *Journal of Development Economics* 19 (1985): 1–24.
25. Conway, "Baker Plan," p. 194.
26. Ibid., pp. 195–196.
27. Fischer, "Sharing the Burden," p. 167.
28. Blanca Riemer and William Glasgall, "Third World Debt: Bill Bradley May Have A Better Idea," *Business Week,* 28 July 1986.
29. Ibid.
30. Ibid.
31. George Kanatos, "Review of Edward Kane's *The Gathering Crisis in Deposit Insurance," Journal of Money, Credit, and Banking* 19 (May 1987): 270.
32. Such a proposal was advanced early by the senior director of national security planning for the National Security Council, Norman Bailey, in "Safety Net for Foreign Lending," *Business Week,* 10 January 1983.
33. Conway, "Baker Plan," p. 201.
34. Ibid.
35. Ibid.
36. Ibid.
37. Peter Truell and Jonathan Cavanaugh, "Peru Outlines Plan to Bolster Better Economy; Bankers, Economists Aren't Impressed," *Wall Street Journal,* 7 July 1987.
38. Lorie Tarshis, "Disarming the Debt Bomb," *Challenge* 30 (May/June 1987): 18–23.
39. Ibid., p. 21.
40. Ibid., pp. 20–21.
41. Ibid., p. 21.
42. Ibid.
43. Ibid., p. 22.
44. Ibid.
45. Ibid.
46. Cardoso, "Latin America's Debts," pp. 17–18.
47. Fischer, "Sharing the Burden," p. 167.
48. Anatole Kaletsky, *The Costs of Default* (New York: Priority Press, 1985).
49. Gavin Scott, "No More Blood in the Stone," *Time,* 2 March 1987.
50. Kaletsky, *Costs of Default,* p. 65. (Emphasis in original.)
51. "Conciliatory default," in Kaletsky's (Ibid., p. 64) sense already has occurred on several occasions. He writes:

    The moratorium on debt repayments declared by Mexico on August 23, 1982, could have been interpreted as a default, as could the buildup of $3 billion in interest arrears by Argentina in 1984, and similar actions by other debtors from Peru to the Philippines. These actions have not been generally described as defaults partly because default is in the eye of the beholder, and creditors found it tactically inopportune in each of these cases to term the borrowers formally "in default." More important, the moratoria announced in the first phase of the debt crisis were considered by creditors and debtors alike to be strictly temporary arrangements, paving the way for cooperative debt reschedulings.

52. Ibid.
53. Ibid., p. 66.
54. Ibid., pp. 66–67.
55. Ibid., p. 66.
56. Fidel Castro, *How Latin America's and the Third World's Unpayable Foreign Debt Can and Should be Cancelled and the Pressing Need for the New International Economic Order* (Havana, Cuba: Editora Politica, 1985).
57. Ibid., pp. 2–3, pp. 28–30.
58. Ibid., p. 3. Castro's data apparently was for 1984, prior to Peru's unilateral decision to limit payments to ten percent of export revenues.
59. Ibid., pp. 5–10.
60. Ibid., p. 1, pp. 34–35.
61. Ibid., p. 14.
62. Ibid., p. 26.
63. Kanatos, "Review of Kane," p. 270.
64. Eugenie D. Short and Gerald P. O'Driscoll, "Deregulation and Deposit Insurance," *Economic Review of the Federal Reserve Bank of Dallas* 2 (September 1983): 11–22 and Gerald P. O'Driscoll and Eugenie D. Short, "Safety Net Mechanisms: The Case of International Lending," *The Cato Journal* 4 (Spring/Summer 1984): 185–204.
65. Stephen Wermiel, "Rehnquist and Scalia Push Conservative Causes but High Court Liberals Still Hold the Upper Hand," *Wall Street Journal,* 26 June 1987.
66. See J.P. Morgan and Company, Inc., *Rethinking Glass-Steagall* (New York: J.P. Morgan, December 1984) and Michael C. Keeley and Randall J. Pozdema, "Uniting Investment and Commercial Banking," *Federal Reserve Bank of San Francisco Weekly Letter,* 19 February 1987.
67. Morgan, ibid., passim.
68. Even today bank regulators have resisted disclosure of information about Manufacturers Hanover and Chemical Bank, financiers of litigation-scared A.H. Robins, expressing worries that the public will *misinterpret* the data, possibly sparking a bank run. See "Fed, FDIC Oppose Request for Bank Records," *Washington Post,* 10 July 1987.
69. "Interview with Walter Wriston," *Euromoney,* October 1983.
70. Victoria Chick, "The Evolution of the Banking System and the Theory of Saving, Investment and Interest," (*Economies et Societies,* Cahiers de

l'I.S.M.E.A. Serie MPn3, 1986, p. 123, emphasis added). Chick's paper develops an interesting model of the historical evolution of banks, where in their most modern stage they become most susceptible to engaging in loan pushing; see especially pp. 112–18.

71. For a recent discussion see P.N. Snowden, "Chicago Schism on Banking Reforms and the Debt Crisis," *The World Economy* 10 (June 1987): 219–26.

72. Anne Krueger, "Debt, Capital Flows, and LDC Growth," *American Economic Review: Papers and Proceedings* 77 (May 1987): 159–64.

73. Charles P. Kindleberger, "Historical Perspective on Today's Third-World Debt Problem," (*Economies et Societes,* Cahier de l'I.S.M.E.A. Serie MON.S, 1985, pp. 109–34).

74. Franco Bonelli, "The 1907 Financial Crisis in Italy: A Peculiar Case of the Lender of Last Resort in Action" in C.P. Kindleberger and J.P. Laffargue, eds., *Financial Crises: Theory, History and Policy* (Cambridge, MA: Cambridge University Press, 1982), p. 60.

75. See Stanley Chapman, *The Rise of Merchant Banking* (London: George Allen and Unwin, 1984), pp. 35–38.

76. See William Darity, Jr., and Bobbie L. Horn, "Rudolf Hilferding: The Dominion of Capitalism and the Dominion of Gold," *American Economic Review: Papers and Proceedings* 75 (May 1985): 367.

Appendix

Table 1.   Interest Rate Spreads (over LIBOR) and Maturities on Eurocurrency Credits to Non-OPEC LDCs, OPEC Nations, and All Nations, 1965–1981 (4th quarter).

Non-OPEC LDCs	1975	1976	1977	1978
Weighted mean spreads	1.65	1.87	1.77	1.06
Unweighted mean spreads	1.82	1.90	1.76	1.04
Weighted mean maturities	5.44	5.14	7.32	9.79

OPEC	1975	1976	1977	1978
Weighted mean spreads	1.67	1.34	1.59	1.11
Unweighted mean spreads	1.65	1.56	1.52	1.14
Weighted mean maturities	5.66	6.95	5.48	8.59

Total Sample	1975	1976	1977	1978
Weighted mean spreads	1.63	1.58	1.48	0.83
Unweighted mean spreads	1.67	1.56	1.41	0.88
Weighted mean maturities	5.63	5.61	6.79	8.88

	1979	1980	1981
	0.76	1.10	1.16
	0.90	0.93	0.95
	10.11	8.06	7.31

	1979	1980	1981
	0.75	0.81	0.69
	0.82	1.16	0.79
	8.42	4.80	9.60

	1979	1980	1981
	0.68	0.83	0.88
	0.77	0.81	0.75
	9.64	7.79	8.11

Interest rate spreads are calculated as percent per annum. Maturities are calculated as numbers of years.

Weights were based on the volume of credits for each country in the current quarter.

Source: Memorandum prepared by Rodney H. Mill, Jr., entitled "Spreads and Maturities on Eurocurrency Credits—Fourth Quarter 1981 and Two-Year Review," (Board of Governors of the Federal Reserve System, March 3, 1982).

Table 2.   Interest Rate Spreads (over LIBOR) and Maturities on Eurocurrency Credits to Selected Major Debtor Nations, 1975–1981 (4th quarter).

Argentina	1975	1976	1977	1978	1979	1980	1981
Spread	—	1.88	1.58	.88	.76	.63	1.09
Maturity	—	4.00	9.14	11.05	10.43	7.65	7.33
Brazil	1975	1976	1977	1978	1979	1980	1981
Spread	1.72	1.95	2.20	1.26	.72	1.79	2.14
Maturity	6.80	5.71	7.76	11.52	12.03	8.87	8.00
Chile	1975	1976	1977	1978	1979	1980	1981
Spread	—	—	1.93	1.10	.92	.93	1.01
Maturity	—	—	4.33	9.57	9.80	7.30	5.06
Mexico	1975	1976	1977	1978	1979	1980	1981
Spread	2.00	2.05	1.88	.91	.69	.90	.60
Maturity	4.76	5.97	7.00	7.93	8.84	6.96	5.41
Korea	1975	1976	1977	1978	1979	1980	1981
Spread	1.47	1.63	1.75	.95	.69	.52	.63
Maturity	3.50	5.32	7.00	9.34	9.61	7.52	7.46
Poland	1975	1976	1977	1978	1979	1980	1981
Spread	1.50	1.50	—	—	.83	1.13	—
Maturity	6.00	7.00	—	—	3.00	3.00	—
Venezuela	1975	1976	1977	1978	1979	1980	1981
Spread	—	1.63	1.63	1.35	—	.68	—
Maturity	—	5.90	6.00	5.70	—	5.00	—

Interest rate spreads are calculated as percent per annum.

Maturities are calculated as numbers of years.

Source: Memorandum prepared by Rodney H. Mills, Jr., "Spreads and Maturities on Eurocurrency Credits—Fourth Quarter 1981 and Two-Year Review," (Board of Governors of the Federal Reserve System, March 3, 1982).

Table 3. Average Spread over LIBOR on Eurocredits, 1975–1980.

	Average Margins (Percent over LIBOR)		Ranges[a] (Percent over LIBOR)	
	Industrial Countries	Developing Countries	Industrial Countries	Developing Countries
1975	1.39	1.59	1.00–1.75	1.25–2.00
1976	1.36	1.62	1.00–1.75	1.00–2.25
1977	0.96	1.42	0.50–1.50	0.75–2.00
1978	0.60	1.10	0.25–1.25	0.50–2.00
1979	0.48	0.78	0.25–1.00	0.25–1.50
1980[b]	0.44	0.74	0.25–0.75	0.25–1.50
1980[c]	0.42	0.85	0.25–0.75	0.25–1.50

[a]Excludes top and bottom 10 percent of distribution.
[b]First half
[c]Second half

Source: Richard Bernal, "Transnational Banks, the International Monetary Fund and External Debt of Developing Countries," *Social and Economic Studies*, 31 (1982): 75.

Table 4.   Estimates of External Indebtedness of Major Developing Country Borrowers, 1985.

	External Public Debt [a] (Billions of U.S. Dollars)	Total External Debt [a] (Billions of U.S. Dollars)	Ratio of External Public Debt to Total External Debt
Brazil	73.9	106.7	0.69
Mexico	72.5	97.4	0.74
Argentina	35.6	48.4	0.73
South Korea	29.1	48.0	0.61
Indonesia	26.6	35.8	0.74
Venezuela	16.6	32.1	0.52
Poland	—	27.0 [b]	—
Philippines	13.6	26.2	0.52
Turkey	17.8	26.1	0.68
Chile	12.7	20.2	0.63
Yugoslavia	9.9	19.4	0.51
Nigeria	13.0	18.3	0.71
Peru	10.5	13.7	0.77
Ivory Coast	5.7	8.4	0.67

[a]Source: World Bank, *World Development Report 1987*, Table 16.

[b]The estimate for Poland is for 1983 from "A Wall Street Journal Watch List" *Wall Street Journal*, 22 June 1984. The source of *Wall Street Journal's* figures are estimates generated by Morgan Guaranty.

Table 5. Estimates of Per Capita External Indebtedness and Debt GNP or GDP Ratios, 1983.[a]

	Per Capita External Debt (U.S. Dollars)	Per Capita GNP or GDP (U.S. Dollars)	Debt-GNP or GDP Ratio
Norway	7,290	13,366	0.55
Israel	7,283	6,264	1.16
Denmark	6,995	11,098	0.63
Iceland	6,383	8,936	0.71
Ireland	5,599	4,967	1.13
Sweden	5,237	10,931	0.48
Switzerland	4,524	15,227	0.30
Canada	4,291	12,083	0.36
Finland	4,208	9,867	0.43
Kuwait	3,450	14,058	0.25
New Zealand	3,262	7,473	0.44
Belgium	3,247	8,392	0.39
Venezuela	2,372	4,893	0.48
Australia	2,115	10,331	0.20
Portugal	1,983	2,083	0.95
Germany	1,963	10,618	0.18
France	1,743	9,576	0.18
Panama	1,712	2,202	0.78
Costa Rica	1,635	1,506	1.09
Chile	1,614	1,819	0.89
Argentina	1,554	2,202	0.71
Austria	1,532	8,863	0.17
Uruguay	1,527	1,866	0.82
Jamaica	1,527	1,527	1.00
Hong Kong	1,510	5,446	0.28
United States	1,400	14,266	0.10
Netherlands	1,258	9,071	0.14
Mexico	1,230	2,033	0.61
Saudi Arabia	1,227	11,401	0.11
Greece	1,225	3,594	0.34
Japan	1,005	9,762	0.10
Poland	745	2,545	0.29
Brazil	734	1,788	0.41

[a]Source: "World Debt in Crisis: Per Capita Picture" *Wall Street Journal*, 22 June 1984.

Table 6. Debt-GNP or GDP Ratio (Highest Twenty Countries), 1983 and 1985.

	1983[a]	1985[b]
Zaire	1.54	—[c]
Ivory Coast	1.17	1.62
Israel	1.16	1.18
Ireland	1.13	—
Costa Rica	1.09	1.10
Jamaica	1.00	1.91
Portugal	0.95	0.71
Morocco	0.92	—[c]
Chile	0.89	1.26
Uruguay	0.82	0.89
Peru	0.80	0.81
Panama	0.78	—[c]
Philippines	0.77	0.80
Sudan	0.73	—[c]
Honduras	0.72	0.92
Iceland	0.71	—[c]
Argentina	0.71	0.73
Jordan	0.66	1.06
Mexico	0.61	0.55
Bolivia	0.60	1.33

[a]Source: "World Debt in Crisis: Per Capita Picture," *Wall Street Journal*, 22 June 1984.

[b]Source: World Bank, *World Development Report 1987*, Tables 3 and 16.

[c]No data was available on total external debt for any of these countries but it is probably safe to say the debt-GNP ratio worsened for all of them. The ratios of public long-term debt alone to GDP were estimated to be 1.00 for Zaire, 0.95 for Morocco, 0.67 for Panama, and 0.73 for the Sudan in 1985. No data on Iceland's external debt was available in the *World Development Report* for 1987.

Several other countries not listed for 1983 had spectacularly high ratios of public long-term debt to GNP. These include 1.22 for Mali, 1.21 for Togo, 1.05 for Madagascar, 1.51 for Zambia, and an astonishing 1.85 for Nicaragua and 2.08 for Mauritania. (See World Bank, *World Development Report 1987*, Table 18.)

Table 7. Total Long-Term (Public and Private) External Debt Disbursed and Outstanding Developing Countries as Percentage of GNP (1970 and 1984) (Top Twenty Debtors).

Country	1984	1970
Mauritania	171.2%	13.9%
Nicaragua	141.8	14.8
Zambia	115.4	37.5
Costa Rica	114.0	25.3
Jamaica	108.8	92.8
Bolivia	108.7	36.1
Ivory Coast	107.5	19.1
Yemen PDR	106.9	—
Chile	100.2	32.1
Togo	100.1	16.0
Israel	99.5	47.9
Mali	95.9	88.1
Papua New Guinea	78.1	33.4
Liberia	77.4	49.9
Sudan	77.2	15.2
Nigeria	76.7	—
Congo, People's Rep.	76.2	53.9
Ecuador	75.1	14.7
Panama	73.3	19.5
Tanzania	69.6	20.7

Source: World Bank, *World Development Report 1986*, Table 17.

Table 8. **Debt-Export Ratios of Major Developing Country Borrowers, 1985.**

	Total External Debt [a] (Billions of U.S. Dollars)	Total Exports [b] (Billions of U.S. Dollars)	Debt-Export Ratio
Brazil	106.9	25.6	4.17
Mexico	97.4	21.9	4.45
Argentina	48.4	8.4	5.76
South Korea	48.0	30.3	1.58
Indonesia	35.8	18.6	1.92
Venezuela	32.1	12.3	2.61
Poland	—	11.4	—
Philippines	26.2	4.7	5.57
Turkey	26.1	8.3	3.14
Chile	20.2	3.7	5.46
Yugoslavia	18.3	10.7	1.71
Nigeria	13.7	12.6	1.09
Ivory Coast	8.4	3.0	2.80

[a]Source: World Bank, *World Development Report 1987*, Table 16.
[b]Source: World Bank, *World Development Report 1987*, Table 10.

Table 9. Debt-Service Ratios on External Public Debt of Major Developing Country Borrowers, 1985.

	External Public Debt[a] (Billions of U.S. Dollars)	Interest Payments on External Public Debt[a] (Billions of U.S. Dollars)	Debt Service as Percentage of Exports of Goods and Services[a]
Brazil	73.9	6.3	26.5
Mexico	72.5	7.5	37.0
Argentina	35.6	3.5	41.8
South Korea	29.1	2.2	15.2
Indonesia	26.6	1.6	19.9
Venezuela	16.7	1.4	12.8
Philippines	13.6	0.8	15.9
Turkey	17.8	1.3	30.8
Chile	12.7	1.0	26.2
Yugoslavia	9.9	0.7	8.2
Nigeria	13.0	1.3	30.8
Peru	10.5	0.1	7.9
Ivory Coast	5.7	0.4	17.4

[a]Source: World Bank, *World Development Report 1987*, Table 19. No data was available on Poland. The debt-service measure in this table is the ratio of the sum of actual repayments of interest made in foreign currencies, goods, or services to external public and publicly guaranteed debt to total exports.

Table 10. Debt-Service Ratios on Total Long-Term Debt of Major Developing Country Borrowers, 1985.

	Total Long-Term Debt (Billions of U.S. Dollars)[a]	Total Interest Payments on Long-Term Debt (Billions of U.S. Dollars)	Debt-Service as Percentage of Exports of Goods and Services[a]
Brazil	91.9	7.9	34.8
Mexico	89.0	9.4	48.2
Argentina	40.2	—	—
South Korea	35.8	2.9	21.5
Indonesia	30.4	1.9	25.1
Venezuela	21.8	—	—
Philippines	16.6	1.0	19.5
Turkey	18.2	1.3	32.1
Chile	17.5	1.6	44.1
Yugoslavia	16.3	1.6	21.2
Nigeria	13.4	1.3	32.1
Peru	11.9	0.3	16.0
Ivory Coast	7.1	—	—

[a]Source: World Bank, *World Development Report 1987*, Table 18. No data was available on Poland. The debt-service measure in this table is the ratio of the sum of actual repayments of principal (amortization) and actual payments of interest made in foreign currencies, goods, or services to long-term public and private external debt (debt with a maturity exceeding one year) to total exports.

Table 11. The Simonsen Criterion and Major LDC Borrowers.

	(a) Average Annual Growth Rate of Exports 1980–85 [a]	(b) Average Interest Rate on External Public Borrowing 1985 [b]	(a)–(b)
Brazil	6.6	9.6	−3.0
Mexico	10.1	9.3	0.8
Argentina	3.2	9.9	−6.7
South Korea	13.0	8.6	4.4
Indonesia	1.1	8.1	−7.0
Venezuela	−5.8	9.5	−15.3
Philippines	−2.1	9.1	−11.2
Turkey	25.3	8.7	16.6
Chile	2.3	9.4	−7.1
Yugoslavia	2.1	9.1	−7.0
Nigeria	−9.9	9.3	−19.2
Peru	1.4	9.4	−8.0
Ivory Coast	1.8	10.3	−7.5

[a]Source: World Bank, *World Development Report 1987*, Table 10.
[b]Source: World Bank, *World Development Report 1987*, Table 20.

Table 12. Country Indebtedness to U.S. and U.K. Commercial Banks as a Percent of Total External Debt, 1981.

	Percent of Total Due to U.S. Banks	Percent of Total Due to U.K. Banks	Percent of Total Due to U.S. and U.K. Banks
Argentina	33.9	14.1	48.0
Brazil	34.5	12.3	46.9
Mexico	37.6	13.7	51.3
Venezuela	38.5	11.8	50.4
Philippines	50.0	11.8	61.8
Chile	54.3	14.3	68.6
South Korea	45.2	12.6	57.8
Poland	7.8	5.9	13.7
Indonesia	29.2	6.9	36.1
Yugoslavia	24.3	14.0	38.3
Nigeria	18.3	20.0	33.3

Source: Andrew F. Brimmer, *The World Banking System: Outlook in a Context of Crisis* (New York and London: NYU Press, 1985), Table 3. No data was reported for Turkey or Peru.

Table 13. Data for the Regressions Analysis.

Country	PG	A	D (%)	G (%)	I (%)
Ethiopia	6.24	1.86	—	2.3	16
Kenya	6.47	1.71	13.2	4.6	20
Malowi	4.89	1.14	7.7	4.2	—
Tanzania	9.34	2.57	11.1	3.6	15
Cambodia	13.37	1.57	5.1	6.8	32
Ghana	1.24	2.86	6.2	−1.3	7
Ivory Coast	17.84	2.71	—	1.2	34
Senegal	13.96	2.29	9.1	2.6	26
Indonesia	7.87	1.86	13.9	7.0	39
Malaysia	26.35	1.57	15.1	7.3	35
Philippines	17.16	1.57	13.6	5.4	36
Taiwan	20.79	1.43	20.6	6.9	27
Bangladesh	—	2.57	—	5.2	13
Pakistan	2.19	2.29	33.5	5.6	27
Egypt	7.70	2.14	12.7	8.8	33
Sri Lanka	5.96	1.86	1.4	5.2	26
Tunisia	5.33	1.57	10.6	6.0	36
Turkey	7.30	2.14	15.2	4.1	33
Yugoslavia	6.58	1.17	50.4	5.3	—
Argentina	12.10	2.43	11.0	0.4	39
Brazil	16.96	1.86	4.3	4.8	35
Chile	2.30	2.43	11.5	2.9	36
Colombia	3.13	1.71	10.7	3.9	28
Mexico	19.81	1.86	1.6	5.6	40
Uruguay	8.38	2.29	13.6	2.5	28
Bolivia	5.19	2.29	7.4	1.5	26
Peru	8.27	2.29	—	1.8	41
Jamaica	11.18	2.29	—	−1.7	34

PG: Growth rate of external public debt 1970–1983 in current dollars (source: *World Development Report*, 1985).

A: Agarwala distortion index (source: Ramgopal Agarwala, *Price Distortions and Growth in Developing Countries*, [World Bank Staff, Working Papers No. 575, July 1983, p. 49]).

D: Defense expenditure as a percent of total public expenditure in 1983 (source: *World Development Report*, 1985).

G: Growth rate of GDP per capita 1972–1983 (source: *World Development Report*, 1985).

I: Percent of GDP in industry 1983 (source: *World Development Report*, 1985).

Table 14. The Regressions Analysis.
Dependent Variable: PG (t-ratios in parentheses)

	Constant	A	D	G	I	R^2	F-Ratio	Degrees of Freedom
(1)	28.54 (4.11)	−9.12 (−2.69)	—	—	—	0.28	7.24	19
(2)	11.25 (3.73)	—	0.09 (−0.42)	—	—	0.01	0.17	19
(3)	5.16 (1.73)	—	—	1.12 (1.91)	—	0.16	3.63	19
(4)	0.43 (0.08)	—	—	—	0.33 (1.88)	0.16	3.53	19
(5)	29.71 (3.98)	−9.13 (−2.64)	−0.10 (−0.50)	—	—	0.29	3.60	18
(6)	26.40 (1.94)	−7.46 (−1.49)	−0.12 (−0.56)	0.26 (0.29)	—	0.29	2.31	17
(7)	21.22 (1.40)	−7.76 (−1.48)	—	0.50 (−0.06)	0.16 (0.83)	0.31	2.49	17
(8)	2.05 (0.34)	—	−0.16 (−0.77)	0.91 (1.31)	0.20 (1.00)	0.24	1.81	17
(9)	21.86 (11.99)	−7.58 (−1.92)	−0.10 (−0.48)	—	0.16 (0.84)	0.31	2.60	17
(10)	20.85 (15.55)	−7.19 (−1.30)	−0.10 (−0.48)	0.10 (0.10)	0.15 (0.77)	0.31	1.84	16

Table 15. U.S. Military Aid and External Indebtedness.

Twenty Major Recipients of U.S. Military Assistance 1983	Percent of U.S.[a] Total of Military Assistance 1983	Amount (Millions of 1983 Dollars)[b]	Debt-Service Ratio (All External Debt) 1983	Per Capita External Debt 1983 (U.S. Dollars)[c]	Debt-C or Debt-C Rat 198
Israel	30.4	1,700.0	156.8	7,283	1.1
Egypt	23.7	1,326.9	77.9	564	0.5
Turkey	7.2	402.8	82.5	516	0.4
Spain	7.2	402.5	53.5	1,033	0.2
Greece	5.0	281.3	46.1	1,225	0.3
Pakistan	4.7	260.8	34.7	133	0.4
Korea	3.3	186.7	—	—	—
Portugal	2.0	111.2	141.2	1,983	0.9
Tunisia	1.8	102.0	30.3	654	0.5
Lebanon	1.8	101.7	—	—	—
Morocco	1.8	101.3	88.8	603	0.9
Thailand	1.7	96.2	49.0	260	0.3
El Salvador	1.5	81.3	—	—	—
Jordan	0.9	52.8	41.1	863	0.6
Philippines	0.9	51.4	199.5	522	0.2
Honduras	0.9	48.3	55.3	531	0.2
Sudan	0.8	44.3	96.7	222	0.2
Somalia	0.5	30.6	—	—	—
Oman	0.5	30.1	6.3	1,112	0.2
Indonesia	0.5	27.4	35.4	188	0.2

[a]A.I.D. *U.S. Overseas Loans and Grants, 1945–1983.*

[b]"World Debt in Crisis: World Debt Ratios," *Wall Street Journal,* 22 June 1984.

[c]"World Debt in Crisis: Per Capita Picture," *Wall Street Journal,* 22 June 1984.

Table 16. The Major U.S. Lenders to Latin America.

	Outstanding Loans (Dec. 31, 1983)[a] (Millions of Dollars)				
	Mexico	Brazil	Argentina	Venezuela	Percent of Total Assets
Manufacturers Hanover	1,915	2,130	1,321	1,084	10.0
Citicorp	2,900	4,700	1,090	1,500	7.6
Chase Manhattan	1,553	2,560	775	1,226	7.5
Chemical N.Y.	1,414	1,276	370	776	7.5
J.P. Morgan	1,174	1,785	741	464	7.2
Bankers Trust N.Y.	1,286	743	230[b]	436	6.7
Bank America	2,741	2,484	300[b]	1,614	5.9
Wells Fargo	655	568	100[b]	279	5.9
Continental Illinois	699	476	383	436	4.7
First Chicago	870	689	NA	NA	4.3

[a]Excluding local currency loans.
[b]Estimated.
NA = not available.
Source: *Business Week*, 18 June 1984.

Author Index

Subject Index

About the Authors

William Darity, Jr., is a professor of economics at the University of North Carolina at Chapel Hill. He earned his B.A. at Brown University (1974) and his Ph.D. from the Massachusetts Institute of Technology (1978). Dr. Darity's research interests include North–South models of trade and economic development, theories of financial instability, Post-Keynesian economics, theories of discrimination and racial inequality, and contemporary developments in classical political economy. His published papers have appeared in a wide variety of professional journals, including the *American Economic Review, Cambridge Journal of Economics, Journal of Money, Credit and Banking, Journal of Development Economics, Southern Economic Journal*, and *The Review of Black Political Economy*. He has previously edited a volume entitled *Labor Economics: Modern Views* and has recently completed an edited volume of the papers of Abram Harris, Jr., entitled *Race, Radicalism and Reform*.

Bobbie L. Horn is an assistant professor of economics at the University of Tulsa. Dr. Horn also earned his undergraduate degree at Tulsa and subsequently earned his Ph.D. from Iowa State University. His research interests include the economics of Thorstein Veblen, the history of economic thought, and theories of the behavior of commercial banks and other financial institutions. Dr. Horn has contributed articles to the *Southern Economic Journal, American Economic Review*, and the *Journal of PostKeynesian Economics*.